Release Your Inner Bitch

(Women Empowering Women)

by

Rose Stadler, MSW

authorHOUSE™

1663 LIBERTY DRIVE, SUITE 200
BLOOMINGTON, INDIANA 47403
(800) 839-8640
WWW.AUTHORHOUSE.COM

This book is a work of non-fiction. Names of people and places have been changed to protect their privacy.

*© 2004 Rose Stadler, MSW
All Rights Reserved.*

No part of this book may be reproduced, stored in a retrieval system, or transmitted by any means without the written permission of the author.

First published by AuthorHouse 09/25/04

ISBN: 1-4184-9843-2 (sc)

*Printed in the United States of America
Bloomington, Indiana*

This book is printed on acid-free paper.

ACKNOWLEDGEMENTS

Dedicated to my mother, Fran, my rock, in the most loving way.

To Dick Stadler, my lighthouse; a beacon on the shores of steadfast reality.

To my children and grandchildren who are always there when the going gets tough,

To Elizabeth Alexander who provided the artwork and logo, and

To Jeff Alexander, photographer, who made me sit still when I wanted to fidget;

To Angie Dick, editor extraordinaire and good friend, thank you.

To everyone who urged me on, literally, when I couldn't take another step due to a broken back.

To Elfie Hook, who may not live long enough to see this in print - - your friendship has taught me invaluable lessons; I love you. and to all the other breast cancer victims mentioned here;

To the women who have experienced first-hand abuse.

To the contributors of this book who knew that if they ever got found out, they might take another beating.

To those who got out, hid, moved on and breathed their own air.

To those who felt the blows and knocks of life, got up, shook themselves off and moved on with determination, courage and empowerment.

To victims of domestic violence everywhere.

To all the bitches who made this possible. Thank you.

If this book helps stop domestic violence dead in its tracks, then it has done its job.

To all the skilled staff at Author House who led me through the publishing process with the precision of trail guides leading me down the Grand Canyon, in the rain and fog, and never once let me fall over the side. Thank you (Michael, Stewart, Scott and all the others) for your expertise.

Bitches don't get abused.

FOREWORD

Who hasn't used the term "Bitch?" We have all been called one or uttered the word at some point in our life. No one prefaces the term anymore by saying the "B" word. The term is now heard on television, in film, in music lyrics and is read in articles, fiction and non-fiction alike. Singer/songwriter Meredith Brooks' solo debut album ***blurring the edges*** featured a song entitled "Bitch" that was a platinum single. The chorus follows:

I'm a bitch.
I'm a lover.
I'm a child.
I'm a mother.
I'm a sinner.
I'm a saint
I do not feel ashamed... so take me as I am.

(Meredith Brooks/Shelly Peiken, Capitol Records, 1997)

Brook's message is all women are/can be bitches. She reclaimed the word bitch and perhaps that explains the song's popularity.

Release Your Inner Bitch is a one of a kind book featuring stories, essays, and poems by women who on their own terms reclaimed the word bitch. These courageous women, ages 20-81, defined the term for themselves.

What follows is a compilation of humor, heroism, and honesty. The reader will find guidelines for joining a bitch club and learn new ways to discover bitches. You'll meet a battered woman in prison for manslaughter who said perhaps if she'd been a bitch, her life would have been different. Bitches often do the unthinkable.

Some are hairdressers, counselors, lawyers, firefighters, teachers, prostitutes, and truck drivers. Some are mothers, daughters, grandmothers, lovers, friends and wives. Some are employed, household engineers, or retired. Some brave bitches find the courage to leave abusive partners and survive breast cancer. Some begin to take responsibility for their own lives.

You will discover bitches you never knew existed. You'll meet a Goddess bitch, a Tsunami bitch, and serial menopausal bitches. The word bitch is incredibly versatile and is used in the essays to express a variety of emotions. As Rose Stadler describes it, becoming a bitch is a process - - an on-going life long process. Some of us began the process earlier than others. Some of us had better bitch mentors than others. You will meet bitches in training and bitchettes. My two year old niece is often referred to as a little bitch. At first I was startled to hear a baby referred to as a bitch, but then she has earned the name because when she is not happy she lets you know in all the ways a two year old is capable of expressing herself.

If ***Release Your Inner Bitch*** brings people together, enables them to celebrate aspects of their lives previously repressed, then the book's success will be far reaching.

There are also stories that will make you laugh, and laughter is a healing element. We need to be able to laugh at ourselves and with one another. However the term bitch for the most part is pejorative and is used by women and men to harm other people. Several of the essays address the negative cultural aspects of the term, but most accounts show what can happen when the inner bitch is liberated - - freed.

Dr. Teri Ann Bengiveno.

By: Teri Ann Bengiveno, Ph. D., assistant professor of American Studies at San Juan University and teacher of women's studies for the past eight years. Dr. Bengiveno is also a featured columnist for ***The Women's Voice*** (A Bay Area News magazine) and for the ***Italian-American Heritage News.***

***

Cover design by Elizabeth Alexander, a free lance artist who lives in Minneapolis, MN.

Author Photo by Jeff Alexander

***

BITCH: <u>B</u>ringing <u>i</u>n <u>t</u>he <u>ch</u>anges.

PREFACE

The **Synonym Finder** lists the following word for bitch: "l) *n* female dog, female canine, 2) *slang*: prostitute, whore, harlot, call girl, hustler; 3) *slang* a complaint, gripe, diatribe, lament, difficulty, unpleasantness, predicament, dilemma, knot, bind; and 4) v, *slang*; complain, protest, object, grumble, bellyache, mouth off, deplore, lament, bewail, and 5) more *slang*: spoil, bangle, botch up, ruin, wreck, make mess of, mess up and screw up."

Webster's Dictionary has the following definition: l) *the female of the dog, a female wolf, fox, etc.,* 2) A woman, especially a bad-tempered, malicious, promiscuous woman, a coarse term of contempt or hostility; 3) *slang:* anything especially unpleasant and difficult: 4) *slang*: a complaint, or 5) to complain. i.e. **bitch up** [botch]; spoil by bungling - - bitchy (adj); bitchier, bitchiest, bitchiness.

Unfortunately, these definitions have set the standard for the word **bitch**.

Here is another definition, rarely seen or mentioned. Perhaps it was deleted from language long before it had the opportunity to mature into greatness. According to **The Women's Encyclopedia of Myths and Secrets** by Barbara G. Walker (P l09), the word bitch has the following definition. "This became a naughty word in Christian Europe because it was one of the most sacred titles of the Goddess, Artemis-Diana, leader of the Seythian *alani* or 'hunting dogs.' The Bitch-goddess of antiquity was known in all Indo-European cultures, beginning with the Great Bitch Sarama who led the Vedlic dogs of death. The Old English word for a hunting dog, *bawd,* also became a naughty word because it applied to the divine Huntress's promiscuous priestesses as well as her dogs. (Potter & Sargent)

Harlots and 'bitches' were identified in the ancient Roman cult of the Goddess Lupa, the Wolf Bitch, whose priestesses the *lupae* gave their name to prostitutes in general (Murstein). Earthy representatives of the Wolf Bitch ruled the Roman town of Ira Flavia in Spain, as a queen or series of queens named Lupa. (Hartley).

In Christian terms, 'son of bitch' was considered insulting not because it meant a dog, but because it meant a devil - - that is, "a spiritual son of the pagan Goddess."

Women throughout the ages have gotten a bad rap because of the first two definitions. **RELEASE YOUR INNER BITCH** offers a chance for women of all ages, races, religions to come forward and verbalize their opinion of one of the most flexible words in the English language. This is a word that can be a noun, a verb, an adjective, a descriptive or a state of mind. This is a word that works overtime, has a wide range and zoom lens, and is greatly misunderstood by humanity. It may be time to change the perception by which women are known.

* * *

Why the book was written:
As a therapist, I volunteered one day a week at a transitional housing facility for impoverished/homeless women and children. Most of the women entered through domestic violence. One day I was working with a young mother/victim, getting her ready to testify against the man who had tried to kill her six times. Her response was to pray for him, which was well and good, but it wouldn't hold up in court. I was trying to make her angry at the violence that placed her young children in the shelter. She had lost her home as a result of the violence, lost her job; was completely displaced, sharing a bedroom with her two small children; and still, she couldn't get angry. I said, "get mad, be a bitch. Bitches don't get abused."

Bingo. It was the *ah ha* light bulb. Bitches don't get abused.

I started taking a survey of my friends and asked, "What makes a bitch? Are you a bitch? What is the exact definition?" There were as many different answers as there were friends. Then it hit me. I could compile bitch responses, and let women finally have a forum to present their own issues. Many of the current bitches have been abused in the past, either as children or as adults - - sexually, physically or mentally - - but once they learned the art of down and dirty bitchiness, the abuse stopped.

Whalla!! Was I on to something? A bitch is not a doormat or a carpet for others. Becoming a bitch is a *process*. It is not something that happens in an instant. It seems to take years of training as an underling, (or an abused spouse, or a battered child) to gain confidence enough to be a bitch. I also discovered that there are good bitches and bad bitches. **Wizard of Oz** presented the good witch and the bad witch. (Perhaps a forerunner, of the B word.) Bitch was certainly not acceptable for everyday use in films fifty years ago, and witch may have been substituted. Who knows? But even children recognize that Glenda, the good witch, was the one who eventually got things done. Good triumphed over evil, and patience prevailed.

I started looking at the difference between me (I wasn't a bitch - - *not me - - surely, not me - -* but the mouse that roared) and them, them being bitches. Bitch is a bad word. It's something that your mother told you never to say. Your father would have tanned your hide if he heard you saying that word. A bitch is a dog in heat: a female dog who has litters of pups in the back yard. *Bitch* is something that you say under your breath when a young beautiful woman passes you a on the freeway doing ninety in a red Jag. *Bitch* is a word reserved for a female colleague who wears too much perfume, makes too much money and climbs the ladder of success on her back.

Look ma, no hands.

It is the art of bitchiness that comes up again and again.

Let's start at the beginning. You were raised to be a nice girl. You were taught to find and secure a husband. Do the right thing, have children and get that pot roast on the table on time. Lord help you if the laundry piles up, or your husband abuses you because you put too much sugar in his coffee.

Your were taught never to sass, cuss or say bad words. You were taught to be refined, cross your legs and sit like a lady. Chew gum with your mouth closed, and if you must pass gas, go outside. If you must be disagreeable, then do it alone, in your room where no one can see you. If you have a different opinion, keep it to yourself.

Smile and nod at appropriate intervals, and you will get along just fine.

A good woman is like a good child, seen and not heard.

A good woman keeps the house spotless, keeps the children clean and happy; and quiet when the man of the house is home. A good wife is a great cook, a slut in bed and an angel in the presence of others. She never discusses religion or politics in public, and never disagrees with her husband, father, uncle or brother-in-law. Stepford Wives and daughters.

That is BS.

God, help us all. There are far too many of us still roaming the earth searching for the great goddess to render us powerful and mighty.

We look to the news anchors of the nightly news and notice that there are more women in front of the camera. Black, white, Hispanic. We applaud them. We see women of all colors and races running and operating their own businesses, and we pat them on their backs. We see more university female graduates and we hail them and their success. But remember, even if you have joined the ranks of the advanced degree, you still have to clean the toilet.

Bottom line. You have to do the laundry, do the grocery shopping and clean out the kitty box. We fought to be *liberated* in the 60's and 70's. Some of us burned our bras. I never did because I would have slapped myself in the chin, but many of my friends did. We challenged equal rights, equal pay for equal performance, and always, in the back of our minds, we did it *nicely.* As a group, we drew attention to ourselves in a nice, friendly manner. Diplomatic, politically correct, always saying the right things at the right times.

In addition, we had to keep our bodies *sexy.*

Stop and take a look at any of the women's magazines on the counter. What messages are we still sending out, and buying? How to please your man in bed, look ten pounds thinner by summer, reduce your thighs, slim down your tummy, how to tantalize him into a frenzy. By this standard, we haven't come very far. Instead, we have become conscious of our femininity as a group; a group of sexy, air-headed Barbie Dolls clinging to a fantasy. Any wonder why romance is still 54% of the publishing industry. Because we want fantasy. We want to escape with Fabio. We want to be caressed and pampered.

We want to be loved and cherished, even if only on paper by the dim lamp after the kids go to bed. We are desperate in our neediness.

But...

We haven't discussed the feminization of poverty.

We haven't discussed the fact that women still work for about 80 cents on the dollar. We haven't discussed the fact that many American industries are moving their factories to third world countries because women will work for next to nothing. This leaves us, as in U. S. - - United States, in a position of having to beg for jobs and industry. There are currently more animal shelters than people shelters. That day care is in a shambles. Child abuse is the second leading cause of death among children and that children are killing children in record numbers (approximately one million children under the age of 18 have died by the hands of other children from the years 1992 to 2002 FBI statistics), or that teen pregnancy is on the rise like an iceberg rising from the depths of the sea.

Why is that?

Why have we become a nation of sexy, well dressed, *nice*, sweet people who are good to each other in public, and meaner than a hungry lion going after Christians behind closed doors? So we have nice abs and buns.... So we drive nice cars and have credit debt up to the lymph nodes. What have we accomplished if men are still abusing women, children are killing each other and violence is out of control? What have we accomplished if females are still considered *dogs*.

Like a bad blind date..... dogs, curs, bitches.

Yes, let's be bitchy. Bitches live longer.

My mission here is to renounce all the prior definitions of the word *bitch* and introduce a new concept. *Bitchiness* in a man would be called leadership. In a woman, it's conniving and cheap.

The next time you don't get paid for a job rendered, say something. Fight back. Write letters and use the same language that a man would use. Stop being a wuss. Next time a client abuses you, take him to court. Next time someone stalks you, turn around and fight. Stomp back. Be a bitch.

I'm not advocating that you go out and arm yourself, and shoot the first person who crosses your path. If you open doors for the elderly, keep doing it, and please continue to put others on the same level as yourself. Do not slink to the depths of being the scum of society. Love thy neighbors as thyself.

This means that if you put yourself lower than your neighbor, you are doing yourself a great disservice. Oprah said that she finally stopped the yo-yo dieting when she learned to love herself. She also said that it took a lot of work, that there are no magic patches or pills for weight loss. The only answer lies in oneself. The same applies to bitchdom. You can't trample all over others. That's the wrong kind of bitch. Being a bitch is a process of growth.

Humility is knowing one's worth, and taking credit where credit is due. It is not wearing a hair-shirt or beating yourself up with put-downs, self defeating behavior or taking a wimpy stance in life. And it may not be *nice* to call a spade a shovel, but there are times when you have to do it. If someone is abusing your child, you would step in and stop it.

Bitch also means, beautiful, intelligent, talented, and charming. A bitch is Murphy Brown. A bitch is Margaret Sanger, Golda Mier, and my dear former boss Peg Subby, who knew how to get things done. When the governor came through, Peg got down on her hands and knees and cleaned the toilets with the rest of us. A bitch is the woman down the street who had the guts to return a refrigerator because it wasn't what she ordered. A bitch is a woman who refuses to pay for a bad haircut. A bitch stands tall and brings up every inch when she speaks, and gets taller as the conversation goes along. A bitch is able to present in front of a crowd, is confident and a leader. A bitch knows her place, and that just might be at the head of the line.

Fran, 81, wife, mother, grandmother, great-grandmother, poet, historian, genealogist, author

THE BITCHER'S CLUB

This is an exclusive club, made up of supervisors, parents, spouses, teachers, nurses, teenagers, and spoiled brats, and covers almost every occupation or profession. The spoiled brats we will ignore because they are minors but they will make excellent future bitchers. Not all of the above can be classified as bitchers, however they must meet the necessary criteria to become certified in bitchomania.

Bitchers meet twice a year. Each gives a report on the following:
1. How many people they managed to get fired,
2. How often their kids ran away from home, threatened suicide, or fought with their peers;
3. How many times they upset members of their family, or others, and made them cry, and;
4. How often they threatened others into submission with haranguing, physical violence, denial of possessions and/or human rights.

However, we must admit that a BITCHER has an important role to play in society. They make it possible to:
1. Keep the factories running smoothly, as they make the best supervisor;
2. Keep the home in top-top shape (not a pillow out of place, not a dust ball under the bed, the hedges neatly trimmed, etc);
3. Keep their spouses from becoming wayward;
4. Have the highest number of kids in the class who need counseling, who have skipped classes, and who were sent to the principal's office;

5. Caused, in themselves or others, high blood pressure, mental problems, heart attacks, and suicides, thereby contributed by supporting the medical profession;
6. Create the highest number of divorces in the country, thereby supporting lawyers, and lastly;
7. Expect the highest standards from members of their family, friends, workforce, etc. In an effort to compete, the victims are often subjects of alcohol or drugs to numb the senses.

HOW TO JOIN THE BITCHER'S CLUB

You must have an affidavit, signed by your co-dependents, stating your qualifications. This can include any or all of the above, plus those listed below:

1. High-pitched voice during bitching,
2. Mood swings,
3. Cussing, name-calling and belittling level,
4. Facial contortions and discolorations during bitching,
5. Physical outbreaks (throwing things, violence, etc.),
6. High self-esteem and total disregard for the feelings of others,
7. Quick retorts to complaints, with added ability to ricochet the blame to others,
8. Ability to manipulate, intimidate, threaten or control others to accomplish their goals.
9. Inability to say "please" or "thank you" and
10. The inability to apologize.

HOW TO SPOT A GOOD BITCHER

1. Bitches are usually single. Nobody can stand living with them.
2. Bitches are fussy about their wear and appearance.
3. They magnify circumstances and events, bordering on lies.
4. They degrade their peers who might be a threat to the bitcher's job security.
5. Their mood swings can cause tears or laughter at the snap of a finger.

6. They are well-versed in body language and make the best actors.
7. Bitchers can be subtle and discreet to gain confidence of their peers. They can draw out the innermost secrets which can be used against the innocent party.
8. Because of their super-bitching powers, they are usually chosen to high position jobs to keep their invisible whip cracking.

If you are one of the foregoing, we welcome you to our exclusive BITCHER'S CLUB. It is a worldwide organization, highly renowned, open to all ages, races, creeds and national origins.

By Fran

Note: It should be noted that Fran, age 81, is my mother, and when I asked if I could dedicate this book to her, she responded with the following letter:

> Dear Rosemarie, Yes, you can dedicate your book to me if you like. It would be a little unusual to dedicate your bitch book to your own mother, but then, sometimes youngsters first recognize bitch-hood in one or the other of their own parents, learn how to cope, and then, like alcoholism, is sometimes passed down to future generations.
>
> Do we inherit our temperaments from our parents? Some psychologists believe that shyness, intelligence (or lack of), alcoholism, mental illnesses, and our whole physical or mental capabilities are either learned or inherited. This includes bitchiness.
>
> You are right though, we must, as individuals, learn to control our tempers (know when to hold 'em, fold 'em) whether they are the result of learning or inheritance. Early temper tantrums in young children can be a sign of later bitchiness in

adulthood, unless the child can be made aware of the consequences early on.

There should be a special name coined for the male bitch; like *mabitch* (for male bitch), or etc.

Love, Mother

* I love the word **mabitch** and have already added it to my computer's dictionary.

***

Martha, age 47

Once when I was standing in line at a car parts store, eight people were served before me. Every time I was about to open my mouth when the question came up, "Who's next?" other people rushed past me. I was beginning to feel stupid and invisible. Finally, in absolute desperation, I threw down the merchandise and stomped to the front door, saying, "I am frigging invisible." By this time I was steaming. Smoke was probably pouring from my ears, but I was angry. Then a clerk noticed me and said, "Can I help you?" I shouted back, "Not anymore," and left the store, wishing that I could slam the door behind me.

The fact that the car parts store lost a potential customer meant nothing, but I never went back to that particular store. The incident taught me something about myself. When you are the only woman standing in male-dominated territory, you have to be assertive. I should have said, "Excuse me, I am next," instead of standing there like a dummy. Had I been the bimbo looking like a stuffed Barbie doll, then all the clerks would have fawned all over me. Had I acted as stupid and used a high-pitched little girl voice right from the beginning, someone might have taken the time to help me. As it was, I was a female customer, buying an air filter and oil, which I had fully intended to change by myself. It was the way I was treated that made my angry.

I have never been invisible since. Now, when setting foot in a man's world, I make sure that everyone knows I'm there, and yes, I've played the stupid female part to get attention, but I got what I wanted. Sometimes I've had to learn a specific language; instead of calling it a *thingamajig*, or a *whatschmacallit*, I use the proper term.

Now it's more like "I was next in line. Or: where are your air filters?" I have learned the art of cutting to the chase and calling a spade a shovel. Am I a bitch now? Maybe. Or maybe just a bit more assertive. Either way, I like the new me.

* It seems that Martha felt insecure in a male environment (car parts store) and made herself invisible. This is a common mistake that many women make. They become invisible, they blend in with the environment, like a chameleon. When Martha learned the proper names of the parts that she needed, she was more self confident, and able to get the response she wanted.

***

Anna, age 37, accountant

I'm a college graduate, intelligent and smart. I work in a professional job; have subordinates and run a pretty sharp unit. However, when I'm in a meeting and say something that should be heard, men start to have side conversations, as if I have nothing to say, as if I'm not there. I get a few sentences into what I'm trying to say, and the mumbling starts. They're talking about their golf game, or where they're going for lunch. One day, I simply stopped talking. After a few minutes of silent frustration, I noticed that the men got silent too. I started talking again, and they started talking again.

So I picked up my briefcase and left the room without another word. I heard laughter coming down the hallway.

I was furious. How dare they not take me seriously?

Two days later, still fuming, I sent out a memo that since I didn't have a chance to speak my piece, I was re-convening the meeting. The day of the meeting, I wore a severe suit that looked like something my father would have worn in the war. My hair was pulled back and I didn't put any jewelry on. I looked like a stiff old maid, rather than the single parent of two vivacious children. If I looked good in a size 5 gym suit, it didn't show. I made sure that my make up was light, almost non-existent.

The men grumbled, but they showed up. I announced at the very beginning of the meeting that I didn't appreciate the fact that they talked over me or had side conversations during something that I considered important, but they shut up and listened. Some of them even thought that my ideas were worthwhile. Afterwards, some of them apologized. The next day I came back to work in my short skirts and black stockings and sling-back heels. My hair was softer and curly and I felt like me again.

I shouldn't have had to look like a man to speak like a man. I got the job on my own merit; not on my bra size.

I grew up being the 'good' girl in my family, but I discovered that in business, 'good' doesn't mean a thing. I had to raise the level of my voice, speak in short sentences. "I want that memo on my desk in two days." Be specific without belaboring a point and address issues directly. No more chitchat about last night's television program. No more small talk about the dog or kids. Just plain old business. Know what? I'm now known as the bitch on the third floor, and I don't care. The guys don't invite me to lunch with them, and the secretaries avoid me, but I get the job done. I guess that's what it's all about. I wasn't hired to impress anyone with my cute little figure or the pictures on my desk. I've uncluttered the personal objects from my office, narrowed it down to one poster that has a wonderful sunset, and says "perfection."

* Anna had been sending a double message to her male counterparts on the job. She cluttered her office with cutesy-*girl* things, then expected to be taken seriously. When she stood her ground, removed the girl clutter from her office, and began to speak in terms recognized by the males around her, she grew as a woman, not necessarily a bitch.

***

Linda, divorced mother of three teenagers, works two jobs to make ends meet, age 42

When my ex-husband left me for a younger, prettier woman, I was devastated. I never planned on raising three kids by myself. It was supposed to be a marriage, a team effort; but he was playing the field. Actually, he was playing in the playpen, with a sweet young thing just barely older than my oldest son. Talk about a twist of fate. She was all of a size two, looked anorexic while I was stuffing myself into a size 14 telling people that it shrunk in the dryer. She had fabulous hair, not a gray hair in sight. I hadn't been inside a beauty parlor for months and used scrunchies to tie up the loose ends. I felt old and used up.

I was depressed for months. The bills were piling up and there was only a hint of child support. I had to do everything by myself; the house, the yard, the car, cooking and cleaning, AND going to work. It was pretty bleak. To make matters worse, the kids started acting like everything was my fault. If I had been a better wife..... maybe their dad wouldn't have left. If I had moved the furniture the way HE wanted...... If I had been better in bed, more often, wilder, louder, WHATEVER........

One day I took a good, long, hard look in the mirror and decided that I had to cut my hair, get a facial, get a makeover and get on with my life. Three months and twenty pounds lighter, I walked into court swinging my hips like I had been doing it all my life. I stood taller, spoke louder, and didn't look down at my feet. I told the judge exactly what I wanted: half the house payment, child support sufficient to feed and clothe three growing kids, the car (paid for), the car insurance (paid for two years), life and health benefits for the kids and myself, and spousal maintenance. I got every last thing on the list! I nailed him in the wallet and felt like a bitch doing it. It felt wonderful. It was the first time in my life that I felt that kind of power.

Maybe I was a wimp in the marriage, but no more. If one of the kids doesn't take out the garbage or do their share of the household chores, I give them two warnings. The third time the garbage is put on their bed, dumped out. Stuff not picked up is put in storage. I've become stronger through this. My kids respect me a little more, and I've got a new man in my life. But marriage is out of the question. At least right now. Maybe later, I'll consider it. But this time the rules are different.

* Linda is newly acquainted to the bitch club, but it doesn't look like she's going to lose her membership. As a wife, she was meek and humble. When she learned to assert herself, she also learned that she didn't have to be a doormat for anyone. She is confident and capable now, able to make strong decisions regarding herself and her children.

***

Dr. Roberta, fifty-something, professor

I have a doctorate in biology; I teach at a major university. I drive a four-wheel drive vehicle and I like camping. My husband is also a professor and we finally have a good marriage. I say *finally* because it wasn't always like this. When I went to school, he complained about helping out around the house and baby-sitting. But when he went to school, it seemed he never noticed that there were clean socks in his sock drawer, or that the sheets were changed. I did everything around the house, worked, and tended the children. If there was a flat tire, I changed it and never mentioned it. I took care of all the finances, the plumbing problems and trimmed the hedges around the house. I was the first one out of bed in the morning, and the last one in at night. There were times I was so damn tired, that I have no idea how I got through the day(s) and months. If he had a term paper due, I typed it for him.

We went where he wanted to go on vacation. We did what he wanted to do; whether it was a movie or out to dinner. We went to his family at Christmas, and I cooked the turkey on Thanksgiving. We had sex when it was convenient for him. This was the pattern for years. All the while, my teaching and academics were making progress, but he didn't seem to notice.

One day, I lost my mind. Our children had grown up and left, so that left him and me, rattling around in the house, not having anything to talk about. "How was your day, dear?" I'd ask, sounding like June Cleaver. He didn't seem interested in my day, but would go on at length about his day. Then I had a tantrum. I picked up his golf clubs and one by one, smashed them against a pole that we have in the basement. Each one curved around the pole, leaving a noticeable dent in the club. I quietly put them back in the bag, knowing that unless he suddenly went blind, he would notice the next Saturday when he went golfing with his buddies.

He came home and said, "Odd thing, all my clubs have a strange angle in them." I smiled, and said, "really?" and went to a motel. I waited for three days before calling home. When I told him where I was, he sent flowers to the motel and literally begged me to come home. I told him no. I got a small apartment not far from the university and lived alone for about a year, with no regrets.

We're back together now, and more in love than ever, but he will never take me for granted again. I should have put my foot down when we first got married, but I was raised to respect my husband in all things. Does that make me a bitch? I presume so. Oh well, no going back now.

* Roberta is a sweet person. She always put her husband's career and professionalism before her own. In the professional position, she is strong and capable; however, in the home, she made the mistake that many women make. They sit closest to the stove and *serve*. When she realized that she wasn't serving herself in her marriage, she grew stronger. It took a year separation to convince her husband that she had worth and value. In that year of separation, she re-evaluated her marriage and the commitment she had made and decided to return home. Had she not taken the time to re-assess herself, she might still be in an unfulfilled relationship. Both she and her husband are happy and content now, dedicated to each other and their marriage.

Linda A. 41, Car Dealer
Late blooming bitch

If you would have asked me this last year, I would have said, "No way, I am not a bitch. A bitch is someone who is rude, inconsiderate and impolite." Now I say, "Yes, I am a bitch and proud of it."

It took a divorce to bring out the bitchiness in me. My husband of 17 years left me for a younger woman. It wasn't so much the fact that she was younger, prettier, had a better education than me, not really that, but that he had gotten "tired" of me and the kids. That was his excuse. He was tired of the same old grind. He said that he had been feeling that way for several years. He never mentioned it, never said anything to me, then suddenly, he was telling me how to do the laundry and manage money. Suddenly I couldn't do anything right. Then I found out why. The pretty Miss Muffet had his full attention, and he said, "he had found himself." It wasn't the idea of raising the kids on my own, they were teenagers and able to figure things out for themselves, and they pitched in and helped where they could. There were never any clues, no hints that he was looking elsewhere or that he was bored with our relationship. He acted like a married man, made love like a married man, and mowed the yard like a married man, then one weekend, he started packing his things. Two bags, that was it. He didn't want pictures of the kids, he didn't want "his treasures" - - he just wanted his freedom. He said that I could throw out his stuff for all he cared, he just wanted to start over, get a new life, and have a little peace.

I walked around in a stupor for the first two weeks, thinking that he would get over it - - whatever *it* was - - he would come home and things would be back to normal. I figured he was going through some mid-life crisis or something. He had given me an address in case of emergencies, and one day I went there, hoping to talk it out. Was I in for a surprise. He had another apartment all along, had all his new furniture to set up housekeeping and even had another dog. He had been living a lie for about a year. I met the other woman, a cute young thing. When she answered the door, I was floored.

I figured I'd find a mattress on the bare floor and some suitcases strewn about. Then I pretended that I was selling insurance, and fled. I was a chicken. I should have confronted her on the spot, but my head went numb and there wasn't a real thought in it at all. I drove around for about two hours, not even paying attention to where I was. Then I recognized the bank building on the corner. We had banked there for years, so on a whim, I went inside and checked out our accounts. They had been stripped. He left about two hundred dollars in each account, and that was it.

The numb was replaced by anger. Instant, eruptive explosive anger. I wanted to kill him, and actually thought about it for a while. But, I didn't. Instead, I got the meanest, nastiest divorce attorney I could, and took him to the cleaners. I got the house, paid for and in my name, the cars, the back money from the accounts, and he got to pay all the bills. I also hit him for alimony, child support and college tuition for my kids.

I understand the sweet young thing moved on. Apparently, it wasn't her idea to live with a man so heavily burdened by debt. He came around, got down on his knees - - for drama's sake in front of the kids - - and begged me to take him back. Sorry, no dice. I'm seeing someone else right now, and don't want to be bothered with a man who after 17 years of marriage, suddenly wanted to find himself.

* Linda's story is not unique. She's not the first to be dumped for a younger woman, and she handled it correctly, in court. Atta girl. Sounds like she's learned the hard way to assert herself.

***

Anita, age 21, secretary.
Am I a bitch? You bet, and I'm going to stay that way. I've got a child to raise by myself, with no help from my son's father. OK, so getting pregnant was a stupid thing to do, but I was 16 and in love.

Dumbest thing I ever did...... every chance I get, I tell a girl, "you are messing yourself up. You are ruining your life...."

Well, I've gone back and got my GED, am taking classes at a community college and can actually *see* a future for myself. Don't get me wrong. I love my child and would do anything for him, but it shouldn't be that way. Now when I've got something to say, I say it and don't beat around the bush.

I stand up for myself. No one is going to stand up for me. It's me and him. I have to stand up for myself and for my child. It's hard being a single parent, with no money and a car that's falling apart, but it's *mine*. I paid for it. I have a checking account, I pay my own bills, I'm responsible for me and my child. No one is going to come along and rescue me. I got myself into this mess, and it's my responsibility to get myself out.

But don't short me on the paycheck because I can't afford it. I found out crying isn't the answer. It serves no purpose. Crying makes your eyes red and puffy and messes up your makeup. If you don't get the paycheck on time, you march right into the boss's office and say so. Don't go asking for an appointment. Don't go saying "please sir, can I have my paycheck." No. I ain't no slave. Those days are gone.

And do I get on my back for some *man*? No. I do not. I have other things that I have to do with my life, and I am not going to get side tracked again. And I am going to teach my son that women are not to hit, not to bounce around, and not to yell at and slam-dunk in the sac. No. Women deserve better. We have a right to be treated with respect, but if there's no one around, then we treat ourselves with respect.

* Anita is a gutsy woman, young, but already has a strong sense of self. She has had to learn a lot of life's lessons the hard way. I'm willing to bet that she doesn't repeat past mistakes. She will go far.

***

Lorraine, age 62
Bitches I have known

Over the years I have had the awesome experience of knowing some of the most sensational bitches ever to cross a non-bitch's path and I have to say, I admire their stamina. Just to maintain their majestic levels of PMS must take a lot out of a person. They control their environment through blatant bitchiness, and tolerate no interference with their plans. Their only direction is Forward; their gear shift is locked in Overdrive; the word "compromise" is not in their vocabulary. If you wish to co-exist with a Bitch, you must "go along to get along".

You quickly learn your place with a Bitch. You always know where you stand since she leaves you with no uncertainty about the overwhelming unimportance of your opinion, regarding her remarks or actions. Bitches know they are always right, and there is never a doubt in their mind that you are dead wrong. They can maintain a fierce confidence in the face of total opposition, with steadfast loyalty to their views, never wavering or (God forbid) giving in.

One prime example springs to mind. A Bitch I once knew (who could have worn the crown of the Queen of Bitches) held her ground through a barrage of complaints and advice from less than 99% of friends and relatives in relation to a really stupid decision she made affecting her entire family - - and emerged from the crapper with a new suit, so to speak. She did what she wanted, damn the consequences, and gladly paid the price. No one could convince her of her folly once her mind was made up. And true to Bitch folklore, she came out of the incident smelling like a rose, with friends and relatives gathering at the shrine to help put back the pieces of her life.

Was she grateful? This was the Grand Dame of Bitches we're talking about here. Her bitchiness entitled her not only to be ungrateful but to actually scorn those who helped her get back on her feet. Amazing! You have to wonder at the tenacity of the woman.

And Bitches find each other. They seem to possess the ability to hone in on belligerent attitudes similar to theirs, and then commiserate with their new-found bitchy buddies about their accomplishments.

Rose Stadler, MSW

It's almost like they emit a bitchin' scent, projected through walls and moving vehicles that can be picked up by other Bitches who also live in the constant state of "that time of the month". Unfortunately, because their personalities clash with every other human being on earth, their friendships with each other tend to be short lived. Only the folks who are the target of their bitchiness seem to hang around long enough to form uneasy relationships.

A Bitch is chutzpah in a skirt. She doesn't need pants to assert herself, no man's shirts or ties. She does quite well in a mini-skirt and heaven help the guy who whistles. She can accomplish in short order what it takes the non-bitch weeks to resolve. A properly geared Bitch can get a mortgage closed in half the time. The underwriter is so intimidated by the end of the process that she is begging the Bitch to name the day. Bitches can get NSF charges taken off their bank statements. Bitches get the lowest credit card rates. Doctors actually come to the phone and talk to Bitches.

The evolution of a Bitch is a genuine mystery of nature. They come into the world like every other human being, innocent, tiny and helpless. What selection process causes that stage to pass quicker for them than others as they metamorphose into their future Bitchiness? Is there a particular Bitch gene that sprouts to maturity when the female hormones kick in and sexual development begins? Are the privileged few, the really primo Bitches, able to convert their PMS into a life force? Are we witnessing the emergence of a distinct and dominant female species?

Finally, it is worth noting that Bitches wear their badge of bitchiness proudly. Make no mistakes, they do not feel the need to excuse their bitchiness. It is their strength. Their mental muscle. Their armor. They know who they are, and we must accept them on their terms. Bitches rule.

Lorraine Mutschler, author of **What Doesn't Kill me**

* Lorraine is one of the sweetest people I know, an author, mother of 12 children, grandmother to some 40-odd grandchildren and still counting, and dedicated wife. She is also highly spiritual. It was a challenge to her to write the word 'bitch' as it is seldom used in her environment. Yet, she recognizes that bitches exist and that they know who they are.

***

BITCH: Beautiful, **I**ntelligent, **T**alented, **C**harming and **H**onest
(Bumper Sticker)

***

Sonia, age 39
Bitch 101

I used to hate being called a bitch. It either meant that I was stupid, mentally ill, or "that time of the month." Well, let me tell you, since my divorce, I'm a Bitch, with a capital B. No one will ever walk all over me again.

I had to learn the hard way, that in order to get what I wanted, or in this case, what was actually mine in the first place, I had to act the part of a screaming shrew. I think my mother would have called it a *fishwife*. I started throwing things and crying; more angry and frustrated than anything. Of course, that just caused my ex to leave, get in the car and drive as fast as he could, saying "damn, that woman is a bitch."

The next day I got out of bed, took a cold shower and gave myself a good lecture in the mirror. What was all that crying and screaming about? Did I want him back? Not on your life. But I wanted the Mazda, AND the stereo, AND the jewelry, AND the bills paid, AND child support, AND AND AND....... I realized that crying and carrying on wasn't the way to go. It just made him laugh.

Then I noticed one of the women at work *always* got her way. She was a Bitch, feared by anyone stupid enough to get on the elevator with her. But there was something in the way she carried herself. She had a firm walk, always seemed to know what was going on around her, her peripheral vision extended about 360 degrees, AND she never had to grovel. Actually, I waited several days before approaching her, but I knew it had to be done.

I gulped back my fear, and knocked on her office door, timidly, like a mouse. When she finally let me in, I was terrified; more of her than what I wanted, but I blurted out, "How come you always manage to get what you want in life?"

"Because I'm a Bitch," was her answer. I started to cry. For God's sake, this isn't what I had come to her for. There I was, blubbering around her office like a baby, while her phone was ringing. She called the receptionist and had her messages held and actually *talked* to me. I couldn't believe it.

"You have to get tougher. Stop acting like a rug for everyone to step on. Get some grit in your life. Change the way you walk and talk. Stand taller, in fact, don't take a chair when it's offered to you. Stand. That way people will always know where they stand with you. Look at your watch every few minutes like you have some place else to go. Always look as if you have a secret date. Have a signature perfume."

I was stunned. The woman was letting me in on her secrets.

"If you're going to cross your legs in a meeting, make sure that everyone sees you do it, otherwise, you look like you are shifting nervously in a chair. And lose the polyester...." When I told her that I couldn't afford a new wardrobe at the moment, she held her hand up like a stop sign. Then she whispered, "thrift stores". "You have to look like a million bucks, but you don't have to *pay* a million bucks to do it. But *always* wear good perfume." Then she waved me away, the audience with the Queen of Bitches was over, but the next time I saw my ex, I was doing exactly what she told me to do. I was wearing an expensive lounge dress, purchased for about $5.00, I had dimmed the lights and had candles burning, and soft music on my stereo, and I acted like a date was about to arrive at any minute.

Take Bitch lessons if you have to, but learn the fine art of being a Bitch, then wear it like a million bucks.

By the way, I got everything I wanted in the divorce, AND I got a promotion at work. The Bitch Queen has moved on, but I have her office. It took me two moves to get it, but it's mine now. If you ARE a Bitch, take time to educate the lesser bitches around you, just a few hints here and there. Don't give away all your secrets in one sitting, but be a little compassionate to the bitches-in-training. I'm still learning about being a Bitch, so I'm constantly on the lookout for new material. It's not like I want to screw everyone else in the world, I just want to be able to get what's mine, what I've worked for, what I've earned. So, you can definitely mark me Bitch, but make sure that everyone knows it. That's the key.

* Sonia's response was typical. Again, bitchiness, is a process of growth. She's right. There is no bitch school that one can attend, then hang the diploma on the wall as a certificate of accomplishment. She had to seek out lessons from another bitch. As a result, Sonia feels that she has come a long way. She got everything she wanted out of the divorce and has learned a few things about herself. She found her own bitch school, and took a course in self-assertion. However, I have known attack-secretaries who have gone to the Doberman School of Charm.

***

Nancy, 54, a non-bitch
I have never been a bitch, but a sweet, kind, compassionate lady. I sat like a lady, held my fork like a lady, always made my home-sweet-home like a lady, did cross-stitch, sewing and made the covered dishes for all the church potlucks. My house was spotless, the children clean. I generally looked the part of a nice mother, nice wife, good Christian, and my fingernails were manicured. The grass was cut and flowers grew in the window boxes in spring and summer. Then one day I discovered that my husband was having an affair. I was stunned. I couldn't imagine what I had done wrong. No dust anywhere in the house, all the meals prepared on time, I had been the perfect wife and mother. It had to be my fault. It must have been something that I did that triggered his affair. I wept, cried bitter tears, talked to him and he promised that he slipped just this once, and would never do it again. So, I thought it must have been a midlife crisis or something, and I would overlook it. Once. Then

it happened again. We lived in a small town where everyone knows everything. The second time was devastating.

That was the day the good wife/mother/lover/house-keeper and maid turned into a raving bitch. I had never been so hurt in all my life. He went to work as usual, and I moved out. That was it, got it all packed and shoved in a truck in one day and left the state. Twenty-some odd years of marriage, wrecked and smashed. I broke lamps in the move, lost dishes and clothes, but something in me snapped. I had been a fool, and the whole town knew it. I was the sweet wife, the good mother.

He used me. Twice he had affairs, and the first time I was able to forgive him. I couldn't forgive him the second time. It hurt too much.

I got to the new city, transferred with my job, and tried to get on with my life, but serious depression set in. I kept thinking of ways to kill my husband, go back to the small town and smother him in his sleep, stab him, whatever. I couldn't get the picture out of my head, and I cried some more. About a year later, I signed myself into a treatment center for depression. There I found out more things about myself than I ever wanted to know. I had been the perfect wife - - and the therapist said that could have been the heart of the problem. I was a Stepford wife, everything was for him and home, I had never asserted myself. If he wanted the sofa by the window, that's where it went. If he wanted chicken for dinner, that's what I cooked. Of course, I had been used, I allowed it all along. I never realized it before. I was the most codependent person on the face of the earth, I couldn't make decisions by myself, I *always* gave up control to him. Always.

I've come a long way since then. Not necessarily a bitch, but more independent. I like the new me.

* Nancy is the prime example of the kind of woman we all sought to be. Married, two children, a nice house in the a small town, the white picket fence and home-grown tomatoes. She thought everything was perfect because she presented the perfect image of the perfect wife. Then she got burned. Since then she has learned to be self-reliant and strong. Still a nice sweet lady, and not a bitch at all. But I wouldn't cross her to see what happens.

Nancy reminds me of a delicate African Violet, you have to baby them into survival. You can't get their leaves wet or the whole plant may whither and die. They need to be watered from the bottom up. Their location, sun and heat, must be consistent. They drop their flowers looking like a sad bunch of posies on the kitchen window. However, one day while I was pulling off old buds from my favorite African Violet, I noticed that you have to pinch the old flowers off to make room for the new ones. The new buds seem to be prettier and last longer than the old ones. Maybe she should have been pruning off the old flowers to make room for the new ones all along. You can't have a pretty flower without a sacrifice. So Nancy's leaves got wet and she lost a few flowers, but she's sturdier than before. Nancy and Linda have a lot in common. Read on, they're not the last women to be dumped for younger versions. It's the other woman who should also be held accountable for infidelity.

***

Carol M. 43, recent escapee

My 20-year marriage ended this last year with me having a fling. I didn't mean to, it just sort of happened. I knew I would be caught, (didn't happen) and it would end in divorce, but what I didn't realize was that I had been wanting "out" for a long time. It simply took another person to show me. My ex had several affairs, but this was the first time I did, and at first, I have to tell you, it was wonderful in a roller-coaster kind of way. Wild, passionate, tender, gentle; then it fizzled just as fast as it started. My husband didn't know about it, but one night, when he was in a drunken rage about something or other, I blurted it out. Then I followed up with "I want a divorce." He looked at me like I had two heads. He never suspected that I would be unfaithful. He raged "you f-g bitch."

"Yes," I said, "and it's about time." That ended one chapter of my life and another one started. The affair taught me about myself. I had goals once, beliefs and ideals. I settled for a drunk because I was pregnant when we got married. His first affair was with an old girlfriend. That should have been the first clue. His second affair was with one of the women he worked with. Did I leave then? No, by that time I had two kids, a lot of bills and no way out. The third time, I let it go. The fourth time, I said something, but I figured that he had been drinking at the time. So on and on it went. We never should have gotten married in the first place. We were all wrong for each other, but I stayed because of the children. They should be old enough to understand that if you make a mistake once, you should be man (or woman) enough to admit it and keep going. So I've moved on, with no regrets. I'm thirty pounds lighter and have gone back to school to get that degree I've always wanted. I kept the house, but I'm thinking of selling it. It's too big for just me and I hate the lawn work, so I'm moving up and away.

My kids think that I ruined the marriage, and one of them called me a bitch. Oh well. I can live with that. The kids will have to figure out things eventually. OK, call me a bitch.

* Carol was in a rut, stuck in an apparent loveless marriage with an alcoholic, then one day, when she let the bitch out, she let it out a little too much. Looks like she's got things under control now. She will soon learn that being single isn't as bad as people make it look. Sure, she will have to change the tires herself, and maybe learn how to do household repairs - - or, she can hire someone. She will breathe her own air, and continue to be strong.

***

Jill. age 45, nurse.
My Mother's Knee

I learned how to be a bitch at my mother's knee. Her voice was drippy sweet, like honey. "Sugar, would you get me a glass of water," she'd say. I'd look up, knowing that she just had a glass of water five minutes ago. Later, I'd ask her about it, and she said, "A woman has to drink plenty of water. Besides, it's the best way to get what you want. *Ask* for something. Be sweet about it. Let men think that they are *serving* you and you just can't live without that glass of water. Be grateful, ever so grateful, thank them. Look into their eyes and smile." She'd pat me on the head, and say, "One day you'll understand."

My mother died two years ago, but I knew that up to the very end, she was sweetly asking for that last glass of water. She was also a Bitch, but she did it in such a way that you were grateful when she told you to go hell. "Have a nice trip, honey." She could suck the socks off a centipede with her sweetness. I began to see her as a phony about the time I was in high school, but I always knew that she'd get what she wanted. Whether it was a new car, or having the kitchen remodeled, she got it when she wanted it. My poor father must have been blind not to see it, but then she was ever so grateful later that he probably smiled all the way to his last heart attack.

Mom wore him down, like she did the rest of us. She wore all of us down with her sweetness. But she always got her way. I never saw her scream and yell, she was always cool and collected; a lot like Scarlet O'Hara. She could manage a discount at the most expensive department stores, pointing out a tiny flaw in the hem of a three hundred dollar suit, and would offer to take it off the store's hands. She never had service charges at the bank, and *always* had someone pump her gas for her, long after self-serve pumps were everywhere.

You could hear her coming down the hallway, with the soft, click-click of her heels, and you just knew that you were going to give up the chair you were sitting in, and be grateful for the chance to do it for her.

"Darling," she said to me once, "it's not what you get in life that counts, it's *how* you get it."

I miss my mother. I wish that I could hear that honey-dripped voice one more time. I would be happy to give up my chair for her, or get her a glass of water. Now I'm doing the same thing to my kids, and it sort of scares me. On the other hand, it makes me proud to be my mother's daughter.

* Jill is a gentle person, full of sweetness and sugar. She is her mother's daughter to the last sip of nectar of life.

***

gael P. Mustapha, author

Releasing Your Inner Bitch

Release her, let her soar, let her fly.
Don't keep her simmering inside.
Say something. Laugh. Let her go.
You'll feel so much better, you know.

Even grandmothers can be bitches. I've learned that first hand this summer. I've always prided myself on trying to be the best grandmother around because I never knew my grandmothers when I was growing up. That was not going to happen to my grandchildren.

Three granddaughters, ages 13-going on 30 (raging hormones), almost 9 and just 5 visited this summer for six weeks. They live across the country and I'm lucky to see them twice a year. We also write, call, e-mail, and have what I like to call a great relationship.

When they're on the spot for a lengthy period, it makes you realize how fast we forget how much food it takes to feed them, how much room for their stuff-toys, books, clothes, colors, crafts, puzzles, games. How fast we forget all that is involved in being a mother. How did we ever do it?

Other grandmothers I know agree we're glad we're no longer mothers; have moved on to this stage of our lives when we can generally give the grandkids back to their parents after a certain time. The noise level can be deafening, irritating, frustrating, distracting.

"Stop already," I yelled one day when the sibling rivalry, pushing, poking, fighting had reached a very high decibel level. I was appalled that I had raised my voice to match theirs. It caught their attention. I had released her - - the bitch inside, angered by my loss of solitude.

Another time, when the almost-nine-year old refused to do her math practice sheets, she snapped, "Leave me alone."

I tried to discover the problem, wondering if she felt scared, dumb, uncertain. She ignored me, repeating, "Leave me alone."

My inner bitch soared. With raised voice, I informed this granddaughter, "I'm in charge here. I need to know what the problem is. Now. Tell me."

She sighed, cried, said through tears, "This is supposed to be summer time, not school time." Once again my inner bitch did fly - - out the window this time. The nearly nine-year-old had a point. We'd do math later.

The 13-year old went to horse camp as a junior counselor for two weeks. Her self-esteem blossomed as she learned and mastered new skills, was praised for her abilities rather than put down. The adults were pleased. She felt good.

Back with me, she talked and talked and talked about her experiences, the boy she met, the boy she fell in love with, the boy she planned to write to, the boy she'd tell all her friends back home about.

"Enough," I covered my ears. "No more about this boy!" I bitched, unable to let my bitch simmer inside. Afterwards, I cried, feeling sad to step on her joy about the boy. I remembered being thirteen.

The five-year old tried my patience too, with nightmares - - a few. One particular night, three times I rose to comfort, pat her back, and wonder why. The third time, I griped, "Go to sleep, damn it. I'm tired of being sleep-deprived." That bitch went from bitchy to bitchier to bitchiest in nothing flat. Then feeling sad, I kissed the little one softly. The nightmares aren't her fault, I sighed.

Next morning, after breakfast, I gathered them around. We needed a fun project we all agreed. We worked together, cut up lots of fruits and vegetables including carrots, zucchini, watermelon, apples, celery and placed them in little bowls. We added raisins and dry chow mein noodles, too.

At the table, we made pictures on paper plates with our food. We took photos. The noodles made great arms and legs and sun rays, too. We all agreed food art was fun.

"Best part," the five-year-old quipped, "We get to eat every bite. We love you, Tutu; you're the greatest grandma of all. The other girls agreed.

What fun. we talked. We laughed, we all let our bitches go - - - until the next time. We all felt lots better, you know.

* gael pointed out the generational aspect of bitchiness. All behavior is a learned response, but her solution was laughter. I have found this to be true with the women I have seen at homeless and domestic violence shelters. The women who have a sense of laughter, joy and cheer, have a tendency to overcome the poverty and abuse of their lives much faster than the women who do not. gael's new book, **Cinderella's Croning** is the first work of fiction to explore the concept of CRONE. This term represents the third phase of a woman's life: maiden/mother/crone.

***

Prayer for working women

"Grant me the serenity to accept the things I cannot change,
The courage to change the things I cannot accept,
And the Wisdom to hide the bodies of those people I have to kill today because they piss me off and also,
Help me to be careful of the toes I step on today,
As they may be connected to the ass that I have to kiss tomorrow."

(Sent by Gayle, gotten off the Internet. author unk)

***

Patricia, age 46, administrator

This is the kind of assignment I've been waiting all my life for. We are bitches, yes, you got it. We bitch during that time of the month, the PMS time or during menopause. Everyone knows to stay clear of us, but it's the other kind of bitchiness that strikes me as odd. There *are* days I'm angry before my feet hit the floor and I *KNOW* it's hormonal, so I take care of myself. I've never really regarded myself as a bitch, but more than likely other people have, because I'm outspoken and assertive.

Let's take a look at the difference between men and women. If a man is a sharp accountant, people pat him on the back for his excellent decision-making skills and money management. The same idea coming from a woman, and she's a tight-fisted bitch.

When a man is assertive or aggressive, that's business as usual; but when we're aggressive or assertive, we're a bitch.

When a man says something straightforward and honest, people say, "people listen when he speaks." When a woman is straightforward and honest, people say, "can't get a word in edgewise with that bitch." Or worse, "domineering bitch, I'd hate to be her husband." Or: "no wonder she's single."

Somehow, the word "bitch" connotes marital status, sexual interest or disinterest. We are pictured carrying a whip and wearing black leather. None of the above is true, but old images die hard. I suppose you could say that I came from a long line of bitches, because the women in my family were survivors. My great-great grandmother helped carve out the Kansas prairie, with eight kids, half of them died before the age of 12. She was widowed at the age of 39. She died at the age of about 50, I suppose that was considered terribly old. My great-grandmother didn't have it much better. As a child, she didn't go to school, but learned how to milk and rope at an early age. She was married off at the age of 14, had her first baby at 15 and had three more children before she was 21. She was widowed at the age of 26, remarried almost immediately to an abusive man, who drank up the farm. She died at the age of 37. She was holding her first grandchild when she had a heart attack, dead before she hit the ground.

Then my grandmother. She was already a third generation American by the time the First World War broke out. She married a serviceman two days before he shipped out and never saw him again. Nine months later she had a child to raise by herself. She eventually remarried, and had more children (I come from this line), but life was hard on her. She endured the Depression, severe abuse and poverty and moved to Texas where it was supposed to get better, but the Dust Bowl ended all her dreams.

My mother got her serving dish, one of the few things that she didn't have to sell off at an auction. I have the serving dish now. My mother was a WWII bride, but my father came home. She spoke of rationing coupons for things that we take for granted: gas, sugar and coffee.

The women had to be strong to bury their babies along the way, to bury their men, and to be widowed early. They kept the home fires burning, and anyone who says it doesn't matter, is wrong. So coming from a long line of strong women, I guess that now you'd call me a bitch instead of a pioneer or a war widow. I can live with that.

* Here again, we have the generational aspect of strong women. Patricia's female ancestors were strong and capable. They were pioneers. Obviously they didn't live long, but they couldn't run to the nearest convenience store when they needed soap, or a loaf of bread. They had to carve out the land, taking from it what they needed. They had to work hard, from daybreak to nightfall, with hardly a moment for themselves. They were war widows, raising children at a time when there was no welfare or social services to assist them. They had to be strong. Patricia feels that her strength is inherent. She also feels that the female ancestors are watching, and encouraging from above.

***

Pam, 37, curriculum planner

Yes, I am a bitch. I've been called a bitch since I was in the 6th grade. Maybe it had something to do with being a big girl - - ok, fat - - or maybe it had to do with getting my period early. Or maybe - - it had more to do with my father, who would sneak into my bedroom whenever he had the chance. I used to lay there and pretend to be sleeping, then one time, he knew I was awake, so he started pestering me to do things, move around more - - but keep my mouth shut. So that one time, I started making noise, I mean really making noise, moaning and groaning, thrashing around. Then he wanted me to be quiet. After that, he never bothered me again. I never told my mother, but I suspect she knew. No one said anything the next day, but I looked at him, and he looked at me, and we had an understanding.

After that, I locked my bedroom door with a butter knife jammed under the door frame. My father died last year and I had a very difficult time at his funeral trying to look sad. I wanted to get on a chair and yell, "you bastard, you ruined me," but it wouldn't have done any good. About a month later, I had a discussion with my younger sister - - just talking, girl talk stuff, and come to find out she had been abused too. After I heard that, I wish I had stood on a chair with a megaphone in my hand and told the whole church what he did. I inherited a portion of his estate, but I didn't have the heart to spend any money on myself. I gave it all to a local shelter for abused children.

I had a brief marriage in my twenties, but it didn't last. It wasn't anything either of us did or didn't do, we just didn't work out. If it makes any difference, we're still friends, in fact, I take care of his dogs when he has to travel. When I have to travel, which is often, he takes care of my dogs, and we water each other's plants. Better friends than spouses. I'm happily single and love it that way. I'm a strong independent woman. I handle my own finances, don't ask anyone for anything, and am self-reliant. I like it that way. If I feel like taking a walk, I walk, if I feel like going to the gym, I go to the gym. If I feel like cooking, I cook, and since I love to entertain, I invite people in. I don't worry about dating, in fact, I don't have time. I'm not looking for a man to take care of me. I have a lovely home, and just recently, I got new carpeting, and my mother asked me, "why do you want new carpeting, you're single?" What does that have to do with anything? I don't get it.

But then, I don't get my mother. My father was an a--hole, he abused her too, maybe not the same as my sister and I, but verbally (and financially) abusive. She couldn't spend a dime without his approval first, then she had to show him the receipts so he would know where his "hard-earned" money went. She worked, but she never had the guts to buy herself a new pair of shoes without his permission. So, yes, I am a bitch. Just for spite, after he died (before the funeral) I took her shopping for shoes. I told her to buy five pair. She couldn't believe it. Then we hit the underwear department. She never had more than two bras at the same time in her life. So she got underwear and a new dress to wear to the funeral. I almost told her then, but it wasn't the right time. Maybe sometime before she dies, we'll have that discussion, but not right now. I don't think she could handle the truth.

* A lot of women report early sexual abuse. You're not alone, but it might do you good to forgive your father. Not for his sake, (he should have been arrested, sent to jail where he would be someone's bride) but for yours. The act of forgiveness clears your spiritual sinuses. I can't explain it clearly, but I know it frees your soul of bitterness. It sounds like you didn't let your past stop your future. You sound like an intelligent woman who knows where you've been and where you're going. Good luck.

**

Frances, 52, college instructor

I teach world history in an upscale community college in New England, and what gripes me is that the affluent parents insist that their kids get A's when the students don't turn in the work, do the assignments and goof off in class. It's a fairly wealthy bed-and-breakfast area, where the parents have either worked hard all their lives to provide for the children, or they inherited the *old* money. The kids think that they deserve a free ride all the way through school, and some of them even threaten me with "daddy's money" if I don't give them an acceptable grade, which to them, is only an A. I love my job and work hard at doing the best I can do at about one/third the money in any student's purse at any given time. One student in particular got on my nerves. She was the typical blond, beautiful, college student with the perfect body, manicured nails and an attitude that wouldn't quit. She goofed off in class the whole semester and when she turned in the one and only paper of the season, it was obviously plagiarized from the internet. I cannot abide cheating in any form so I confronted her. I failed her on the paper, and the next day, her father was in my office. He was having an adult tantrum, insisted on my resignation, which I laughed at. No wonder the daughter was like him. I guess I had had it that day and told him that his daughter's options were to either withdraw from class while there was still time to salvage her GPA or take an incomplete. He actually pounded his fist on my desk, treating me like an unproductive employee in his large firm.

Perhaps it was the difference in economic scale that bothered me, or perhaps it was the fact that he was throwing his weight around like he was used to people bowing down to kiss his shoes. Maybe it was because I truly loved my job and have enjoyed teaching history for over twenty years, or perhaps it was the fact that his face was turning purple at his own rage. I quietly picked up the phone and called security and had him removed from the building. He apparently called the administration from his cell phone and within minutes the head of the department was in my office. She agreed with my decision to fail the daughter and remove the father. I've never done that before or since, but the girl showed up in class the following day a little more subdued and finished out the semester with a B.

I suppose that we're both considered bitches now, but so what? The way I see it is that parents provide the tuition for the education, but it's up to the student to make the grade. This was a spoiled brat who was used to getting her way.

* Frances demonstrated that it is possible to stand one's ground without losing one's temper. Good job for a professional woman who is in control of her own destiny.

***

Bernadette, 48,

I grew up in a house full of bitches; grandmama at mother's throat; mother at my aunt's throat; mother-in-law down the road; my sisters at each other's throats; husbands and sons trapped in the middle. The women went to church, or to the great gospel revival tent that came to town a few times a year. There would be moaning, weeping and general gnashing of teeth as bodies rolled in the aisle. For weeks afterwards, people spoke in 'tongues'. My father called it bitching and grabbed his fishing pole and hid out. On his way down the dirt road, he'd call over his shoulder, "Girl, don't you ever turn out that way."

I'd yell, "Take me with you." A few paces up the dirt road, he'd pull the old truck over, and I'd climb in. We'd go fishing for the day, listening to the sound of the brook, talking, scaring the fish away with our laughter (mimicking the bitchy relatives), and then he'd carry me up the steps at night, asleep in his arms.

Well, guess what, daddy? I am one fine bitch today. Times have changed, women have changed. Blacks don't have to have picnics in the park because they couldn't get a seat in a restaurant. We can (and do) go anywhere we want. We've become an educated lot, teachers, lawyers and movie stars. We are a bitchin' race, daddy. You'd be proud of your little girl, with an MD after her name. Too bad you didn't live long enough to see me graduate at the top of my class, or marry another doctor. Too bad you can't see your beautiful Black grandchildren. One of my grandchildren does modeling for a department store, and you'd be so proud of her. She's adorable, and loves fishing. She'd be your little girl.

I'd love one more time for you to yell down the dirt road at me, "Hey, girl, wanna go fishin'?" Daddy, can you see me? We've come a long way. We live in a nice house, not a shack on the Black side of town. I am proud to be Black, proud to be your daughter, and prouder still of the way we hold ourselves.

* This is a love letter to a deceased father, sounds like Bernadette and her father had some very good times with that fishing pole. I'm sure he can see her now and is very proud of her accomplishments. I'm also very sure that this woman has raised her children to be strong individuals with goals of their own. Neat lady, I'd like to meet her.

***

Andie, short for Andrea, age 66, retired secretary for a large bureaucracy; now does taste tests (sample lady) in a grocery store.
I got tired of trying to impress the young bucks at the office, and the new breed of females there. I call it the Queen Bee Syndrome. The farther up the ladder those women go the farther they get from where they started. We all put our pantyhose on one leg at a time. You'd think that someone like me would have been a valuable find in the government, but no; I got put out to pasture because I couldn't do all the fancy computer stuff. Does that make me any less of a person? No, it does not.

Some of those young women must be the bitches that you want to write about, but I've got a few bitches up my sleeve too. Take my husband now. We've been married close to 45 years, and we know each other pretty well by now, so I don't take no crap off him, and he's doesn't take no crap off me, but every once in a while we both feel the pent up need to have a rip-roaring good old-fashioned fight. That's right, lots of hollering and fussing, then we make up. No hitting. He tried that once and woke up with a frying pan sticking out of his head. But we do make up. That's what we're supposed to do.

He'll say to me, "Andie, isn't it time you got a little bitchy with me so we can make up?" Then I get a little bitchy, complain about this and that, then we make up, and he's as happy as a lark. Truth is, whatever I'd be complaining about was something that I was going to complain about anyway. He just likes to think that the idea is his and I let him have his way, because we're too old and comfortable to change anyway. One of my granddaughters - - now there's a bitch for you. That girl pitched a fit because a dress was the wrong color.

When you have a fit about something, it has to be important; like the roof is leaking on your bed or something like that. But the color of a dress isn't important. Life is important. Loving each other is important, but if you want to call me a bitch because I don't want to argue with her, then fine, so be it; or maybe you'd call me a bitch because I don't agree with something or someone. That's fine with me. Just make sure you get the name right. Andie

* Andie is a tough cookie. When she retired early (she felt that she didn't have a choice), she had to find another source of income. It wasn't beneath her to take a job at the local grocery store passing out samples. She feels that she was born at the wrong time. She didn't go to college, and feels that might have made the difference in her life all along. She raised five children. Her husband was often gone from the home because of his job, but she did a fine job. She feels that she taught her children right from wrong and they all grew up to be capable adults. The bitchiness displayed between her and her husband is more of a game they play, foreplay if you will. Apparently ,they both understand each other and enjoy their marriage, and the intimacies it brings.

***

Pat J., age 5l, assistant director of a transitional housing facility for women and children.

Am I bitch? I don't have to tell you.

Actually, I am a bitch, but I'm confident enough with myself that I don't have to define myself to anyone. I say what I mean when I mean it, don't back-track, apologize when I'm wrong, but don't take any guff from anyone. I was always confident and self-assured. I never had to pretend anything. It's my way or the highway. Bottom line, if somebody doesn't like what I say or do, they can move on.

I can make small talk when I have to, or engage in silly stuff, but what matters is me. Maybe I'm selfish. Actually I don't care what the word is. I know who I am and that's enough for me.

I give bitch lessons.

* Pat agreed that bitchiness is a process of self-determined worth. She is a strong, capable woman and knows exactly where she has been and where she is going in life. No-questions, no-excuses type of person.

***

Jean T. (pseudonym) no age given.
You have the power

I had this dream the other night, and the next day I saw the flyer for "Calling all Bitches" and I knew I had to respond. This isn't about my life, it's about my dream. In my dream everything went wrong, it rained when it was supposed to be sunny. The shoes were too tight, and the money was tighter. My life was falling apart (and in this respect, there may be a similarity) but that's where the reality stopped and the dream took on new meaning. First of all, everything was in vivid color. Reds were redder and blues were bluer. Everything was stunning. In reality, I hate going in crowds, but in my dream, all I had to do was blow a little and a gentle wind came up. It was so pleasant that everyone went outside to enjoy it more, leaving the whole store to me. Then my real-life husband appeared looking like Homer Simpson in a tee shirt, clutching a beer in one hand and the remote in the other hand, and I blew on him. He disappeared. I blew on the old furniture, and it disappeared. I blew on the dust, and it was gone. I blew all over the house, drapes, old chipped dishes, cluttered closets; and like magic, it was gone. I blew on everything except the kids. I was down to the bare walls, and there under one of the old picture dust frames, I saw a lock and key in the wall. I had never seen it before, but then the pictures had been up for ages and all that was left was the darker dust frame. It made sense that I never saw the lock and key before. I remember feeling cautious, like Alice in Wonderland, thinking "should I?" Then I heard a voice. "You have the power," It said. A female voice that seemed ageless.

So I turned the key in the only direction it would go, and in my dream, a new world opened. It was sunny and warm, lively, in living color, with the brights brighter and the colors more colorful. I stepped though a portal of some kind, and found myself on the other side looking at my life. I kept hearing, "You have the power. You have the power." Like a chant, a mantra, it prodded me on.

I walked through a lush green garden on a path that was surrounded by beautiful rock walls. Not the kind of walls to keep one in, but the kind of walls that add beauty and serenity to a setting with lots of open-ness about it. I sat on a stone bench looking at the absolute tranquility of it all, and heard one last time, "You have the power." Then, "Take the time to breathe. There is power in every breath, power in life, power in living."

I woke up immediately, fully awake, not needing coffee to get me going. I worked out for twenty minutes before I hit the shower, then I sat down to make a list of things that needed changing. It started out as a shopping list, get toilet paper, paper towels, change the walls, paint, get new pictures, get a different job, go back to school and finish the degree I started years ago, lose weight, and get rid of the overstuffed dust-mite ridden sofa. None of it was up to my husband. He would have to do his own changing. I felt like a new me, revitalized, energized and ready to face whatever I needed to face to make changes. The chant on the way to work was "I have the power, I have the power. Breathe, breathe." The first thing I did when I got to work was call the University and asked about getting into school. I found out that I only need six more classes to finish, so I registered by phone, and paid for two classes with my VISA card that was on the edge of maxing out. I'll pay it off when I get a different job. I can see it now, the new me is coming, and I already love her.   When I got home from work, after stopping at Home Depot for new paint, I changed into old jeans and started ripping up the living room. I jacked up the stereo and put the kids to work. I can't wait to see what happens.

As for Homer Simpson, I don't know. His choices might be different than mine, but suddenly, without warning, I am a much stronger person.

* Wow, this is one of the most remarkable pieces I received. I wish I knew who sent it. I would send that woman a bitch cup. One dream. What insight. She knew (must have known all along) that she needed to change her surroundings, but she also knew that in order to do that, she had to first change herself. Inside. You can't change the outside until you are comfortable with the inside, and with that inspiring dream, she started to make the changes beginning by working out and getting new paint. She also knew that you can't change anyone else. The amazing message, "You have the power," should be on every billboard in town, and on tee shirts across the world. The power is in all of us, unfortunately, unless we get hit by the cosmic 2x4, we fail to see the things that are important. I love this one. I am truly impressed, and you notice, not once was the bitch word mentioned. I applaud her, and hope she keeps it up.

You have the power - - all of us - - use it wisely.

***

Bitsy Mama, over 60, rancher

You might have guessed from my name that I'm on the small side of life. 4'9" but I've always packed one hell of a wallop when I needed to. Five children, two husbands, six grandchildren and I ran a ranch. I can rope and ride with the best of them, and have never let an ornery horse stand in my way, but there were plenty of times when I had to have a step up to get *on* the horse in the first place.

My first husband was 6'3" and he'd lift me like a sac of potatoes. We had good times and bad times, but he never beat me or raised his voice to me. When he died, I was devastated and couldn't get on with my life for nothing. The kids would come over, and say, "ma, you have to do such and such," but I couldn't breathe for the grief that was consuming me. Later, I met and married my second husband, a widower, and he moved into the ranch-house. Keep in mind, that I really didn't have much experience with bitching because my first husband was so loving, but this man was a different breed. Took about a year to get him trained, but he's all right now. (I shutter to think what his wife must have put up with.) He'd bunk down in the hired-hand house a few times, but now I think that we're on the same track.

* Bitsy Mama validates the saying that 'good things come in small packages.'

***

Mary Ann, 50ish, adoptions expert, counselor

You are speaking to the Bitch Queen! I have a Bitch Woman coffee cup that I use every day. Generally, I'm easy-going and get along great with just about everyone, and I can kiss up when I need to, but most of the time people know exactly where they stand with me. I have never had a problem speaking up for myself or getting my point across. I am a hard worker and the primary breadwinner in my family.

I was widowed at the age of 21. My husband was killed in Viet Nam. I had a baby girl to take care of. That makes you grow up pretty fast. My second husband had a different agenda as a musician. Marriage and children were extreme opposites in his life so we divorced. By that time I had two children. It was my choice to be a single parent. I've done whatever I had to do. I bailed hay and ran a day care center. Finally I went to school and got a degree. Eventually I got a master's degree in social work because that was the only way to succeed in the field I'm in. So I did it even if it meant working grueling hours and going to school part-time for four years.

I've been around enough to know what I want out of life. When you have to be the only one to bring home the bacon, you have to do what you have to do. You can't hem and haw around with your kids' lives.

I think that I've done a pretty good job of raising the kids. They both know how to turn a dollar sideways and they both are making good money now, so I can be proud. I never let my daughter think that just because she was a girl that she had to do whatever 'girls' do. She runs a bar, and does a damn good job of it. My son makes more money than I do. They both are outspoken people, good adults on their own. They both own their own homes and have good jobs. And they're good to me.

I'm tenacious, and will keep up a good fight, but when it's time to back down, I can tell that too, and will be gracious about it. I'd say that I'm pretty well-adjusted, but if someone thinks that little old Mary Ann is going to back down, they've got another thing coming. I don't back down, in fact, in the face of adversity, or a really good challenge, I make it a point to be as articulate as possible, both in writing and in my speech. There usually is no doubt about an issue when I say something. I have a good sense of humor too, and I wouldn't intentionally hurt anyone with my opinion or ideas.

Once in a while you have to rock the boat to stay alive. I wouldn't have it any other way.

Being a bitch should never be harmful to others, not like people who abuse their children or beat their wives; no, it's a matter of strength and courage in the face of adversity, the ability to get something done when it has to get done, and believing in yourself. Sometimes you are the only one to believe in yourself, and that's all right too. It's when you stop believing that you have a problem.

* Mary Ann is a rock in a soft shell. She is compassionate and warm, has been there and done that, is easy-going and enjoys a good belly laugh; but don't cross her. She can hold her own with the best of them. She pointed out that belief in oneself is a primary aspect of life. If you know yourself, your strengths and weaknesses, you are more apt to succeed. This sense of self didn't just happen. She had to find her strength in sorrow. She admits that she could have folded into herself when she was widowed at a very young age, and she could have allowed welfare and widows' benefits to support her, but she went back to school. She knows the value of a good education and has fought hard to get where she's at. I suspect that she will go all the way to a Ph. D. She has attained every goal she's ever had, and it all came down to believing in herself, hard work and a goal-oriented plan. Right now, she's planning on opening a therapeutic horse ranch for troubled and/or disabled children. Trust me: it will happen.

***

Georgia, 50, banker
This year I became a bitch

Don't blame me, chemo did it. This year I passed the 50 year mark, a goal that I didn't dare dream of because a tiny lump in my left breast got my attention about two years ago. Of course, the first thing I did was see a doctor, and numbed by the diagnosis, I became a statistic. The second of ten women. I didn't smoke, didn't drink, ate wisely - - I always had a weight problem, so I had to keep that extra ten pounds off - - didn't have breast cancer in my family. But there it was, a small lump the size of a pea. While I slept, it grew. I had a needle biopsy, all the tests, and sure enough, it was cancer. Tiny, hardly noticeable, cancer. I had a lumpectomy, chemo, everything short of a mastectomy. If it came down to that, I would give up the breast, but the doctor didn't think it was necessary, so we just took out the lump, and a lot of breast tissue. "Thank God we got it early," he said. I went bald, lost my eyebrows, and eyelashes. Friends didn't know what to say to me. Some were sympathetic, others thought it was contagious. Then just as the peach fuzz was growing back, I noticed another lump in the other breast. I remember that day, I was looking at my face in the mirror. Shallow cheeks, sunken eyes, dark circles, a little nest of gray peach fuzz on the top of my head. I immediately called the doctor and said, "take them both off today." I made arrangements to have surgery, this time a total mastectomy, both sides. My husband was supportive all the way, and so were my three children. They said, "do what you have to do, mom."

I used to love my breasts. They were a part of me, I knew I would grieve their loss. I would be flat-chested, but cancer free. They were a small price to pay for life.

So far, knock on wood, I am cancer free, but every morning when I get dressed I look my vacant chest in the mirror, and see the terrible scars. Then I strap on the "bra" - - that cost a small fortune - - and go about my day. There is nothing in life that saps you more than almost losing it. Nothing is harder than facing death square in the face, and say, "come and get me, you bastard. I dare you." I fought back, which means throwing up for days at a time when the chemo got me, getting through the pain, having to face my husband without a shirt on, making love for the first time afterwards, and seeing myself in a bathing suit that was totally appalling. I have a lot of living left to do. Cancer made me stronger, gave me a better appreciation of flowers and the smell of cut grass. I used to be a work-aholic, but never again. I've learned my lesson so I look for rainbows and pennies from heaven.

The insurance company was going to cancel me half way through the procedure, and that's when I turned into a bitch. I had worked all my life, paid premiums etc, then suddenly they called it a pre-existing condition because of the lump in the left breast. Oh no, I wasn't going that route. The cancer in the right breast was a continuation of the cancer in the left breast, it had spread. I had to argue, write letters, get the doctors to write more letters. In the meantime, the medical professionals were turning me over to collection agencies for unpaid amounts in the hundreds of thousands. (Cancer treatment is very expensive.) My credit rating was ruined. My thinking was, "You can take my breasts, you can take my energy, you can have my hair, but don't you dare touch my good credit rating that I worked so hard to build."

In the end, I had to file a lawsuit. As if I had the stamina to go ahead with everything, wear a high powered suit to court, and testify against the insurance company. That's like going up against God; they have ten lawyers for the one piddly little guy you hired - - more expense - - and they have volumes of books on all of the tables. My guy only had three boxes of my medical records and bills. I thought it would never end. At the end of each day, I'd be so weary that I could hardly stand up, but I kept at it. We're nearing the end of the ordeal, and it looks like I'm going to win, but here's the clincher. My doctor has to ensure the insurance company that I'm going to remain cancer free for the rest of my life - - and no one can make that promise. So if it comes back, we'll have to go through this all over again. I don't know what was worse: the cancer or the court battle.

* Bravo, Georgia. A good friend of mine is going through breast cancer now, she's at stage 4, terminal. She eventually had to file bankruptcy, go on public and medical assistance, and fight the same battles that you did. I know court battles are bad enough, cancer at the same time would be tougher than anything I ever went through in my life. You have courage even if you don't have breasts. Your spirit is strong, encouraging, and inspiring for other women. Thank you for your story. I hope you live a long and prosperous life, with good credit and comfortable tee shirts.

***

Beverly, age 33,

Hell, I don't need to know how to release my inner bitch, I need to learn to put her in a cage. This bitch needs to be contained. I often yell, shout and make myself heard, but people still ignore me, saying "there goes that loud mouthed bitch again," and I don't accomplish anything. I have truck-driver's mouth, because I drove a truck for a long time. Also worked for carnivals. You have to be a bitch to get things done when you're a female truck driver. You can't let people steamroll over you. It's *after* I got off the road that I was still a bitch.

* Apparently Beverly needs to learn the fine art of when to fold and when to hold. She says that she's still a bitch and nothing is getting accomplished. Well, Beverly, why do you yell so much and at whom? Is a fifty cent issue worth five dollars of emotion? Exactly *what* are you trying to accomplish? Put your priorities in order, *then* if the situation warrants, resume old habits, but its not necessary to be a bitch all the time. Life is short; use it wisely. All behavior is purposeful and learned. It can be unlearned as well.

***

Sandra, attorney, age 57
Abandon All Hope, Ye Who Enter Here.

That could be the stone tablet on my office door. I love the effect my voice has on an entire room. I love to see people run for cover when I enter a courtroom. They know, aside from my camouflage suit and flak jacket that they're in for a hell of a battle. I generally win, not because I'm a bitch, but because I'm a good attorney and I know the law. I'm fast on my feet and think like a Doberman in a junk yard.

It wasn't always like that. I had to work darn hard to make it through law school. I was a mother, and someone still had to clean the sink and do the dishes. I'd be studying with a law book in one hand and the diaper bag in the other. I went to law school at a time when it wasn't popular for women to do much outside of the home, other than waitress or teacher. You had to have a 'nice' profession, not something like mine. It was all right if you were a nurse, something admirable like that. Women were taught to be mothers first. Home and hearth came ahead of everything. My parents, God love them, tried to talk me out of law school. My friends, lovely brides all, nice-stay-at-home mommies, tried to convince me that I was making a big mistake. My husband thought that I had lost my mind.

No one actually thought that I'd make it, even though they gave me lip service like "you can do it, you can do it," so when I did it, they were surprised.

I lost my share of cases, and learned from each case I lost. I would grill myself on the court transcripts until I knew exactly where I screwed up, and was more determined than ever not to screw up in the future.

Now the law is my lover, my universe. It's not me who's the bitch, it's the law. It's black or white, not gray. The gray cases are the lost cases, the ones that can convince a jury either way. I like the black and white. Firm, dense and thick. I see things in terms of legalities and logic.

I dress the part of bitch too. Black and silver brings out the bitchy, witchy woman in me. I wear expensive suits that last and still manage to look like a female. I wear good makeup and jewelry. I'm into comfortable shoes now, or sometimes I go barefooted, but that makes me more human. Who cares what I have on my feet? It's my head they want, and it's my head they get. When I'm done for the day, I go home and put my feet up and turn off the phone. I don't do business after 6 PM. That's my bottom line. If people want me, they can call my office during the day. If they don't like my terms, they can go elsewhere. At home, I paint. Watercolors, oils, whatever. Or putter in the garden. On weekends, I hike in the Mountains near my home. I have two dogs for company, and that's just fine. They understand me, and I understand them. Come to think of it, they're females. The original bitch concept is a female dog in heat.

* Sandra sounds like an impressive bitch to me. It also sounds as if she knows exactly where she has been and where she is going. She knows what she will tolerate, and what she will delegate. This is a strong woman, sincere and forthright in her comments. She is someone we could all admire and want to know for her honesty.

**

Anna, age 50-ish, administrator
From Martyr to Bitch

Women go around proclaiming "I am not a bitch," perhaps because the word indicates the worst possible female in the world.

According to the dictionary, it's either a dog, or a malicious woman, an evil woman, a woman with a fast and mean tongue. I think that we all grew up with the golden rule drummed into our heads, "Do unto others," etc; and if we were good girls, we didn't question, didn't challenge; we grew up to be good mothers and knew how to can the tomatoes and iron shirts.

Well, those days are long gone. I make strawberry preserves, and that's about it. I have worked outside the home for as long as I can remember, and frankly, I don't remember the last time I ironed *anything*. Many times I don't have time for the niceties in life. I'm in a hurry, rushing to get to my job, rushing to get home. I'm not necessarily rude, but if someone cuts in front of me in the checkout line, I tell them that I was there first. I've learned to speak up for myself.

I used to be the kind of woman who was a doormat for everyone. My kids, my husband. Anyone selling vacuum cleaners door to door. I would listen to strangers on the phone selling lightbulbs while my dinner got cold. I was raised to serve with a smile, be kind in all things, practice charity every day of my life. Do unto others.......

Not anymore. Actually, not for a long time. I don't have time for everyone else. I do the things that have to get done, and don't knock myself out anymore. I think of it as *evolving*.

There are times when I feel a twinge of guilt, not often. It passes quickly, but there are times when I think that I am still doing too much; chairing this committee or task force, writing a proposal myself when I could delegate. Then, I have to stop and take a deep breath, and say, "wait a minute, I haven't seen the inside of a beauty shop for a month, I need to get my nails done, I need a facial, I need a day off...." and I take the day off, go to a movie, stop wrecking myself with the needs of everyone else.

The biggest battle was the battle with breast cancer. I lost a breast, but I won the battle. This was the thing that made me stop and take a good look at myself. I was doing for everyone all my life, cheerfully, with a smile, in the good Christian manner of life. Then I needed time for me, time to heal, time to grieve the loss of my breast. Time off work, time away from the kids and grand-kids, time away from my husband, time to stop dusting the living room. It was hard for me to relinquish that power and authority to others, because they didn't do things the way I wanted them to. There was always a tiny dustball that caught my eye, or a picture that was crooked, or the broom wasn't hung the way it was supposed to be.

It was in the support groups that I learned that I was a control freak. I had to have things *my* way all my life. Even when I said I was doing for others, it was on *my* terms, with a smile on *my* face. When in actuality, I was a martyr, causing myself undue trouble and internal hardship, wanting still to be the good girl. They teach you all kinds of things in a cancer support group; there is closeness, companionship and an understanding of the internal you. You go from passive to assertive; from silent to outspoken; from alone to with others.

Breast cancer doesn't care if you are good or bad. It will take the breast and come back for the other one.

You have to learn to eat right, sleep, rest, stop dead in your tracks in the middle of the day and take a nap. The chemo makes you sick. There is nothing pretty about breast cancer. It consumes your every waking minute.

You don't have time to do for everyone else. You have to take time for yourself. This was the hardest lesson for me. Letting go, letting others, letting God. So if this makes me a bitch, I can't do anything about that. I am constantly on guard. Every minute of my life. I wonder what's left of it. I have taken time to put my house in order, so to speak, but I have stopped giving and doing for everyone else around me.

I had to learn the art of self-ishness. I had to put me first and I didn't know how.

Some of the people closest to me don't understand. I used to make the best bread, "Mom, how come you don't make bread anymore?" (Honey, I stopped baking bread fifteen years ago.... I'm surprised you still remember. I had to work.)

Then I found myself making excuses for the things that I have to turn down. (Sorry, I can't make that conference in Toledo..... then I hunt for a reason...... my cat has diarrhea..... when the truth is that the conference last year was a total bomb and boring. the chairs were hard and material covered was the same old hash.....) Now I say, "Get someone else to attend." No more talking. End of discussion.

I still don't think of myself as a bitch, but I suppose people who don't know me or my history do. They might say, "There goes that bitch again, who does she think she is?" I don't have time for hurt feelings. Life is too short.

* Anna survived breast cancer. After that, all else is secondary. It must have been a tough battle, and if I had a Bitch Cup in my hand right now, I would raise it and say, "Here's to you, Anna."

***

Roberta, 33, firefighter
Super Bitch

Don't call me a bitch because I might be saving your life one day, and you could regret it. I go into hazardous duty all the time, smoke and flames. I can haul a water hose, climb a ladder or get into a burning building as fast and hard as any guy, wearing 80 pounds of gear. You try it. Then call me a bitch.

Actually, the physical demands of the job are easy for me. It's hard to see what's inside the burned out homes or structures. It's real hard for me to try to resuscitate a drowned child, or see a baby that's been battered by it's *mother* or *father.* That makes me absolutely want to hurt the parent, in the worst possible manner. Then I am the soft female, vulnerable, thinking of my own children (two: a boy age 9 and a girl age 7). Yes, I am married, I have an active sex life with my husband, who is also a firefighter. I am not a lesbian. I am not a dyke, I just happen to be physically strong. I am hard and lean.

I have always had a sense of adventure; camping, hiking, running track, anything physical and outdoors, that was me. Tomboy growing up. Yes, I had a date for the prom, but I drove my father's truck because my date didn't have his license yet. The dress got stuck in the door and had grease and oil all over it. I took that piece up and tied it in a knot, no one noticed.

I was a head taller than all the other girls (and boys) in school. I'm almost 6 feet tall in my stocking feet, so I could never get away with the things that 'girls' did. Big girls don't cry, remember. So I didn't cry, never whined, never whimpered about anything. I got on with life early.

I get called a bitch all the time, mostly by my team. We love each other, and when one of them says, "If I get stuck in a building, send in the bitch. She'll get me out." Now *that's* trust.

* Roberta, Super Bitch, Firefighter; now this is one woman I would want on MY team in the event of a fire, or other disaster. She is strong, both physically and mentally. A neat lady.

***

Roady (nickname for the past 25 years)
I only use my real name on legal documents and then with great trepidation. I'm not sure what the statue of limitations is on certain crimes. I get creative when I have to.

I guess you could say I was a child of the 70's. I was into free love, drugs, rock and roll and as much sex as I could get. I had a child early in the 70's but my parents took her away from me. I've had contact over the years, but for all practical purposes, she is their daughter, (although they are getting a little old to be pretending... another story... another time.) They were right, by all standards, I was an unfit mother and didn't deserve my child. I found myself homeless, living out of tent in the middle western states and winter was coming on. I was just about out of money, had no future, had done as much pot as I could in a day's time, so when I was "rescued" by a motorcycle gang, it was as close to heaven as possible. They took me in (and passed me around) then made me one of them. For the next ten years I rode with them (and won't give up my loyalty under any circumstances.) I admit that during that time, I was the toughest bitch this side of hell. I looked and acted the part. Black leather, torn jeans, vest, gun, you-name-it and I wore it. We traveled light so I didn't keep much of my stuff. One night here, another night there. Sometimes we'd spend a month in one city, then the boss said to "ride," and we did. We were loyal to each other.

By the time I was 30 I had so many tattoos on my body that I didn't know where one started and the other ended. The one on my back is really pretty, I have some full color tats that I really love, because there's nothing like a backless dress with a green-eyed tiger looking back at you. I have flowers, animals, dancers - - nothing too tacky, but I also have track marks on my arms. They aren't nearly as pretty as the animals. I hooked up with a body artist for a while, and with him, I learned to do all the heavy drugs, including the stuff you shoot. That was my undoing.

By the time I was 38, I looked 50, with the wrinkles from the sun and wind, the tats on my body like a roadmap of whoever I was with at the time. It was one messed up drug party, on the road all the time, switching partners, being owned, but like they said, "I chose it, I could walk away any time I wanted."

Right. Like you can walk away from the Mafia. You can't. Once they own you, they own you. They might put you up in an apartment once in a while, pay the rent and buy the groceries, but that also means that anyone they want can come over, when they feel like it. You have "roomies" you don't know. No one asks questions of bikers, we honor the code. You're there, you must be all right.

I was owned by several men, but the last one knocked out my teeth. "Who the hell needs this?" I asked. He told me to go, so I did. I walked out the door and didn't look back. By now I was 40, homeless again, scared out of my mind because I always thought they'd come looking for me (they did, but that's another story.) You don't cross them and they'll leave you alone. You don't go to the police for any reason, you don't rat on your brothers and sisters and if someone ends up dead, you keep your mouth shut and ride. What was I supposed to do with my life? I was 40, didn't have any skills and no way to make a living. Who would hire me with no teeth, and a body full of tattoos and no resume? (and track marks). I ended up on welfare, got my teeth fixed and wore long sleeves all the time, summer and winter. I found an entry-level job and worked my way around the insides of a large bureaucracy until I found my own cubicle. Gradually, I started wearing 3/4 length sleeves, handled the looks from the matrons and eventually made my home starting from one small efficiency to a small one bedroom apartment.

I'm still loyal to my friends, but I can't ride with them anymore. I'm straight now, have taken on Hep, (hepatitis - - the deadly kind) something that comes with past needle use - - either dirty needles from the drugs or tattoo needles. Who knows where it came from? I was wild, a bitch, I rode with the meanest bunch, but we're still family. There are others that I know of with Hep too, but we still stick together. I'm just not up for the ride. I've lived fast and hard, but at least when I die, and I probably will if the interferon doesn't work, I'll have insurance. I wasn't much of a mother to my child - - who is now an adult, making her own mistakes, but at least I can leave her a life insurance policy worth the equivalent of a college education.

If I had it to do over I'd never have taken that first hit. If I knew what hard drugs could do, I'd never have done the first joint. My parents were right: I was a F---up from day one. And if anyone asks, there is no glamour and romance in riding with a biker group. You're on the road for four days, your butt hurts. Your legs, back and shoulders ache but you can't stop. You stink but don't get a bath, you sleep on the side of the road in a small tent, and you pee where you squat.

* Roady, your life sounds raw-boned and hard-core. I'm sure you've been there, done that beyond our wildest imaginations. I have absolutely no advice to share with you, because by now, you've heard it all. The best thing you said was in your last paragraph, "If I had it to do over, I'd never have taken that first hit." That is the most profound statement in your piece, and I thank you for it. Good luck, I wish you well.

Bernie, age 42, hairdresser

In my business, I see bitches all the time. Women complain about the smallest detail. A hairdresser is a type of counselor. I see women from all walks of life and it always amazes me that so many women can't decide what to do with their hair, much less their lives. They don't know if they should be blond or reddish-gold. My God, it's their head! They should have an idea of what they want. They come in and say, "Fix it," but then they're not satisfied with what I do. So, they complain to the management. Well, honey, I am the management, and if you don't like the way things got done, go someplace else.

A lot of the women I see tell me about their personal lives, their marriages, their kids in trouble, the husbands not paying support, or the ex-husbands not visiting the kids, whatever. It seems to me that women are still waiting for Prince Charming to come along and rescue them. I make women beautiful on the outside. It's their job to make themselves beautiful on the inside.

I tell women to be strong, take a stand one way or another, don't back down. Know what has to get done and do it. Don't make excuses, don't buy the lies or excuses from other people. If a kid gets himself in trouble, make that child responsible. Don't cover up for others, and that includes husbands and kids.

Get strong on the inside; that's my advice. If you can't be strong, then stay home and shut yourself up in the house. Don't bother going out, or getting beautiful on the outside because it won't help. You'll still be a wimp.

Be the total woman, on the outside *and* the inside. Don't sit in front of the television set all day and except the world to come to you. Get out and exercise, walk, do something that will make you stronger. Take time for yourself. Don't be a floor-mat for everyone in your life.

In this job, I've had to hire and fire other hairdressers. I had one girl who tried walking all over the others, she would call in late, not show up on time, complain about her take, do a bad job then cry about the way she was treated. I had to let her go. I gave her three chances. Then the fourth time she called in late, I told her not to bother coming in at all. It was her choice. And it was my choice to let her go.

When I make a decision, I stick with it. I don't dilly-dally around. I've been married and divorced twice, the first time I was with my husband for ten years, and he bounced me off the wall a few times. I stopped being a battering ram for his inability to be a man, and since then, I have become stronger. I don't complain about life. I take it by the horns and deal with it. Right now. When the second husband didn't pull his share of the household expenses, I kicked him out. It was my house, my electric bill, my furniture, my car he was driving, and my checkbook that he screwed up. I was a fool twice in my life. No more. I make good money and I work hard. My kids each have a summer job and have responsibilities around the house. It has to be that way because we're a team, but I'm the team leader at home too. What I say has to go. I can't depend on anyone but myself, both in business and in my personal life. I've made mistakes, but I learned from them.

Being a bitch is a responsibility that all women should have. Be responsible for yourselves; then others. If people don't like it, that's too bad.

* Bernie pointed out that being a bitch is taking responsibility for your own life. She indicated that she can't wait to be rescued by Prince Charming, or any other male. She has taken life by its ears and made it *her* servant. I agree with Bernie, a good haircut can make all the difference in my attitude. Bernie is saying that women should take responsibility for the outside, *as well as the inside* of their personal environment. This goes back to empowerment and self determination.

This is learned behavior.

This is having the self confidence to say exactly what you want. We've seen this quite a few times. Speak up, ladies. What you have to say might affect only you, as in the color and shape of your hair, but it also might affect the lives of those around you. Verbalizing your opinion does not guarantee that others will listen to you, but it will make you stronger for the effort.

***

Alexis, 34,

When I found out that my live-in boyfriend of three years was seeing someone else, I took all his clothes and threw them out of a three story window. Felt great. Then the street people came and took whatever they wanted, and he was left with a few socks. Whew! I was magnificent. However, there was one minor glitch in the event. I didn't want to pitch the stereo because it would probably hurt someone, so I left it on the landing. But I did toss out the compact discs. They fly like Frisbees, so I was able to send them soaring over parked cars, across the street, down the block and into the night. I felt so much better once I had cleansed my environment, but I noticed that things were slightly different than the way I had envisioned it. In my rage, I threw out *my* CD's and left his on the bookcase where he had moved them the night before. By the time I realized what I had done, it was too late. I was stuck with Clint Black and Patsy Cline while my *Best of the Beatles, Eagles,* Rod Stewart and many others were gone.

Moral of the story: be careful when you throw something, it just might be yours. Too costly to replace. Now when I get really angry, I take a few minutes to blow up two or three balloons, then pop them with a pen. Sometimes I pop helium balloons that you buy in a store, but they don't make as much noise. I need a little explosion to validate my anger.

* From the music you described, it sounds that you were probably too different anyway. Abrupt separations have a way of bringing out the bitch. A sudden disruption is like an aneurysm, it's a little explosion, but it could be deadly. Stick to the balloons.

Rose Stadler, MSW

***

Cari, 37, sales
Life's Hard Lessons

I have four kids and my old man is in jail. What a bummer! I'd say that it was a hard luck story, but it was drugs, plain simple drugs. He was dealing and I was too dumb to see it. We were having a lot of debt problems, both of us were working, but the last pregnancy was too hard on me, what with getting the kids ready for day care - - that cost an arm and a leg as it was - - and everything else. We talked about it, and decided that I would quit my job because the insurance benefits came from his job, and we could afford the delivery. I was busy with the kids, and pregnant with the fourth child, sick as a dog, and constantly tired, so I didn't see what was right under my nose.

When the police busted the door down, they found drugs all over the house. I was amazed. I never suspected a thing. He was hauled off to jail immediately, fired, and bingo, that left me, pregnant with the last child, no hospital benefits and nothing in the cupboard. Suddenly catapulted into poverty, with house payments, car payments and credit card debt stacking up, I didn't have a clue what to do. He said he thought it would be a way out of debt, that as soon as the baby was born, he'd stop dealing. I had to go on welfare, had two of the cars repossessed, and eventually put the house up for sale - - to avoid foreclosure - - and filed for divorce. It was the hardest two years of my life, but I don't want him back. If that was the only way for him to support us, then I don't want it. Or him. Right now I have four kids, they are my responsibility, and my life. They motivate me to keep going, and it's really hard, working every day, getting them off to day care, doing all the chores, getting back on my feet, but I can do it. I'm stronger than I ever thought. I have a new strength. I'm tougher than I thought. I can do this. I feel like the *Little Train That Could.* I'm not sure if bitchiness or a new-found courage added to the new me, but I will never be blind again.

If I had it to do all over again, I would take a much more pro-active stance and know about all the finances. I would watch the debt closer and not buy a new car every year or two, and I certainly wouldn't have gone in over my head for a house just because it had the double garage with the utility rooms by the separate entrance. I live in a small, down-scale house, on the blue-collar side of town and have only one car. My kids wear used clothing, and so do I, but I have learned a lot about me. I can stretch a dollar until it begs for mercy, and I always know exactly how much cash I have on hand and where it came from. I write down every expense, no matter how trivial it might seem (school lunches, field trips, Dairy Queen, etc). Lastly, I don't expect a man to take care of us. I'm not looking for another man in my life right now, maybe later, but right now, I've lost all trust and confidence, and have finally figured out that the only one I can depend on is myself. I've gone back to school, part time, only one class a week right now, but it's a start.

* What a lesson in life! Like so many other women in here, they have been terribly disappointed by men, but Cari also has four children to take care of, be financially responsible for, and be the mainstay in their lives. Her financial burden was due to the ignorance of her husband, who thrust his wife and children into an uncertain future with his actions. I'm sure this wasn't what she was envisioning on her wedding day. But it sounds as if she's toughened up and has gotten on with her life. One day at a time, one foot in front of the other, you can do it. Get that degree, one class at time, and eventually you will be wearing a cap and gown. Hats off to Cari.

***

Elizabeth, age 38, elementary school teacher
Empowerment

Wow, what an amazing opportunity to say what I want to say. You know, if a man is assertive, it's called leadership. If a woman is assertive, she's called a bitch. When a man speaks up for himself, he's right. When a woman speaks up for herself, she's called a bitch.

Rose Stadler, MSW

It took me years to figure this out, and you can't go to a bitch school and learn how to be a bitch. You have to be soft spoken and nice. I'm sick and tired of being nice. All my life I've had to be nice, to say *please*, *thank you* and *may I.* I had to ask permission to go out, to stay out, to spend the night at a friend's house, to drive, do this or that. I had to ask for approval when I went to college, and I had to take the classes that my father wanted me to take. If I wanted any help with the tuition and books, I had to please him every turn in the road. Then later, I *still* found myself having to turn to him and ask his advice and basically, get his permission, for whatever it was I was doing. "Daddy, should I take this job? Daddy, should I marry so and so? Daddy, what kind of car should I drive?"

Then one day, he turned to me and said, "What's the matter with you? At the age of 30 you can't make a decision by yourself. I always though that you were pretty capable, but you generally ask me what I think." I was stunned. He had been waiting for me to make my own decisions all along. With my brothers it was different. He *expected* them to make decisions at an early age and even taught them how by playing ball in the backyard. I guess he raised us differently. He still wanted me to be sweet, but he expected the boys to be boys. He expected them to ruin their pants and wreck the car at least once. I didn't realize that I had been looking for approval where none was needed.

Then I learned the word *empowerment*. It means making your own decisions, taking the consequences and doing for yourself. Mostly, it's a strong word that makes me responsible for myself. Yes, I am responsible for my children, but I am the only one responsible for my happiness.

If it's *my* car, *my* car insurance, *my* car payments, then shouldn't it be *my* choice of car? My husband and I had that discussion. He really wanted me to get a small truck, I wanted a mini-van. I bought the mini-van but we live in a state where both the husband and wife have to sign on the loan agreement, and he was still sort of grumbling, but the payment was being deducted from *my* paycheck, not his. So we got the mini-van. A few weeks later I found a used trailer in the paper for about $300 and got it for his birthday. Now we're both happy. I guess *empowerment* also means compromise. It doesn't mean asking my father *or* my husband for permission. It doesn't mean being nasty to get my way. I don't have to walk on other people to make my way in life, but I don't have to seek approval either. I'm much happier knowing that I am responsible for myself, my happiness, my spirituality, and eventually, my life. I think that other people around me are happier with the new me as well, because now they see me as strong and capable.

* Like a lot of women, Elizabeth was turning to the men in her life to make her decisions for her, starting with her father from early childhood, then moving to her husband. It was a startling revelation when her father finally said, "Elizabeth, can't you make your own decisions?" Perhaps he didn't realize that he was treating her brothers differently than he treated her, but the pattern of seeking daddy's approval was set in motion. When she married, she looked to her husband to make the decisions for her.

Here was an accomplished teacher, a woman who obviously went to college and was capable of graduation, and an eventual career; but who was not capable of making *life* decisions for herself. It wasn't until the incident with the mini-van that she started to make her own decisions. She was a people-pleaser, more specifically, a *daddy* pleaser, and didn't realize until she wrote the submission, that she might be raising her daughter to be a *daddy* pleaser (don't wake daddy, daddy likes your hair in a pony-tail, you're wearing daddy's favorite dress.... etc.). She shuttered at the thought that her daughter would grow up to be a female wimp, and vowed to change her ways.

***

Sam, 46

Originally, I was Samantha, cute little girl with sausage curls. Daddy's girl; the perfect child. Then in school I became Sammy with the tight cheer leading sweater, pom-poms, and the letterman boyfriend. Then I became Samantha again, married and mother of two; little Susie Homemaker. Apron, buns in the oven, Tupperware and white knee-boots.

Now, plain old Sam, on the second husband, lost the cheer-leader whipper-snapper grin. I suspect that I am becoming the menopausal bitch but I have reached a point in my life where I really don't give a damn. I've spent all my time on my kids and husband(s), worked just as hard as they did, paid half the bills and now when I want something, I feel that I have a right to get it. Husband number two will say, "I see you went shopping again." (Yes, bras and panties, a few T-shirts and a pair of jeans.) "We can't afford it." (Sure we can, I pay for it out of my salary.) "No, you charge it, and we're *both* responsible for the charge cards." (Oh, like *you* never charge anything.) "I only charge what's necessary, like tires for the car." (Right, Mr. Perfect...... this is about the point where I remind him of the new BBQ grill we *had* to have, the screen television set and the new set of tools....) Before you know it, we're off and gone on another fight. We always fight about the same things: money, kids and sex. He has his kids, I have mine. We don't have any together, but *his* kids are perfect. Mine are not. Some days it seems like a constant struggle, and I'd just as soon not go home from work at the end of the day. I can't stand fighting any more, so I take the easiest path. Be a bitch right off, and he leaves me alone.

* Sounds like the two of you need a weekend away in a nice motel, where you can lay around the pool, have a drink or two, and have a *discussion* (a real conversation - - with *listening*). Or: you could always go on Dr. Phil and air out the laundry in public. Personally, I think a weekend away would be preferable to TV cameras watching your every move. Work to improve your personal communication skills. There's no doubt about it, men and women are different. He sees the shopping bags. You see the new underwear. Different point of view. If you take a rock and put it in the middle of the room, and have several people around the rock describing it, they will each see the rock differently. It's the same rock, but it has different angles and appearances from different focal points. Each person will describe the rock differently. Finances are the rock in the middle of the marriage.

***

Kelly, 34, bar-back
Bad Ass Bitch

Interesting that I should have seen this flyer when I did. Just last night on the job some guy grabbed my butt, which happens a lot in this line of work. I'm a bar-back, which means that I run to the basement and get more liquor when it's needed. I was hired to be a bartender, because females do a better business than males, and we look good in wet tee shirts. We also get better tips, and I need a decent tip day, every day of the week to make ends meet. (Hey, you do what you gotta do. I got two kids. It's me and them, babe, know what I mean.) So this guy grabs my butt, and I ask him not to do that again. He does it again, and I grabbed his hand in one of my 'moves' (if you grab the thumb, the whole hand follows) and tossed him out of the bar. He called me a bitch. Like: "whatareya, bitch, some kind of licker?" (that's slang for lesbian - - which I'm not.) We get called "bitches" a lot. I don't even know what the word means anymore, but I can tell you this much: the guy is lucky to still have all his teeth. We get propositioned all the time. Just because I work in a bar doesn't mean that I'm a slut. I work here because the pay is good and I have two kids to support.

* I wouldn't mess with Kelly, sounds like she can release her inner bitch on a dime. Where do guys get off thinking that they can play grab-ass any time they want with a woman in a wet tee shirt? I'd say he started it. She finished it. I wouldn't dream of playing the therapist with Kelly and say something like: "why not go back to school and do something else?" She apparently knows exactly what she's doing, and like she said, she needs the money. Who am I to judge? But I would say this much, if you're going to wear wet tee shirts, then you can expect to be grabbed once in a while - - but no, that's like blaming the Central Park Jogger for running in the park. No one has the right to grab your butt without your permission, wet tee shirt or not. But the move, grabbing the thumb: where'd you learn that and would you like to teach it to some of the more complacent women out there? Sounds like Kelly has taken a self-defense class, something I recommend to all women. She is certainly not a victim. Atta girl, Kelly.

***

Anon. ageless
Goddess Bitch

Bitch is one of those amazing words that can be a noun, (Now there's a real bitch for you.), a verb (She's bitching again.) and an adjective (Wow, bitching!) It is also a state of mind, an attitude, a lifestyle. It is also a learned response, a set of behaviors, a fine art and the entire magnitude of things to come in one's life. Bitches are a breed unto themselves. A species of the female. There is the lone bitch, like the lone wolf, who hunts alone, stalks her prey alone and devours the carcass of her defeated alone, taking victory alone. This might be the bitch in the mirror (Mirror, mirror on the wall, who's the fairest of them all....)

Then there are bitches who run in packs. They draw attention to themselves, let everyone know that they are dangerous, have switch fingernails that draw emotional blood, and never get caught being bitchy. They leave few witnesses to their destruction. They see no need to fight a battle twice. Once is enough. It gives them the taste of blood drawn in competition. They put another notch on the lipstick tube and move on to lesser prey.

A bitch never stays in the same place for any length of time. She tires of the battle, having won, she moves on.

A bitch is a strong ally if she's in your corner, but if she's your ex-wife, look out! She wants your soul hung as a kite. She will use your socks as the kite ties, and use your intestines for the string.

Release Your Inner Bitch

A bitch is great if she's your mother, but if she's your teacher and you haven't done your homework, you might as well 'fess up right away because that woman has eyes in the back of her head; her pores are eyes and there is no escape for you. She will track you down like Dianna, the huntress of the night.

A bitch is a marvelous employee, she delivers the goods on time, with no explanations of her success, but woe to you if you cross her on her sales records.

A bitch is a great lover in bed, giving as good as she gets.

A bitch is a hard worker, loyal unto herself. She is the goddess, the mother, the sun and the moon in all of us. She is our mother, our daughter, our daughter-in-law, our cousin and our grandmother. She is the step-mother, foster mother, adoptive mother, she is the womb from which we all came.

She is courageous, strong, mighty and merciful when necessary. She is not a fool. She is good with weapons, using words as arrows and a look as a spear. She has no need for violence, and abhors physical abuse of others. The bitch will endure. The bitch will bleed once a cycle, and will have children and will breed other bitches. This is both a warning to mankind, and a blessing that the cycle will continue, for if not for the bitch within you, life would cease.

* I wish this individual had put her name on this. Judge Judy comes to mind with this one.

***

Rebecca, 41,

I never went to school to take self-confidence lessons. When I was a teenager, I was self-confident and pretty sure of myself, but after I got married (age 19), my self confidence waned badly. I didn't realize it then, but my husband was the possessive controlling type. I had to account for every minute of my day, what time I left for work, where I went on my lunch hour, who I went with. He'd get home from work before me, so he always knew exactly when I got home. Then he started controlling all of the finances. He gave me an *allowance*, because he said that he was better at budgeting the money. If I needed a new dress or shoes, he would *take* me shopping and pay for my purchase with our checkbook. At first I didn't see anything wrong with this, then one day one of my friends asked me how come I never had any money for a birthday party at the office, or a baby shower, or any of the other incidentals that popped up.

I told her that my husband controlled the finances. She looked at me and laughed, and said, "I'll bet he tells you what underwear to wear too." I was so ashamed, it was as if she was looking right through me. He did. Every morning before I got out of the shower, he would lay out my clothes for the day. At first, when they were laid out on the bed (already made) I thought that he was being nice; but he wasn't being nice.

Shortly afterwards, things started nagging at me. I felt like I had a leash around my neck. One morning when he was selecting my skirt, I told him I didn't want to wear that skirt, because it felt tight around my waist. (I had been gaining weight by leaps and pounds.) He insisted that I wear the skirt that didn't fit, and called me a fat bitch.

The words stung. I felt as if he had slapped me. I got dressed, waited for him to leave then called in sick. I took off the clothes and threw them away. I stood looking at myself in the mirror for a long time. I had gained at least 50 pounds since we got married, everything about me had lost its luster. I had lumps and rolls all over the place, in truth, I looked like a lumpy pillow.

How could I have let myself go like that? Sure I had had a baby, but there was no kidding myself. This was not "baby fat". This was eating fat. Then I thought of all the things that he made me eat. He'd serve me, putting food on my plate, telling me what I needed. Just like the finances. Just like all the times I had to account for my whereabouts. Just like him selecting my clothing. He wanted me fat, childlike, dependent, convinced that I was stupid. He was a controller, possessive, jealous of any man who looked at me. Then it hit me like a ton of bricks. *That was it.*

I spent the day going through cupboards and refrigerator shelves. I threw out everything that was fattening. Then I went through my closets. I took out the things that I could still get into and put them aside. I put all my "skinny" clothes at the back of the closet, I would wear them again.

He got home early that day. He had called my office at least three times and knew that I wasn't there. When he saw what I had done, he was furious, and raised his hand to hit me (yes, he had hit me in the past, but I let it go..... he said that he loved me, blah, blah, blah), but this time, I looked at him and said "if you ever do that again, I'm calling the police." He laughed at me and told me I didn't have the guts to pass gas, much less call the police.

In short, it got ugly that night. In retrospect, it was the first time I ever really stood up for myself. I told him I wanted my life back. I wanted my checkbook, my clothes and the right to come and go as I pleased. I wanted to select my own food and clothes.

We lasted about a year after that. I kept trying to grow and he kept trying to stop me. One day, I had prearranged with the after-school program to keep my child a little longer. I had been stashing money aside, writing checks at the grocery store for groceries, then asking if I could get $20 in cash over and above the amount. Then I would take that money and put it in my credit union the next day. Some of the cash got hidden behind air vents and under the drain in the refrigerator. By the time I left, I had over a thousand dollars in savings and about $500 in crinkled twenty-dollar bills.

Nothing else. I didn't go back for the furniture or clothing. I left the toys, dirty laundry, everything.

When I picked up my son, I had our birth certificates, school records, immunization records, medical records and most of the important things that I would need to begin a new life. I didn't know where I was going, and it was scary, driving alone at night. My only thought was that I had to get away, and that meant leaving the city, my house, and my job. We drove about 100 miles, then I stopped and got a motel for the night. In the morning, I called my boss and asked for leave time. (I had about a month accrued so taking time off wasn't a problem.)

Rose Stadler, MSW

I still didn't know where I was going, but I pointed the car west and ended up in the city I'm in now. I don't want my ex to know where we are, so I'm not saying. West of the Mississippi is good enough. No child support or welfare because I don't want to be found. I've legally changed my name.

That was five years ago. I'm back down to a size 9. I am financially secure and independent, and yes, single as the day is long and loving it. I now have a degree in business, and just got accepted to the master's program for my MBA. I have learned to be a bitch, but I started out as a frail, fat, lonely person, afraid of my own shadow. Know what? I like and admire the new me. I heard that he got married again. Pity.

(For $50, I'll send the new wife a list of all the hiding places in the house........)

* Rebecca's story is typical of battered, abused women. They are abused physically, but they are also abused mentally and emotionally. Those are the hardest scars to see, But they are the scars that remain with the battered woman the longest. We can say that Rebecca *should have seen* the intimidation and abuse coming when her husband was selecting her clothing for her, but when something is done *nicely* it hardly seems abusive. Yet, her husband was the controller. He wanted his wife to look fat and frumpy, because she was a possession, not a person. She had to account for her time, exactly how long it took her to drive the distance to and from work; had to account for every dime in her purse, and had to please him sexually when he wanted. She was a slave for him and his ego.

Luckily, she got out. Thousands of women aren't so fortunate. Most women are abused (stalked or killed) by the most immediate male in their relationship. Rebecca had to move and change her name to obtain her freedom, and to this day, she is still looking over her shoulder in case he's following. She doesn't trust the fact that her ex-husband is remarried, but she knows exactly what kind of woman he married - - someone exactly like her (old) self; someone wimpy and passive, someone scared of her own shadow, and someone who hasn't learned the art of standing up for herself. Rebecca has started a new life for herself and her child, and she will never be the same again. She is still fearful and distrusting of men in general, but has learned to stand up for herself. She has also made it perfectly clear that education and financial independence are key elements in female survival.

There were four million reports of domestic violence across the United States in 1998. By these statistics, you'd think that four million women had the courage to report abuse, but that also means that there are probably three times that much who haven't learned the art of empowerment. People are not to hit. Period.

(See back of book for statistics on domestic violence.)

***

Regina, 41

I used to be a well-rounded person, have a good sense of humor and be able to cope on all sorts of levels. Then I got married which included instant step-children, three dogs, a broken-down truck, a pregnant cat and the mother-in-law from hell. It took less than six months for me to realize that I might have made a mistake. It took about three years to work out the bugs, but we did it; and now I am the beautiful, wonderful step-mother who lets the kids go to a concert on a school night. The dogs curl up to *me* now because I slipped them doggy treats from the start, the cat ran off with the first tom that came along and the truck has been traded. I've had bitch moments, but it was a survival mechanism, not the real me. My mother-in-law is *still* a bitch, but that's not my problem. I've had to set limits. No, she cannot come over and rearrange the kitchen, or cook for 'her son' unless she plans to cook for all of us. That includes paying for the groceries, setting the table and cleaning up afterwards - - obviously, she doesn't do that a lot anymore. But there was a time when she was driving me crazy because she was the only one who could cook for her son. She'd come in and take over, telling me that I didn't have enough or too much spice in the sauce;

the gravy was lumpy, the meat should be more tender; if I'd cook something on a lower heat, or if I'd cook on a higher heat, or let it bake longer, or not long enough (etc.) One night, with an audience of the *step*children watching, my husband holding his breath, and the dogs peering out from the hallway, I told her that she could gladly take over the kitchen. Take the laundry room too. The living room, and the fire place, and she could take the vacuum cleaner, the pots and pans and the laundry soap, *because I was leaving*. My voice rose about three octaves, I pushed back a chair, (that fell over in the process) and grabbed my purse.

She has since referred to the day I *knocked* over the chair, but she's left my kitchen alone. Everything is fine now, and I smile sweetly when I offer her another cup of tea.

* Two women cannot occupy the same kitchen without one of them having a fit. It's been known to cause wars. The son/husband could have stepped in when he saw trouble rising, but it might have been wise to let the women settle it in their own way. He might have had good reason to fear mom.

Thank God it was only a test. Regina did well.

***

Fiona, alter-ego, age 37,

Actually, my real name is something else, but I have always referred to myself as Fiona, red-headed temptress. I am a red-headed temptress, but I am also a mother, home-maker, laundress, taxi driver, lost sock finder, cleaner of the potty chair, dog feeder and walker, soul-mate and wife, mother, daughter, daughter-in-law, cook, baker and candlestick maker. The fact that I have a degree in engineering has very little to do with who scrubs the floor in my house. I generally do, and wait until the footprints walk across the house on their own. When the kids (three of them) want something, they come to me, as their father is a *busy attorney*, with briefs to read, proceedings to write, clients to meet and cases to win.

I took my framed, leather-bound degree and hung it up in the laundry room. It makes more sense to have it there rather than in a fancy office someplace. When the plumbing backs up, I take care of it. When the vacuum cleaner eats a sock, I take it apart. When the car breaks down, I handle it. I take care of the bills, the meals, the dog and his buddy from down the street, the hamster and the Gila monster in the glass cage that one of the kids brought home from school for a summer foster home. I am wonderful. I know where the stamps are, know where the lost shoe is, can find the rectal thermometer in the sofa pillows and can estimate the exact moment when a check will hit the bank within milliseconds of a deposit.

Truthfully, I am an unfulfilled bitch. I long for the day when the kids are grown and will no longer need me to fish Hot Wheels from the toilet, or when they have stopped papering the walls with each other. I long for the day when my husband and I can go off by ourselves, without diaper bag, water bottles, moist towelettes, frogs, dead insects in jars and chewable vitamins that look like candy.

Actually, I have had power suits, and jobs that meant something, but the cost of a nanny was too much. The woman ate me out of house and home, stole my jewelry and beat the dog. I tried day care, but I didn't like the idea of strangers taking my place as a mother. As I see it, I was spending twice my salary to make sure that my children were cared for, so I quit the mommy track, and now am on the home track. I do a bit of consulting from the back room, which is the office, play room, computer haven and the last place the hamster was seen alive. It pays fairly well, and as long as no one really knows that I work in my pajamas in the middle of the day, or that I have just unstuck the peanut butter sandwich from the computer screen, I'm all right. However, I am still the unfulfilled bitch. I want to be a seductress, I want to wear fishnet stockings and six inch hooker heels. I want to seduce my husband in a motel where children won't say, "mommy, can I sleep with you?" Every now and then I have to do something to release the inner bitch, and I can't do what I want.

So, when the kids are sleeping, I lie naked in the bathtub, stroke my body, pretend that I have a male harem of sex slaves, and I become Fiona, the red-haired temptress; and I seduce them all, one at a time, or in hordes. Then the phone rings and it's a telemarketer wanting to sell me tickets to the policeman's ball and I'm back to reality, still looking for the hamster and wondering when the Gila monster will escape.

* Every woman needs an escape once in a while. No wonder the romance book market still outsells every other market.

***

Morgan, age 49, therapist

I am the gentle bitch. I don't cuss and swear or make a fool of myself in public. I know what to say, when to say it and exactly how to say it. I teach self-esteem to my clients, and empower them to make decisions in their life. My practice has enhanced me. Or the other way around, I'm still not sure, but it is a circle of self-assuredness.

I wasn't always this way. At one time I was married to an abusive man who continually told me that I was nothing except his wife, had nothing, would be nothing, and couldn't count to ten without his help. I bought it for about five years, then one day, I reared up and rebelled. Who the hell did he think he was? Who was I for believing it?

That was the end of that. I filed for divorce, went back to school and hung out with other welfare moms on campus. It was tough going, and anyone who says food stamps and welfare is a way of life should try it for year. Oh yes, I taped my shoes back together and wore them for another month. For a week I walked around with the safety pin in my glasses.

It wasn't a pretty picture.

But I survived. Got one degree, then another, then another. Got scholarships, funding, grants, bought used books, borrowed books, stood on my weary feet for hours copying books at the library because I couldn't afford to buy them. I took the bus when the car died, and I stole the grocery cart from the store when I needed it. I had yard sales, I collected cans, I sold old blue jeans, I made Christmas presents and I learned to cook noodles five hundred different ways. Finally, I borrowed my cap and gown, and knew that I had arrived.

By this time, I had worked my way off welfare, and had gotten a decent job, and began to pay society back You have to give back to society. When you see a woman and child down and out, you have to help. That means listening, giving a shoulder to lean on, maybe even giving her a box of toilet paper and sanitary supplies for a month. Now I teach other women the fine art of empowerment. Ok, being bitchy. Let's say it. Let's call it what it really is. I teach women how to get what they need in life. If they get what they *need*, the *wants* will follow closely afterwards.

I'm a strong believer in the Erickson and Maslov models of development.

You can't achieve much if you are grubbing for food and shelter. Once that is taken care of, you move on. I know, I've been there. It's the grubbing for food and shelter that makes you tough. It either breaks you or makes you stronger. It's at this base stage of development that you have to make a decision to survive or go under. If you have children, and the food and shelter is a handout that is designed to keep you UNDER the poverty level, then you have to do something else to survive. I've seen women sell their food stamps at this stage. This is the stage where a woman will do whatever she has to do to make sure that her children are safe, unharmed and fed. Some women turn to crime; drugs and prostitution. This isn't an answer at all. This is only a bleak response to a bleak situation.

Other women suddenly develop teeth. They gnaw and chew their way back up. You'd have to be homeless to understand exactly what it feels like to dig through a garbage can behind Pizza Hut........ You'd have to be damn hungry to do that, pick out the biggest pieces of pizza for your child...... Pizza places are better than any other place for handouts because the food doesn't get runny or slime together.

I'm not sure other therapists understand this, but in terms of Erickson, it's the bottom of the rung; it takes you right back to the womb and your entry into the world.

* Like so many others, Morgan has been there and done that; she has experienced the feminization of poverty that millions of women experience. She has eaten out of dumpsters, *forgodsake*, and fed her children the biggest piece of garbage pizza. This is a woman who will do what it takes to protect her children. This is a woman of incredible strength and courage. I defy anyone else to do this, and say it doesn't affect you. I dare you to live on the streets!

As a therapist, I understand exactly what Morgan is saying about the Erickson and Maslov models of personal development. One must have life, in the basic form. Food, clothing, shelter. Only after that has been provided (or obtained by guts and courage) can one move on to the next stage. She is absolutely correct in stating that if you take care of the needs, the wants will follow closely behind. Some needs; like food, water, clothing and shelter; are paramount to survival. Then other needs follow. Her assessment of education and personal choices come *after* the food and shelter. Apparently she never gave up hope, and never gave in to despair. She saw in herself a strength, that she now shares with other women.

The word *empowerment* is a word that she uses often. Women *must* learn to make their own decisions. They can change their minds later, but they must set goals for themselves. If that goal is to get out and find a different job, or to learn a new skill, the goal must be set in writing. Once it is set in writing, it is set in motion. Once it is set in motion, it has become a reality, even in its infancy stage.

***

Marsha, (pseudonym), age 47
Bitch on Wheels

I'm a bitch on wheels, literally. I broke my back in a car accident coming home from the prom when I was senior in high school. I want my dancing legs back, but that won't happen. Actually, I got married in a wheelchair, got pregnant (in bed) and actually have a child (delivered by C-section). I can't feel anything below my waist, so I have to have a different lifestyle. People think of disabled people as asexual, but we're not. We have sex, children and all the other things in life, we just do it differently.

At first, I was grateful to whoever gave me help; and believe me, twenty-four years ago, I needed plenty of help. Opening doors, getting up steps, getting in and out of cars, getting a job!!!! Now that was a tough one. Going to school! It was all very hard.

One of my classes at the university was on the third floor. That was before ADA (Americans with Disabilities Act), so I had to bitch about not being able to get to my class. The building didn't have an elevator and the university wouldn't change the class location, so two very strong men had to haul me up and down, every class. Three flights up and three flights down, twice a week, and don't drop me.

I learned to speak up for myself in the seventies, when women were burning their bras and talking about 'liberation'. My liberation never came, because I didn't get my legs back. My parents remodeled the house, adding a waterbed in my bedroom because I couldn't get in and out of the bed easily. Some of my friends stopped coming around. I guess they weren't friends after all.

I learned to drive with hand brakes, and my dad turned an old VW bus into a 'handi-van'. That was long before all the new equipment came along. I had that bus literally torn apart, had a bench in the back, so I could rest between classes, and I learned to do everything with my arms. I have the world's best biceps. Now I wear racing gloves and have a new three-wheeler that I use on wheelchair races. I work out, on the floor, every day. My arms and hands are extremely strong. Other people need their whole body to do what I can do with my arms and hands.

On the job, I have to be twice as sharp as other people, because people will say that I got the job because I'm in a wheel chair, and they *had to hire the handicapped.* Some of that is true. Some of that isn't. I don't necessarily use my handicapped status to get promotions, but I have to admit that it helps, and yes, I *have* had to speak up when something wasn't done properly. I needed a wheelchair ramp to the parking lot, and I got it. I needed personal parking. I got it. I had to have a handicapped parking spot in front of my house, and I got it.

There are lots of conveniences now, drive-up banking, drive-through junk food, but the thing that bugs me is the post office.

I still have to go in to mail a package, that means getting out of the van, getting the package, getting the door open, (three of them) and waiting in line. I was told that I could call a 1-800 number and have packages picked up at the house, but I get a robot on the other end of the line. I can do the grocery shopping, clothes shopping (some stores put circular clothes racks too close together and my wheel chair gets stuck) - - but I don't bitch about it. I write the manager a letter instead and let them know that I was forced to spend my money elsewhere, and why. Usually, when I go back, things are generally rearranged. Most of the time, if I ask to see a particular item or use a particular dressing room, clerks are most accommodating.

I have to depend on other people to get along in this world, so being bitchy (yelling screaming and having a tantrum) is out, but I have learned to throw my voice across a room when I need to. Living your life from a wheelchair doesn't have to be the worst thing, but not being able to see your goals and dreams; *now that's a bitch.*

I have to get ready for a race, so that means I have to work out and put at least ten miles on the 3-wheeler. Timing is everything. I'm shooting for about 8 minutes a mile, at a steady pace; but I can't keep that up for more than three miles. I'm good for the first mile, then I start to slow down. I have to be able to maintain that throughout the entire race. I won a five-mile race six months ago, with my daughter riding her bike right next to me. It was one hell of a rush.

* Marsha has learned empowerment, self determination, goal setting and courage, and has learned it all from a wheelchair. She doesn't like to have anyone say that she is *in* a wheelchair, but that she is a disabled person who happens to *use* a wheelchair. She will make sure that we are all politically correct when she is finished with us, and she is one person who will stand (or sit) on her own courage and make the rest of us aware of her and her disability. Marsha indicated that she probably would not be this strong if she had never had her accident, and while she wants her dancing legs back, she wouldn't trade places with the walking population. She is assertive and strong.

***

Tina H., 39, Hair stylist
Love is not enough: The enabler.

I grew up thinking that love was the answer to everything, that when I got married, starry-eyed and dreaming, that it was my job to make things right. You make your bed, now lie in it: isn't that the way we were raised? We were good girls, doing the good-girl thing. We married for love, and love would fix whatever was wrong. It was a mistake to believe that. I was married for years to an alcoholic, who was also a drug user. I thought I could/would change him. No, instead, I was a first class enabler, suffocating in denial, anger, rage, guilt, loss of respect, and embarrassment. We'd fight, make up, he'd make promises that he never kept, then I'd get angry when he went out and got drunk all over again. It was a two-step dance. Two steps backward for every one step forward. He was also abusive, and I have a scar on my forehead as a lasting memorial to my gullibility, but I loved him, and being naive, I thought it would make all the difference in the world. I thought he would change, or that he was going through a phase. His phase lasted all the while I knew him, and little by little the marriage ended. It eroded over a period of time and loss of trust.

Then it came apart in one day when I had to escape because my son almost died when he ate one of "daddy's candies." The candy turned out to be morphine pills, not only did it almost kill my son, (age 2 at the time) but that was the end of the line for us. That was the breaking point; it was bad enough that my husband didn't value us enough to stay straight and sober, no, he was an abusive drunk, using whatever drug was handy, and love didn't mean a darn thing. Love was not enough to change him, but it sure opened my eyes. My son was in the state of a coma, unresponsive, but breathing on his own. In the ER, we didn't know what he had ingested, but at the last minute I realized that my husband had used morphine, and told the doctors. They gave my son a shot and he came out of it. That was my breaking point, or more precisely, that's when I changed and became strong. I had left my husband before, but he always found me, with more promises to change, to stop drinking, to stop doing drugs - - he had been in and out of rehab - - I put him there - - but this day, I knew I was going to leave. That was the last straw. That day I learned, absolutely, and without doubt, that we were not as important to him as his drinking and drugging. It wasn't about him anymore. I realized that he was not my world, my children were. I woke up that day. I got strong, and looking back, I can clearly say, that was the moment that I changed from victim/enabler to strong, independent woman. It tore me up, but the thought of burying my child was even more tragic. I wouldn't have been able to live with myself if my son had died.

That's when I got out. It took me months to realize that peace and serenity were mine, that all I had to do was listen to the silence. I didn't know that I had been so traumatized living with him that stress seemed like the only normal course. After the separation, our lives (my children and I) literally depended on my ability to focus on the future and not the past, however, the past still haunts me. I've learned from it, and am working on a book directed at other women. The working title is **The Enabler or Love is Not Enough.** I don't know what will happen, but it's one day at a time for my family.

* Tina is one tough lady. She's been there, done that, the hard way. Like so many women who devoted years to an abusive, alcoholic, drug-using husband, she balanced her life between sanity and insanity. After the divorce, she pulled herself up from the bootstraps, bought herself a 'fixer-upper' house, invested in a hammer, nails and a good screwdriver. She knows which end of the drill to use and isn't afraid to get her hands dirty when it comes to overhauling a house. You will notice that never once was the word "bitch" used, but for Tina, it represents self-confidence, independence, the day when she made a move to save her own life (and her child's), and the willingness to take a good look at her life and move on. She hasn't looked back. Get that woman a bitch cup, she deserves it, and all the good things that life has to offer. She's remarkably strong, resilient and like a weeping willow, she bends in a storm without breaking. I will watch for her book, and love the idea of women empowering women.

She still believes in romance and love, and is writing a romance novel, but you can bet that her protagonist will be a gutsy woman who won't fall in love with a weak man. By the way, she's planning to write that novel on the wrap-around porch that sits on the house she bought, by herself, with her own money and down payment. Way to go!

***

Anon.
B Stands for Bitch
B stands for Bitch as we all know
    a woman of course
    who doesn't go with the flow.

She isn't soft-spoken all of the time
    dares to disagree and speaks her
    own mind.

A true bitch, of course, is the Dragon Queen
    an in-law she is and
    a hideous dream,

Who's on the prowl looking for gossip and dirt
    and spreads her venom to maim and to hurt;

The male of the species struts and
    crows and tells all who'll listen
    of husbandly woes

Rose Stadler, MSW

His wife won't have sex (he's a lousy lover)
    spends all his money
    on food, clothes and the like.

His breath smells of tobacco and stale beer
    like no other
    sometimes he reminds me of his mother.
        Keep 'em barefoot and pregnant he says
        with a sneer. Time for a beer!

        All of you bitches stand up and fight
        what's right is right. The hell with the might!!!

* I have absolutely no idea where this one came from, but it indicates that this woman is fed up with having sex with a beer-drinking husband. There are several things that she can do: she can confront the husband on the beer consumption that is apparently a problem, she can do nothing, or she can close her legs on those nights. I suppose that she could keep a bottle of mouthwash on his side of the bed, but he probably wouldn't use it. This strikes me as a woman who is searching for her own identity and strength. I assume that she has already taken the first step by sending this submission out. Good luck, lady.

***

Polly, 46, strong bitch

    I say that I am a strong bitch. It didn't always used to be this way. For most of my life I've live well over the 250 pounds mark, probably closer to 300 pounds if the truth were ever really known. I didn't plan on getting *that* fat, it happened over the years. With each birth, I'd add 40 pounds and it wouldn't come off. Finally, one day, I was laying on the sofa, watching television, and eating junk - - more like a six pack of Coke and a whole box of Twinkies - - and suddenly it felt like an elephant was sitting on my chest. I couldn't breathe.

I couldn't move. One of the kids called 9-1-1 and the paramedics came; it took four of them to lift me. I was mortified, I didn't have any underwear on because you can't get them that big, and I couldn't raise my legs to get them on anyway. So I was in this huge tent thing, barefooted because you can't get shoes that big, and my feet were black from walking barefooted - - and you can't get in the tub any more, so you have to take a shower when no one is home - - and my fat was rolling and pitching like waves on the ocean, and the firemen were sweating and breathing hard. Hell, I was breathing hard. Later, the doctors in the ER told me that I either had a heart attack or was working up to one, and that I had better take the weight off **RIGHT NOW**. A whole slew of doctors came in to see me, a cardiologist, a gastroentrologist, every possible doctor in the world. They all said the same thing. Lose weight or die. They didn't mince words.

See, I always blamed my husband for walking out on me - - but who would stay? I was fat and ugly. My kids were embarrassed, they didn't want me to attend school functions. My family basically ignored me and didn't invite me to Thanksgiving, making jokes about not having chairs strong enough to hold me or having to roast too many turkeys to feed me. I didn't go shopping for new clothes, but salvaged the Goodwill for ex-extra large stuff that might go over the blubber. I was a wreck, and I continued to eat. I ate and ate and ate, stuffed myself all the time. Any excuse was a good reason to eat.

The ER thing scared me enough to follow the doctor's advice - - have gastric bypass surgery. The words "Morbidly obese" means that you can die from being too fat. Morbid means death. It scared me so much that I made out a will. Not that I had anything much to leave except for the seventeen bags of chips in the cupboard. I had the bypass and in the first two months I lost 67 pounds. In the next three months I lost another 100 pounds, and finally, I was able to see my feet. I learned how to eat properly, how to exercise, work out, take time for myself. In short, I've lost more than half my body weight, I'm down to a size 7 and I'll stay there for the rest of my life.

Rose Stadler, MSW

A few weeks ago I saw a woman in one of those all-you-can-eat places. She looked like I did a few years ago, with terrible wads of ugly fat that rolled down over the top of her shorts that didn't come up to the waist - - if there was a waist, and her blouse was open. She was sitting alone, in the far corner of the restaurant, shoveling the food in like there was no tomorrow. When I saw her make the 6th trip to the trough, I had to say something. Very casually, I approached her table and asked if I could sit down. I know she had heard all the ugly jokes and remarks that strangers make. I know she felt terrible about herself. I know, because I've been in her size 58 dress. I told her my story, told her that I understood why she was eating her way to an early grave, and how lonely it can be. I gave her my phone number and the doctor's business card that I always carry with me. I told her that there is hope, that she doesn't have to look at life from the tong end of a fork. A tear slid down her face, then she put the numbers in her purse and left. She hasn't called me, but she might because I didn't approach her in hostility or as a mean gesture. I honestly wanted her to be strong and beautiful, maybe not right away, but in time. She doesn't have to be so fat that people make rude comments about having to widen the doors to their home to have her over.

I'm not sure how this relates to the bitch theme, except to say that while I was learning about the new me, I also had to unlearn about the old me. I had to part ways with old habits, stop blaming others for my misery, make my own plans and decisions and stick to them. I had to help others along the way, and I do every now and then when the opportunity presents itself. I also lecture for weight loss centers, and tell people that they don't have to settle for their old habits, that they can change. If I could lose about 170 pounds, then they can change anything that they want to change.

* To be honest, I never expected this one to arrive in the mail, but it certainly is worth putting in the book. Weight in excess is a problem pertaining to health matters, but it also has a huge effect on self-esteem. It sounds like Polly had a problem with more than just her eating. When it finally took an emergency to convince her to lose weight or die, she lost the weight. She couldn't do it alone,

and I imagine, she had tried every diet on earth, so when she finally had to resort to surgery, she did. Her courage had to come from inside her, and I don't mean her stomach. It had to be a matter of will power over Twinkies. It's remarkable that she speaks out to other obese people and that she will take the time to talk to them. It's kindness and compassion (and certainly empathy) that give her added strength. I assume, never having met her, that she continues to work out, and continues to look good. Atta' girl, Polly.

***

Debbra, age 43
Letting the bitch out: Flushing Mom

I have a terrible story, being locked in closets as a child, being abandoned by my mother, tossed from one care-taker to another. I was sexually abused, physically abused. Finally I became a princess in my step-father's eyes, and he provided the best care ever. But that didn't always last. My mother would find us, take us, run off again and start the whole process over again. Then I married an abusive man, had a daughter, then got divorced. Then my mother, the Queen of Bitches, took my daughter and wouldn't let me see her. She had convinced the court that I had sexually abused her, I had to fight to get her back, but by that time, it was too late. I had remarried another abusive man, and lost contact with my daughter. By then I had moved, but always on the lookout for my mother. She turned up in the oddest places. We'd go for years with silence between us, then she'd call and find me again. I had gotten too old (and fat) to physically abuse, but her abuse was constant, evil and directed at whoever I was with.

Then I got single, and by this time I had a son by another abusive man. My son's father drowned. I have very poor taste in men, and generally pick a loser. The last few years have been extremely difficult. My weight went down, then up, then down; so did my health. I broke my neck and battled disabilities. This time its fibromyalgia and a whole host of others. I've been in counseling for years with in-home therapy because I can't get out. (I use a walker and a cane, and have a scooter to get around.)

My turning point came when my mother committed suicide. She had checked into a motel/casino and locked herself in her room, then shot herself in the head. It was the day before Mother's Day. Some Mother's Day! When I got her ashes, I didn't know what to do with them, so I flushed them down the toilet. She always wanted to take a cruise... but that was my independence day. She was dead, probably on her way to hell. I grieved, but there was more joy and relief than anything else. I realized that I had always been abused due to her. The men I picked were extensions of her. I never was able to do anything right for her, and eventually, for the men in my life. I was in my 40's when the Liberty Bell rang. Since her death, I have learned to live alone, with my son, but some would say that I am still dependent on others to do everything for me, because I have doctors who come to the house, and I have a care-taker who helps me get dressed and do the grocery shopping. It's very hard being disabled, but its even harder being bi-polar, and MPD (just one diagnosis). I don't really know if this is true or not, but people have told me that at times I act like a total stranger and use different names. Maybe it's true. Maybe not. I don't know. But I know this: I never have to be afraid of my mother again. I've moving to another city, another state, and this time I'm doing it for me. I'm not following my mother (again, with a different school three times a year) or for a husband (to abuse me), but for myself and by myself (and my son.). I'm going to get in the car and drive across the US. I can do it, because there is no one to stop me from living the life I deserve.

* I know Debbra; there's a whole lot of anger there. She is a woman who has suffered severe abuse in early childhood and later in adulthood. The damage that has been done to Debbra is immense. Debbra lost herself in the process, and is just now beginning to locate her soul. She has to be willing and able to let go of the past and let the future shine. One of her shining bitch moments was after her abusive mother committed suicide. Debbra went through all the grief that was possible for an abusive mother, but the final moment

came when the ashes arrived. Not knowing what to do with them, she flushed them. *Flushing Mom*, now that's a book waiting to be written. (How is it possible to be such a hateful mother?) Perhaps after Debbra makes the move on her own, for herself, by herself, she will have proven that she has always been capable and strong. Three cheers for Debbra. She's come a very long way.

***

Serial Bitches, Anonymous

A bitch is the vindictive ex-wife who won't let the father of the children see his kids despite years of child support, then tells the kids that dad isn't paying support. Then she raises the daughter who has a magnificent wedding, calls her dad to let her know about it, then adds, "Please don't come, it might upset mom."

A bitch takes the tags off the Christmas and birthday presents from the father and puts her own name on them so the kids think that daddy doesn't care.

A bitch is the woman who seduces her husband in a slinky red teddy, then serves him with divorce papers the next day.

A bitch is the office manager who has a snide remark for everything and everyone.

A bitch is the catty woman in a sharp Anne Klein suit, whose shoes click the floor with each step, like an executioner.

A bitch is a woman who steals another woman's ideas, takes the credit for something she didn't do, and always seems to be one step ahead of other women when it comes to getting a raise or a promotion.

A bitch is the woman who smiles sweetly while slowly poisoning the office or department against other women.

A bitch is the woman who sidles up to men in a cunning way, who can't stand another woman in the room.

A bitch is the woman who will lie, cheat and steal her way to the top, maybe even brag about it later, adding a lock of hair from each victim to her scrapbook. She likes souvenirs of prey. Speaking of souvenirs, a true bitch is one who refuses to return personal effects to the biological children of her deceased husband merely for spite, or to pull rank on them. It's some kind of revenge that only she knows about, but like a cat with a dead mouse, she will never let those things go that have no meaning to her.

These could be called Serial Bitches.

A bitch never forgets, she can hold a grudge forever, and will bring up the smallest incident at the most inopportune time. She is the one who will tell the new daughter-in-law, at Thanksgiving, in front of 25 people, that the turkey is dry, the mashed potatoes are runny and the gravy is lumpy. She is the one who will point out that the dress you borrowed came back with sweat stains under the arm pits, or the phone was disconnected.

A bitch is the woman who castrates men and demeans other women, smiles sweetly, then lies about it.

A bitch is the shame of all women, she brings a bad reputation to the word woman. She is a slimeball with breasts, a cunning beast with a uterus, and the female version of ASSHOLE. She is unforgettable, to be avoided, nasty and mean. She is the female Tasmanian Devil, the banshee of the human species. Bitches eat their young, devour their spouses like Black Widows and torment everyone in their environment. They die alone.

* There is a difference between a serial bitch and a purely honest bitch. A bitch can be an honest women, yet is capable of bellowing orders and still maintain her integrity. What is described here is a monster. As stated, this particular type of bitch is the shame of all women. These women are callous, cold and uncaring; perhaps not illegal, but lacking moral and ethical values. They are out for number one, and God help the person who gets in their way.

***

Karen S., 50+,
MENOPAUSAL BITCH

A big surprise awaits the unsuspecting woman when she approaches fifty. A seemingly normal, well adjusted and happy female will find herself sliding on an emotional rolling-coaster. Laughing and giggling one minute, at some inane cause and then dashed down to hopeless despair on a crying jag. When asked why she was crying is unable to come up with a logical reason. It is then that the Menopausal Bitch raises her ugly head.

Problems that were at one time easy to cope with, have now become giant hurtles to overcome. If our Menopausal Bitch is married "HE" becomes her focal point and she is sure he is the culprit who has placed all these aggravating problems on her. Screaming, name calling, sulks and tears become her standard armor. This poor, innocent, naive, and unsuspecting male becomes the target.

It's "His Fault" she is falling apart. No amount of cajolery, reproaches or words of love will make our bitch reasonable. At night she is restless with hot flashes that cover her body, off goes the blanket, then it's cold, back on goes the blanket. This is repeated all night long. Now not only is our heroine riding up and down her emotional waves, she is not getting enough sleep, increasing her frustration. Questions arise in her mind about her validity as a desirable woman. (Touch me and I'll break your arm. Don't touch me, and you're dog meat, mister.)

Generally, it is around this time that the children have left or are in the process of leaving and the anguish she feels is only compounded by her emotional instability. Questions plague her, "What will I talk to him about when the kids are gone?" "What will I do with my life?" This may be the time she decides to join the younger generation in dress with short shirts and platform shoes and purple nail polish.

This is the most stressful time of her life. There was a time when she could handle five small children, wipe one child's nose, help another child do their homework, separate two that are pulling each other's hair, with a child on her hip and cooking supper with no trouble at all. Now she shrieks when the phone rings. If she is not knowledgeable about what is happening to her she is likely to think she is losing her mind.

Once the Menopausal Bitch passes this crisis, either through a doctor's intervention with hormones or just time, she quietly slips away unnoticed and leaves the woman wondering why her spouse is so pissed off!

* Ah yes, the menopausal bitch strikes again! Sooner or later, it will happen to all of us, and sooner or later, some unsuspecting male will sidle up and ask a stupid question. "What's for dinner, honey?" and the bitch is throwing pots and pans out the door. If the man is smart, he'll leave flowers on the table, run to the nearest McDonalds for sustenance, and embrace his wife and mother of his children as a good friend who just needs a minor tune-up. This is not a life-threatening event, but it gets more publicity than male menopause or mid-life crisis in other individuals. It's a mature rite of passage that is not to be feared. Menopause is a Croning event that draws down blessings from the four elements: air, earth, fire and water; draws down the power of the universe and *herstory* of all females.

***

Bridget, 46, new to the bitching game.

My husband of 20+ years and I finally had an understanding -- we don't like each other. Apparently we never did, so we've both moved on, and now we're friends. He's my best friend and I am his best friend, and I will dance at his wedding, and he at mine, but as husband and wife, we were a very bad idea. At first, it was one of those things, we got married for all the wrong reasons, had the house and kids, bought new cars, new houses, stayed together for the kids, had fights and made love, but still, it was all wrong. The bottom line is we don't like being married to each other, and finally, once the words were said, it seemed like the calm after the storm. The rest was simply shanking hands and wishing each other the best, and moving on. I'm confident now, not a little whimpy girl or an uncertain child looking at a fork in the road, wondering which one. No, I can make a decision and stick to it, or change my mind, as I see fit. I wasn't always like this, no, I wasn't. I always had to ask him for his opinion, which car should we buy, where should we live, what should I wear to work - - the brown suit or the blue dress? Do you like my hair short or long? Does this make me look fat?

The old me was three years ago. The new me is on-going and growing. I have new wings, I travel, date, roller-skate, dance in slinky dresses and sling-back heels and have colored my hair with wonderful highlights that I wouldn't dare get before. I'm a new me, I like me. But I have to say it took a long time to find me, I was always hidden in the closet or under the laundry. Make way, here I come. I'm going to dance, travel and keep doing what I love to do. Actually, there isn't another man in my life right now, but my ex thinks there is, and that's fine with me. We see each other and the other night he was over for dinner, and honestly, it was nice to see him, but it was also nice to give him a peck on the cheek and send him home. We should have separated years ago instead of prolong the misery that we were both obviously living.

* Bridget, welcome to the world of single women. Sounds like you have already arrived. Not once was the b word mentioned.

***

Marlene, 55, retired from retail sales

Being a bitch can mean different things to different people. When a woman is aggressive about things that go wrong, or about family members, or situations at work, she is being a bitch. When a man is aggressive, he's being powerful or a leader.

As a retired sales person, working with the public for over 25 years, I know that you can't speak your mind. You'd lose your job if you did. When an irate customer comes in to complain about waiting in line too long or not getting a sale item (when they bought the wrong item), nine times out of ten, they will go to the management if you say anything. You have to be discreet. I would have loved to be a bitch, but bit my tongue instead.

On the home front I tried to stick to my guns, but it wasn't easy when my husband sided with our three boys. I finally put my foot down and said, "This is how things are going to be around here...". My husband was a good parent, but he wanted to be more like a buddy. When the kids started treating me badly, I had enough. I had been accused of being a bitch, but too bad. Now I say what's on my mind and stick up for myself. I don't want to hurt anyone's feelings, but I get my point across.

I'm not unreasonable, but sometimes people think I am because they haven't seen the new me. The kids are adults now, and I don't back down. My husband still says that I say stupid things, but I fixed him. Once we had gone to play cards, and he said that I was stupid, so I got up and left in my own car. Went home and enjoyed my own company. He never did it again.

Being a bitch is great. I had to learn how. Sometimes it's hard to be aggressive and still have family and friends who don't hate you. I bought a little card "license to bitch" and carry it for a joke, and every now and then I bring it out and hold it up for everyone to see. Now that I'm retired, there isn't much to bitch about the work place, and the kids are out of the house, so that leaves me and my husband. We have a better understanding now.

There are good bitches and bad bitches. The good ones are friendly and care if they hurt other people's feelings, but the bad ones are opinionated know-it-alls.

* I have had the honor of knowing Marlene all my life because she is my sister. When we were growing up, I would have called her a bitch because she had more guts and courage than me. She was older, so I looked up to her to break the ice with the first tube of lipstick. It was easier being the younger sister, because she paved the way for boyfriends, curfew, clothing, dress codes and how to 'manage' the parents without punishment. Thanks, Mar.

***

Pauline, 36, airline ticket counter

"Do unto others before they do unto me," is my motto - - in my personal life only. At work, I am the picture of sainthood or the airline would get sued and I'd be fired. First, I can't afford to lose my job because it's the only income here (2 kids, single, divorced). I was abused as a child, not whipped or beaten with barbed wire or anything like that, it was more like emotional abuse. I know, I know, everyone is claiming to be some kind of victim these days, which excuses all behavior. I was a typical middle daughter, a mistake according to my parents. They always said, "she won't amount to much. Don't expect Pauline to pull her weight. She's a little slow." I suppose I was a little slow because I didn't walk and talk as fast as my sister, a fact that my parents point out to this day. (When my son wasn't walking by a year, my mother said, "well, I don't suppose you can expect much, can you, considering his mother didn't walk until she was 14 months old.") I couldn't read in school, and to this day I am dyslexic and when I get anxious, I see things backwards and upside down. I was probably Attention Deficit Disorder, but we didn't know about things like that when I was growing up. I couldn't read, but I didn't dare say anything because both my sisters excelled in everything they did. Finally, when I was in about 6th grade, someone noticed that I had difficulty.

I can read now, but it was a difficult time getting through high school and two years of college. I had to prove myself over and over. It was embarrassing to have to take the driving test orally, or to take tests in college orally, privately, because I couldn't read them fast enough to pass. I have a pretty good auditory memory, so if someone would have taken the time to read to me, I would have been able to remember. That's history now. Other kids made fun of me all the time because I was overweight, wore glasses, had braces and couldn't read. I never was picked for anything on the playground. I was bullied and beat up at different times, so I suppose that makes me a bully, which doesn't excuse bullying behavior on my part, but I'm always waiting for someone to make fun of me, to joke around at my expense, so I get them first. I know I shouldn't, and I've promised to stop, because now I can read, have contacts and have had the braces taken off a long time ago. But there's something in me that has to get in the first one-liner. I'm the first one in the elevator, and the first one through the door at a store. I'm mean and pushy, and I don't mean to be. I do something, like run my cart over someone's foot in a store, then tell them to move. I don't apologize. I know I should, but it's very hard for me to say, "I'm sorry." So that makes me a bitch, and sometimes I care, but most of the time, I think that they get what's coming to them. I may not say it, but I think it.

* Pauline, you're not a bitch, you're a bully, and there is a difference. Bitches are wise, responsible and confident. They are not unkind for the sake of putting notches on their lipstick tubes. Wake up, sooner or later it's going to catch up to you on the job and you will get in trouble for being insulting. You can't wear a mask all the time. I'll bet your co-workers already know that you are the first one in line for the coffee and donuts, and the first one out the door at quitting time. They already know, and if customers at the ticket line haven't noticed yet, they soon will. You'll forget that you're at work, and it will slip out, something small, but demeaning and insulting to others and you might find yourself looking for a new job. Stop blaming others. Grow up.

So you're dyslexic? Big deal. So is Cher, Whoopie Goldberg, Tom Cruise and a whole gaggle of other successful people. So you got bullied on the playground? So what? You can't take that to the grave with you. It's time to forgive the bullies and stop being a bully yourself. Move up and on.

Go out of your way to be nice to three different people every day. Open a door for a stranger, put a quarter in a parking meter, pick up a stray piece of garbage on the street. No one has to see you being nice, but I guarantee that after a week or two of secret good things, you will start doing them in public. It will become second nature for you and at the end of a month, you'll wonder why you were such a bully in the first place. Or go on Dr. Phil. The choice is yours.

***

Jennifer, age 37, waitress

I am a bitch only when necessary. Tips depend on being nice, so I don't dare be a bitch at work, in fact, I am the sweetest person on the face of the earth. A lot of people think waitresses are airheads, but that's not really true. We work hard, we're on our feet all day, and we can't walk off when we feel like it. We have to take a lot of crap from customers, but I still bite my tongue and be nice. I have to say, "I'm sorry sir, I'll take care of that right away," but in my mind, I am thinking "I hope the SOB chokes on his BLT." At home, it's another story. My husband thinks that because I wait on people all day, I should jump up and serve him. Wrong. He can get his own water or salt. Otherwise we have a pretty good relationship, except when finances are concerned. He thinks that I should automatically put all of my money in the family kitty. Wrong. I keep the tips. That's *my* money; it buys new shower curtains, takes the kids out to dinner, and bought Christmas and birthday presents. Sometimes I even get new shoes. My money, my tips. My sore feet. I suppose that qualifies me as a bitch, but I don't really care. I work hard, I earn the tips and I get to keep what's mine.

* Jennifer obviously has put her sore feet down on a sore issue of tips. She earned them, she should be allowed to keep them. I know for a fact that I would make a lousy waitress, and admire the work they do. I would probably get fired after the first day for throwing the soup on a customer's lap. Waitresses are unsung heroines who make the world go around, they *do* work hard and should be applauded for their efforts. For every business man who's gone out to lunch with the boys, for every deal that's closed in a restaurant, there's a waitress with a full pot of coffee and more water. She's the one who clears the table and cleans up the messes that small children make. She's the one who gets the orders right and makes sure that everyone is happy. I'm a tipper in restaurants, and I hope that others appreciate the hard work, effort and contribution that waitresses make to society.

Rose Stadler, MSW

***

What do you call a woman with PMS and ESP?

A bitch who knows everything.

***

Shawna, age 37, profession unk.
Being a bitch has many meanings. First off, I could be a bitch because I'm outspoken and call a spade a shovel. I say what's on my mind, and have gotten in trouble for talking before I think things through. I've corrected that, wait a few minutes, then blast forth. I don't know why women have to take garbage, stuff it, sit on it, let it stew and then get ulcers and migraines just because they haven't got the courage to stand up and speak for themselves. A lot of my friends say, "you ask for it - - ticket refund, bad meal in a restaurant, exchange a purse because the strap broke, etc - - I'm afraid to." That's BS. Why should we be afraid to talk?

I suppose in retrospect, my mother was afraid to speak up to my father. He was always putting her down, saying stupid things, and he hit her a lot. I think the last time he hit her was when I was about 14 years old. I took my brother's baseball bat out of the hall closet and took after my dad, saying that I would kill him if he ever hit my mother again. I don't think that he did after that, at least not that I ever saw. I left home when I was 17 years old, and wouldn't you know it..... the guy I hooked up tried it on me. Once. I fought back, and left the same day. No thank you. If I'm going to get hurt, I can do that myself. Don't need a guy to break my nose or put a new crease in my cheeks.

I've seen men verbally abuse women all the time, and by the same token, I've seen women stand by like mutes, not saying a word. Not speaking up for themselves. Once a man that I worked with started groping one of the new girls. She was about 19 years old, pretty and very naive. She didn't do anything, which sent two messages.

One: It was all right to grope, and two: she would welcome further groping. Neither of the messages was right, but she was powerless to do anything about it. (Later, I found out that she had been sexually abused as a child, so it was probably her thing to just stand there...) I waited until the guy was alone in his office and I started to grope him. I had my hands all over him; feeling him get hard, then I started laughing. "How do you like that? You bastard." Then I sat him down and told him exactly what I thought of him groping the new girl. He never did it again, and I notice that he avoids me when I happen to see him walking in the hallway. Once he did a U-turn in the middle of the office when he saw me. I laughed again. I laugh every time I think of him.

I've moved on from that job, and so has the girl he was groping. I've heard that he's still groping females, and one of the these days, a woman will slap a lawsuit on him so fast that it will make his head spin.

I've had some very fine bitch moments, but that one stands out in my mind. I have never taken a back seat to anyone or anything. I am not afraid to try something new and I have taken jobs to prove a point. One other thing: I am five foot four, weigh 110 pounds and have a very fine body. I work at it, otherwise, I suspect that I'd be inclined to be fat. Fat females run in my family, and I don't want to drop dead of a heart attack at the age of 40. I keep myself fit for myself, not to attract the attention of a male in heat, but for me. I feel better when I work out. I am not a lesbian, and I generally like men. But I will never be a victim to a man.

* Shawna said what I've been saying all along. Bitches don't get abused. They are not victims. They have learned to speak up for themselves. Obviously Shawna is in the category of SuperBitch, in cape and tights, crusader of the under-female, zipping through the night, slaying gropers. She could give lessons on assertion.

If we had a Bitch of the Month club, she would get her own parking spot in front of the door. This is a woman who will never have extra service charges on her bank statement. Get this woman a bitch cup!

Rose Stadler, MSW

***

BITCH: **B**lack, **I**ntelligent, **T**alented, and **C**harming.

***

April, 25, adoptee

I was adopted when I was three months old. I love my adoptive family and wouldn't do anything to jeopardize my relationship with them at all, but I resent not being told that I was adopted. I feel that I have a right to know about my biological parents. When I was about 13 years old, I started acting out - - staying out late, skipping school, running with a wild gang - - and my father let it slip that he didn't know where it came from. He said something like, "I wish we knew more about you," then he shut up. He was probably frustrated at the time because I was such a handful. We had counseling and my parents always went in first, then I went in and we'd hash out the week, what happened and who did what to whom. It wasn't until after I turned 18 that my parents sat me down for a heart-to-heart chat. That's when I found out that I was adopted. I was stunned, but it made sense. It explained why I didn't look like my brothers and sister. My eyes are very dark brown and I have sort of olive skin, more Mediterranean, but I learned that my biological father is biracial and my biological mother is white. My parents said that they never met her and didn't know anything about my biological parents. I wanted to find them, at least look for them and find out why they didn't want me. That was one time I went on a real bitching spree. It lasted until I was about 20, then I calmed down. I wanted to know why they didn't tell me, or what other secrets they were keeping. I made life pretty hard on my parents then and accused them of all sorts of things. I've since apologized for being such a bitch.

Later my mother showed me paperwork, but it didn't really tell me much of what I wanted to know so I contacted an adoption agency and found out where to start looking. I don't know why I want to know, but I do. Since then, I've discovered that my mother was very young, and that probably explains a lot, but I'd like to know anyway. I mean, why do I like certain things and hate other things. Now that I'm married and have a child, it's more important than ever to know about things like diabetes, arthritis, cancer, etc. Every time I go to the doctor, they ask questions like "Are your parents still alive? How's their health? Do they have cataracts or glaucoma?" I always have to say, "I don't know. I'm adopted." It feels like I'm missing half of myself. I don't think I'm explaining it right, but it feels like there's a hole in my history. I'd like to find out before I have another child because my daughter seems to really like building things, so maybe there's an architect in her background. I'm not really a bitch, but I do get depressed and cry for long periods of time and wonder what kind of heredity I have. My daughter is the love of my life, and so are the parents who raised me. They are grandma and grandpa, and I absolutely adore them. But I'd like to know more without hurting their feelings.

* April, yes, there is part of you missing. You need to connect the dots and have every right to do so. You have a right to know medical history, race, ethnicity, age of the parents at the time of your birth and what they liked to do for hobbies or what they excelled in. I've done adoptions as part of my social work career, and know how important Non-Identifying information is. That's what you need to get your hands on. The adoptions workers (today) are very vigilant about filling that out but I don't know what the rules and regulations were 25 years ago. You might start by asking to see the adoption papers and your birth certificate. Go back to the county and look up the records of all baby girls born on your birthday. If that's not possible, ask your parents if there was a private attorney involved (or was it a state adoption?) and start looking there. There is also an organization called SEARCH where you can register your name, date of birth and other information about yourself. Perhaps your biological parents are also looking for you, and if they are, they would have been directed to the same organization. They have an excellent cross-reference data bank and do most of the work for you. There are other agencies available to you as well. Hit the internet and start by doing a basic search for agencies that may or

may not have participated in adoptions 25 years ago. It sounds like you would be looking in the late 70's or early 80's. Those were strange times. Interracial relationships were just getting off the ground, and if your biological mother was young, there may have been extenuating circumstances for placing you for adoption. I've always regarded it as a very brave thing to do, so when and if you do happen to cross paths with your biological mother or father, be kind and understanding. It's also possible that your biological father didn't know you existed, so a little tact (if you find him) would go a long way. Put yourself in their shoes, but always love and cherish the parents who raised you. Obviously they loved you enough to want you and protect you until you were of the age of majority. Good luck.

***

BITCH: Big, **I**nteresting, **T**riumphant, **C**reative, **H**urricane

***

BITCH: **B**abe with **I**ndividual **T**raits of **C**harm and **H**onesty

***

BITCH: **B**old, **I**nexhaustible, **T**op banana, **C**ustom-built **H**oney

***

BITCH: **B**abe who gives the **I**llusion of a '**T**omacina' **C**at on a **H**arley.

***

Kim, age 41, Japanese-American descent, real estate broker
Tsunami

In my family we did not use the word 'bitch' but with three generations of women living under the same roof, certain considerations were given. We lived the traditional lifestyle, for the most part, bowing respectfully to one another and always treating our parents and grandparents with the utmost veneration and admiration due each member of the family. We were silent children, smiling instead of laughing out loud. We walked single file or held hands, subdued children. When I was about seven years old, I overhead a conversation between my father and my mother. They were quietly referring to my elderly aunt as *"tsunami"*. I was surprised.

She didn't look like a giant tidal wave or earthquake, or something that caused terrible destruction where ever it occurred on earth, so my confusion was doubled when I asked her what my father meant. He was embarrassed later at dinner when she confronted him, over turning the soup and hitting the flat of her hand on the table. My grandfather laughed quietly in his rice bowl, careful not to draw attention to himself, and my father sat red-faced with my mother. They both bowed their heads and ate in silence.

Later, I learned why they were so embarrassed. I should have kept my childish mouth shut, but I had been caught eavesdropping in a private conversation. Later the word was "Americanized" to bitch, but my relatives would rather endure physical pain than to utter it.

Now, I am in large development real estate, and I frequently hear the word directed at me. I am a self motivator, have a degree in marketing, and am now using it to make huge sums of money. I am happily married and have two children, so I am a little concerned that the word is made in reference to me. Mostly it is made by fully Caucasian men, and some unhappy customers who might not qualify for a very expensive piece of property. My daughter called me a bitch last year when I would not let her 'be herself' as she said, but she was 14 years old, and a parent has a deep responsibility to children who are not capable of making their own decisions. I felt bad that she called me such a terrible name, then I thought of my auntie. *Tsunami*. Perhaps it runs in the family, and my daughter has more of her blood in her than she knows. This will make it hard for her later, to be disagreeable and unbalanced in life, but she will eventually learn.

For me, the old ways linger in my heart and mind long after the relatives have died. Maybe I am also a tsunami, because I get things done, but I am always respectful to others.

* Kim pointed out that there is power in silence. She also indicated that personal responsibility should always include respect of others.

***

Sharon M. 35, Administrative Secretary

Seven years ago I got out of an abusive relationship. That made me strong, and when I heard that this book was that bitches don't get abused, I knew I had to say something. My relationship began like so many others, at first my boyfriend was controlling, which I misunderstood to be love. He watched my every move, even when I went to the bathroom. At first I thought it was strange, and people warned me. But I didn't listen. I argued in his defense. "He just loves me," I'd say. Then he shoved me a few times, then he hit me, and gave me a black eye a week after the wedding - - yes, I married him despite the numerous red flags. "If he hits you before you get married, it will get worse," people said. I didn't listen, and even made excuses for him. It got worse. By the time I was pregnant, he was hitting me almost every week; nothing was ever good enough for him, and he would always say, "look what you made me do." Then he'd make me apologize for whatever it was I did wrong, and we'd end up in bed. He'd say, "Now apologize like a good girl and I'll forgive you. If you didn't do such and such, I wouldn't have to hit you." Our first child was born, and within three years, our second child was born. When he started to abuse the kids, I left. That was that. He went to work and I packed three or four suitcases, took the car and split. He wanted to get back together, but I wouldn't. It was one thing to hit me, knock me around for whatever offense he made up, it was another matter to hit the kids. I've had to get a restraining order on him and he stalked me (and the kids) for a while, but now when I see his car, I call the police. He's been put in jail a few times, broke probation and keeps stalking me, but now I carry a gun. I haven't seem him in a while, I heard that he has another girlfriend. I still have a lot of issues to deal with, and still see a therapist for the abuse that I think is coming every time I blink, but I'm getting better. I wasn't a bitch when I should have been, but this book is right on, bitches don't get abused. If I can help other women, I will.

I'm in a good relationship now and my husband wouldn't think of abusing me or the children, but there are times when I flinch if we have an argument. All my husband has to do is raise his voice, and I hide in the bathroom. It's like a ghost that's still there no matter how much holy water I sprinkle. I'm terrified of being abused again, but I know this, if there is ever a next time, the man doesn't stand a chance. I've taken self defense classes. Next time, if there is a next time, I would fight any way possible. I would gouge the eyes, do whatever I had to do, but I wouldn't take it again. And to any woman in an abusive relationship, I say, get out no matter how. Just go. You can begin again, you don't need any of the furniture, you can get new dishes. You can do what you have to do, but leave, and if you have to fight back, then fight dirty.

* When I interviewed Sharon, she had all the same PTSD displays that a woman can have. Post traumatic stress disorder isn't just for vets, abused women and children have it too. She's seen a counselor on a regular basis, but still flinches if you simply remove a piece of lint from her shoulder. She reacts with fear if the volume goes up a notch, and has not learned freedom from abuse. The man who abused her has been gone from her life for seven years, but she still sees him around every corner. They've been separated longer than they were married, but the abuse lingers. She was literally tortured for periods of time when her husband locked the bathroom door and wouldn't allow her to use the toilet, or he put a pad lock on the refrigerator to make sure she stayed the same weight. He counted her sit-ups, made her run three miles a day to stay fit, and if she didn't run before he got home from work, he would run with her, then he'd make her run five miles - - even when she was pregnant with the second child. If she ate an extra piece of toast, he tacked on twenty more sit-ups and another mile. Once he beat her because her period was late. He wanted to make sure she wasn't pregnant. Once he woke her up in the middle of the night because she left the newspaper on the coffee table, he only punched her that time.

If any of this sounds familiar, get out of an abusive relationship. If your man is controlling: i.e., has to know where you are every minute of the day, gives you a cell phone and makes you call in when you're out, goes to the beauty parlor with you to make sure you get the right hair-do, picks out your clothing, and checks the mileage on your car when you go to the store, you might be in Sharon's shoes. If you are, get out. Don't tolerate abuse in any form: verbal abuse, physical abuse or controlling behavior. Abuse isn't love, and bitches don't get abused. Sharon said that she needs to learn more bitchy behavior, but doesn't want number two husband to suffer for the sins of number one husband.

***

Connie, 53, restaurant owner

Right now I'm a scared bitch because last week I was diagnosed with the beginning of breast cancer. The doctor recommended an immediate lumpectomy but my daughter's wedding is Saturday, so I've had to put it off. I have flowers, photographers, the church, gowns, hair styles, cards, RSVPs, the dinner, and all rest to think about. Now I wonder if this will be the last time I get to look drop-dead gorgeous in my satin designer dress that I had made especially for the wedding. With everything going on, I haven't told my husband or the children, especially not my daughter: she'd go ballistic and cancel the wedding. She's a nervous wreck the way it is. After the wedding will be soon enough to tell the people that I have to tell. But I'm afraid. I know that the wedding photographs have to be special, so I'm getting my hair and make-up professionally done, get my teeth whitened, and smile like I've never smiled before. All will be well. I will dance, toast the couple, and everything will be perfect, then I will collapse. I'm too young to be thinking of dying, but behind this happy face, the mother-of-the-bride face, is a terrified little girl. It's a small lump, and the doctor assured me that I will be fine, but all I can see are scars and special bras in my future. And chemo, turbans and hats to hide my bald head. I'm afraid, but because I have good bitch training, I know that I will be able to ask all the right questions, and get the right answers. This may be the biggest test of my life.

* Connie, you have the courage that you will need to face all the things that are in your path right now. I've talked to a lot of women who either have had breast cancer or - - and this one is tough - - who didn't beat it, one because she was afraid to undress in front of a man, and another who let a small lump grow to the size of an orange through denial. Be brave, and know that there are millions of women out there, like you, who thought it would never happen to them. Women, get those annual mammograms and do the self check monthly, and if you find a lump, no matter how small - - even if doesn't hurt - - and most cancer lumps don't hurt - - get yourself to a doctor. TODAY. Don't wait until a little lump becomes a large lump. You will be in my prayers.

***

Joy M., age 61, mother, grandmother, great-grandmother, cashier in a coffee shop, poet
Bitch Ball

In my college days, I was a SOTA (Slightly Older Than Average) student. I facilitated a group for women. One group consisted primarily of student-mothers, formed as a support group to discuss ways of avoiding stress, attending to household needs while at the same time creating good study habits while raising a family. In this group I discovered how bitchy women can be.

Single mothers helping other single mothers was great at giving all kinds of tips for college survival with children. Still these mothers acted in an unfriendly manner if an eligible male stumbled into our group. These women showed claws and cattiness.

One session gave me an insight of how sarcastic women can be. As I listened to angry women bouncing insults off each other, my head visualized a beach ball bouncing back and forth. Wham. Bam. I could see the motion of the ball. The motion appeared as a string of light that tied each member to the group.

Today, 27 years later, the light image sticks in my head. I do not belong to any self-help group due to fear and distrust of sisterhood and a union of women. I don't need the negative communications in any circumstance.

However, one of my daughters works in a factory without air conditioning. The heat affects the female employees and tempers flare. A few will mutter and bitch, suddenly with one bitching remark, loud verbal outbursts are heard. The verbal abuse explodes as the women continue their work. My daughter indicated that the heat and the pressure of packing and checking each part of a weed-puller is boring and tempers fuse sparks quickly. My other daughter indicated that the remarks in a more professional setting are more coy and subtle, while male remarks are snide until the female confronts the males for an explanation, thereby earning the 'bitch' title among males. The ball still bounces, but the way it is caught and sent back varies from non-bitch, to bitch, to queen bitch and back again, still tying a web of frustration around women.

* I have known Joy for about 26 years, and she doesn't have a mean or jealous bone in her body. She could no more be a bitch than a rabbit can be a wolf. Joy is a loving woman, giving to those around her, often at the expense of herself. She is the kind of woman who always remembers birthdays, holidays and anniversaries.

***

Beth Lavryk-Alexander, age 33, mother, talented artist, cover design for this book
Wolf Bitch

I looked up the word, 'bitch' in the **Women's Encyclopedia of Myths and Secrets**, by Barbara G. Walker and was amazed that I found the following: (p. 109)

"This became a naughty word in Christian Europe because it was one of the most sacred titles of the Goddess, Artemis-Diana, leader of the Seythian *alani* or 'hunting dogs.' The Bitch-goddess of antiquity was known in all Indo-European cultures, beginning with the Great Bitch Sarama who led the Vedlic dogs of death. The Old English word for a hunting dog, *bawd,* also became a naughty word because it applied to the divine Huntress's promiscuous priestesses as well as her dogs. (Potter & Sargent)

Harlots and 'bitches' were identified in the ancient Roman cult of the Goddess Lupa, the Wolf Bitch, whose priestesses the *lupae* gave their name to prostitutes in general (Murstein). Earthy representatives of the Wolf Bitch ruled the Roman town of Ira Flavia in Spain, as a queen or series of queens names Lupa. (Hartley).

In Christian terms, 'son of bitch' was considered insulting not because it meant a dog, but because it meant a devil - - that is, a spiritual son of the pagan Goddess."

For many independent women, if not all, the word "Bitch" as a title should be carried with our heads held high, like a crown. What does it matter that most people who would throw this title at us with spite and hatred, only to find that it is because of our strong desires and drives that it is, indeed, a proper and proud title we bear? All I truly know is that the farther you succeed in life, the more likely this title will come your way.

We are not stupid, thick-headed beasts of burden to be led about by a string in the direction others would gladly choose for us. We are strong-minded, opinionated, smart women who have, in our own ways, decided what path we would walk and where we would follow. This should be a choice made by the woman and no others.

All my life I have always had strong female friends and relatives. None of them have even been offended at being considered a 'bitch', in fact, many considered it a compliment. They decided their own paths, their own ways, and their own time. To this end, I and all of my female friends wear this title proudly where ever it applies.

* Beth refers to the word bitch as a title to be worn proudly. She certainly does, and would never take any garbage off others. She is outspoken, strong and caring. She lives by the rule "harm none," and that includes herself. It is an honor to know Beth, as she is my daughter-in-law. My son chose well. My grandsons will grow up in a home that is filled with light, love and respect in all things.

***

* **Bitch**, **B**ringing **I**n **T**he **CH**anges. Excellent way to approach the word. To Bronwynn, Beth and Anita, the word indicates strength and courage. The same with Mary Ann. They all know something that a lot of women don't know. Chances are, these women will never be abused, or place themselves in a situation where respect is not given to them. They will work hard, and should be rewarded financially. They are courageous and outspoken. They have learned to communicate with precision, stating exactly what their needs are and in Bronwynn's case, bringing about change as she goes. Very fine submission. Note the word *tsunami*. Heavy tropical storm that sweeps up from nowhere and ends with destruction.

***

Beth Lavryk-Alexander again.
Ready, Set , Go
Work, work, work, work, work,
It never stops. It gets so bad sometimes you just start lashing out at anything in sight. Because it's there, you have reason and license to lash. A friend of mine told me that "sometimes you just have to have some cake and let the bills go a little longer." Of course, there's my father's facts of life. You are only a few weeks away from being

homeless. In this day and age, it's all or nothing. You either work hard and get rich or you work hard and just get tired.

I never thought that I would be so low on the totem pole. I suppose my own fears keep me in a lot of places I would rather not be.

Bitchiness: where does it come from? *Life*. By learning to deal with life we learn from those around us, both mother and father. At first unconscious, then we relate it to those closest to our level - - our siblings. You cannot yell at mom or dad without major consequences, so you turn it on (you guessed it....) your siblings. Why? Because there are a minimal amount of repercussions. Later, it's to friends who have a good ear to listen, then to our acquaintances at work Here you'd better be careful whom you choose.

In the end, it is the one you are supposed to love the most. Or because of it. Because no matter what: he should always be there for you. Of course, most of the times they don't understand why they are the target. Men can't figure it out, but other women can.

***

Virginia, the Big 5-0,
Better Late Than Never (not really a bitch, but learning about myself)

Ever since I was a child I had a dream of being an artist. That was the thing I wanted to do more than anything else. I would take a pen and piece of paper and draw at the dinner table when I was three years old. I would rather be alone with an old sketch book than go to a movie. Later, in school, I got in trouble for constantly doodling on my homework and school books. When I was a freshman in high school, one of the teachers recognized a tiny bit of talent and encouraged me. That was all I needed. I drew, painted, volunteered to do the sets for the drama class, did whatever artwork I could. My parents were also encouraging - - to a point. They continually said that it would never pay the rent, that I was wishing down a well. They bragged about my talents, saying "what a wonderful hobby." They would show off my work, enter my paintings in the local county fair contests, and when I won, they would hang the painting on the living room wall with the blue ribbon on the frame.

But when I went to college, I had to 'settle' for something more practical - - because they said that I would need a back-up job, and they were right. So I studied math, economics, and all the things that bored me to death. That was me: bookkeeper, accountant, CPA, MBA and eventually worked my way up to top CEO of a major corporation. My parents were right to insist on something that would pay the rent. It took me through marriage and children. I was the practical one with numbers clicking off in my head.

Then one day when I was looking in the dark recesses of the attic for something for one of the kids, I found my old dried-up art supplies. It got me in my heart, like a dream that had passed me by. I sat down and cried. I was consumed with a combination of guilt, remorse, loss and grief. I had done everything for everyone all my life, and given up a very important part of me. When the kids were little, we did all sorts of crafty things at the kitchen table, but by the time they were in high school, we all had different things to do. I never got the easel set up in the spare bedroom when the first one moved out. I never set up a studio like I wanted to. It was a dream in the back of my head, something to do when I was old and gray.

For my 50th birthday present, I bought myself all the art supplies that I thought I would need. I cleaned out the "storage/pantry" room off the kitchen and had sun lights put in, then finally set up the new easel. My husband and children were surprised and honestly thought that I'd be turning out some paint-by-number piece just to show them that I could do it. My first work was a little clumsy but I got the hang of it. I don't know why I let art slip away from me but now that I've got it back, I intend to keep it. Now I know the value of following a dream. I gave it up once, I will never give it up again. My husband can generally find me in my studio, with different colored fingers and a paint smudge on my nose, wearing one of his old shirts, smiling happily at my work. I have small grandchildren now, and have also set up small easels with large pieces of paper. I hope to share the vitality of art with my little people.

Release Your Inner Bitch

I don't think that this qualifies as bitchiness, more like finding myself in my old box of supplies. I had forgotten the joy art brought me.

* Virginia, as an author, I know exactly how you feel. When you put a dream on hold, you lose a part of yourself. I can understand the need to have a practical job, but when you give up a living, breathing part of yourself, the rest seems to be lacking something vital, like air or water. Giving up a dream is like sleepwalking past your goal. However, your parents had a point, you needed to have a back-up to get you through life and would urge everyone to have at least three different options for paying the rent, never just one. The more versatile a person is, the more doors open to him or her. I've always said, "learn more than one skill, five are better, but excel at two or three." Remember Sammy Davis Jr.? At one audition, someone asked him if he could tap-dance. He said "yes," and immediately learned. His book was called, **"Yes, I can."** I've subscribed to the "Yes, I can" theory (within reason) ever since. What you don't know, you can learn.

Good thing that you found your old art supplies. You must have put them aside because they were a life-force part of you, and knew someday, when you were ready, you'd find them. Persistent patience pays off eventually and now you have little ones to teach. Enjoy their company. Good for you. It's never too late to follow your heart/dream/goal/passion. You will be more 'awake' from now on by using the right side of your brain (creative side) as well as the left side (logical). You will be perfectly balanced and the envy of all the rest of us who either can't draw a straight line with a ruler, or can't add. I'm the reason calculators were invented.

***

Jane, age - - undetermined, retired Air Force
HOW DID YOU GET HERE??

"How did you get here," he said between clinched teeth. I had already told him that I was a fully qualified photo interpreter with over four years in the intelligence business. He did not want to accept that I knew what I was doing. He seemed to be locked on the fact that I wore a skirt. I had explained that I ranked high enough in my class to pick my assignment, and I wanted the new B52H's. He was still in shock and muttering as he tore my file cabinets apart. This was my introduction to the dread ORI -- Operational Readiness Inspection, or SAC's answer to professional self-esteem.

I understood his feeling - but I did not like his display of "attitude" in front of my boss -- already shaky about having a WAF (Woman in the Air Force) Officer on the Wing Intelligence Staff. I had been one of the first to report to Wurtsmith AFB as part of the relocation of a SAC B47 Wing in Florida to B52H's in Michigan. We were co-located with an Air Defense Squadron, and my first duties were as supply officer for Intel as we tried to get old buildings rehabbed, and new blockhouses finished and furnished. The Sac inspector was not happy about my choice of colors in the Wing Hq - but the painters had asked what colors I wanted, and the supply people told me not to bother them, so I had picked shades of blue and beige rather than "government green". I felt it was far more energizing for the Air Crews we had to work with, and they liked it. Ah well, I had been warned I would be written up for SOMETHING, and I could live with "paint" on the list.

The Wing Commander had looked a bit stunned when he saw a WAF on his operational staff, but smiled and mumbled something about "great". As I seemed to know my job he rapidly became more confident, and I stayed. The crews had accepted me, as had most of the staff. But this SAC inspector wasn't helping at all! As the ORI progressed, I scored navigation legs, confirmed bomb scores, briefed and trained crews with the radar predictions I had drawn, and in general was a good little Intel Puke. But everything I did was accompanied by the muttering of the SAC inspector who now considered it his mission to replace me with a navigator (male - as were all aircrew in those faraway days). His mantra became "How did you get here?" and as his constant comments got to me, I was terrified I would smart off at the wrong time.

The crews were wonderful - they gave me some of the credit for their high scores, and the Wing was headed for an excellent rating. Everybody was happy - including my boss - which made me happy. Then the Wing Staff gathered for the out briefing - and I did hear about the paint color, and everything else possible to attribute to "having a girl in the Wing". He was a Lt. Col, and I was a 1st Lt. - but the third time he pointed to me and demanded "HOW DID YOU GET HERE!"

I blurted out "I drove - there is only one bus a week " By the time the laughter subsided I was accepted in the Wing, and we all looked forward to more exciting times! I stayed there four-and-a-half years, and survived all the ORIs.

Oh yes, I was the first WAF in an operational job in SAC, and the first female launch officer for Nukes - but those are other stories!

*Jane is one of the strongest women I know. As a Chaplin, she is also very compassionate and seems to understand the human condition more than most. She has been there and done that more times than anyone else I know, yet she finds time for the details in her life, and has a throng of followers from every corner of the globe. One fine lady.

***

Lily, age 35,

Like all young married couples, my husband and I had our share of disagreements, but one time it got into the knock-down-drag-out fight. My husband slapped me. At first I was totally surprised, caught off guard. I looked at him without tears or hysterics and said, very slowly so he would get the message, loud and clear, "If you ever do that again, one of us is leaving in a body bag." He never hit me again. Other than that one moment, I don't think that I've been a bitch, but by standing my ground there was never a second time. We're still married, happily.

* Lily was right to stop any future abuse by addressing it the very first time it happened. Another woman farther on down the book said the second time a man hits you is when you lose your soul.

***

Teresa, age 43, administrative assistant

I'm not quite the bitch I should be. At work people are passing me up right and left. I have a degree and am qualified for higher positions, but my applications seem to get lost, or when I have an interview, it seems that either I'm doing something to negate myself, or they already have someone in mind for the position. My question: how do I get ahead in the work world? I look and act right for every interview, but I can't seem to get past the pre-selected line of bitches in front of me.

At home, I have to ask several times before my husband takes the car in to have the oil changed. If I want new wallpaper or paint, or to remodel the kitchen, there's always a reason not to. It really doesn't matter what I want, or how I ask, the first thing he says is "no," or: "are you out of your mind, we can't afford it." Doesn't matter if I'm asking for a trip or a new sofa. The answer is always "no", so it doesn't matter what the question is. This makes me feel that I am nothing, either in the work place or the home.

I know that I have to be doing something wrong, but I can't figure out what it is. Maybe someone can give me a few suggestions about how to run my life a little better.

* First thing, Teresa, go take care of the car yourself. It doesn't take more than 20 minutes to have the oil changed. If you are not responsible for your car, and the engine blows up because the oil has been neglected, it will probably be your fault. Sounds like your husband would say, "What's the matter with you? Can't you change the oil?"

Then go get the wallpaper samples and tape them where you think the changes should be. Take charge in the home. Learn which end of a screwdriver to use, then use it. Same with all the other tools. If you have to learn how to do-it-yourself first, then surround yourself with home improvement books and tapes, take a trip to your local hardware store and ask questions. Then get rid of the fingernails, and dig in. That might mean that you have to move all the furniture yourself or hire some teenagers to help, but in the end, you will have achieved a major accomplishment, with or without your husband's help.

As for the finances, start keeping a budget book. Log income vs. outgo, for both of you, even if you have a joint checking account, joint savings etc. (It's better if you have your own checking account, but one thing at a time.) Make sure that you know where the money is going. Take responsibility for the finances as well, then when he says, "No, we can't afford it," bring out the budget book and show him where you *can* afford it. If mutual debt is a problem, seek the services of a financial counselor, but either way, take charge of your money. You work. You put in 40 hours a week. Why should he decide when and where you spend your share?

Speaking of work, you say that you are qualified and degreed for a higher position, but haven't gotten anywhere. Is it possible that the same type of constant "no you can't" attitude that you get in the home environment is carrying over to the work environment? Maybe you just *think* that you can't succeed because you have been programmed to believe that you are less than qualified.

As a therapist, I really would like to know more about you. I would want to see what kind of clothes you select for an interview. I would want to look at your resume, or job applications.

Humility is knowing ones worth. I coined this years ago when I was going through difficult times, and things were as bleak as they could ever be. Humility is not wearing a hair-shirt or looking at the floor when the boss speaks to you. No Mamm'm. If you can type 95 words a minute, you have to say so. If you have mastered every program on the computer, you have an obligation to bring it to the attention of the person in charge. If you can run or facilitate a training seminar because of your expertise, then say so. If you have the ability to chair a committee, then do it. I have learned that no one will speak up for you. You have to do it yourself. If you have a particular skill or talent, its your responsibility to point it out. Everyone excels at something, and it is your job to discover your area of excellence, then share it. I suspect that you are sitting on your talents, waiting for others to discover them. (It won't happen. Trust me on this.)

Take a more active role in your life, from the kitchen counters to the desk or cubicle at work. Know everything there is to know about a subject, learn, do your research, and please, stop assuming that others will take care of you. The first thing you have to do is stop *asking* (Captain May I...) for things (or situations). When you ask, you automatically open the door for a "no" response. Just start *doing*.

You might also take an assertiveness training course, or hit the library or book store in the self-help section. If this doesn't work, and you still find yourself on the losing end of life, then seek the services of a therapist or counselor to help you unlock the inner workings of your mind.

***

Nichole, age unk, administrative secretary.

People call me a bitch all the time, and I admit that I am a bitch, but it's too late to change now. Besides, I wouldn't want to change. Underlings fear me, and I like it that way. Don't mess with Nichole, that's my motto. People can take it or leave it, that's my attitude and my way of life. I don't owe anyone an explanation for anything. I never apologize and never make excuses. If people don't like it, or me, that's not my problem. My first husband abused me, my second husband was a mamma's boy, my kids have grown up and gone. I live alone with three cats. That's the way it is. No apologies, excuses or explanations. Take it or leave it.

* That's pretty clear. No apologies, excuses or explanations. Take it or leave it. Nichole rules. However, I would hate to have her for a supervisor, it doesn't sound like she's open to new ideas or suggestions. I'll bet that she's left a trail of former employees in her wake; sort of like Sherman's march to the sea. If I thought it would do any good, I would tell her to lighten up a bit, but I doubt that she'd listen. Seems to me that there has to be a balance between total bitch and situational bitch.

***

Campbell, 46, self-employed

You bet, I'm a bitch. My bitch was released when I was about 4 or 5 years old. I have learned a long time ago that if I didn't speak up for myself, no one else would. By the time I was 7, I figured out that I was pretty much alone in the world, and if I wanted to live, I would have to "just do it." I leaned to take what I wanted. Food, clothing, anything. I knew very early on that I couldn't count on my parents - - both parents at first, then a single mother, who was a wimp and couldn't do anything to save herself, much less us kids. We had to fend for ourselves, so we did. I was the oldest so I took on the role of caretaker for the two younger siblings. I hate to admit it, but I learned to steal very early - - food and candy bars at first, then later, bigger things. By the time I was 13, I had gotten away with pretty much everything. By that time, I had run away, had sex, was a fighter and scrapper, and could stand up for myself. knew that if there was a world out there, I had to have my share of it.

By the time I was 18, I carried a knife with me at all times. I know how to handle myself. I will not be backed into a corner, and I've done my share of backing. No one will ever lay a hand on me.

I am self-sufficient and proud of it. If there is something I want, I go after it. If I see a job that I want, I don't mind "enhancing" my resume, wearing a tight blouse or doing whatever I have to do to get that job. I don't really care who is in the way or if I have to step on toes to get ahead. I admit that I've lied and cheated to get ahead. I've run red lights all my life, literally. I don't let anything stop me from getting what I want. Nothing, or anyone stands in my way. Ever. I take what I want from life. If I hurt anyone along the way, that's too bad. They can look after themselves, I look after me, so call me a bitch. That's what I am. I have no regrets.

* Let me guess: your yearbook read, "Most likely to die in a prison riot."

Sorry to disappoint you, Campbell. You fit the description of someone who is either a psychopath or has an antisocial personality disorder. Let me fill you in: The diagnostic criteria for Antisocial Personality Disorder (***Abnormal Psychology***: Barlow/Durand, page 529). "There is a pervasive pattern of disregard for and violation of the rights of others occurring since age 15 years, as indicated by three or more of the following: 1) Failure to conform to social norms with respect to lawful behaviors as indicated by repeatedly performing acts that are grounds for arrest. (running red lights, fighting,); 2) Deceitfulness, as indicated by repeated lying, use of aliases, or conning others for personal profit or pleasure; 3) Impulsivity or failure to plan ahead; 4) Irritability and aggressiveness, as indicated by repeated physical fights or assaults (carrying a knife); 5) Reckless disregard for safety of self or others (running red lights, carrying a knife); 6) Consistent irresponsibility, as indicated by repeated failure to sustain consistent work behavior or honor financial obligations (Good thing you're self-employed. No one could stand to work with you. By your own admission, you've lied and cheated to get ahead.) 7) Lack of remorse, as indicated by being indifferent to or rationalizing having hurt, mistreated, or stolen from another. (I have no regrets.); The individual is at least 18 years old. There is evidence of Conduct Disorder with onset before age 15 years of age. The occurrence of antisocial behavior is not exclusively during the course of schizophrenia or a manic episode."

So, Campbell, you are not a bitch. You are a treacherous psychopath and it would be a good idea to stay out of your way.

***

Janet, age 44, nurse practitioner

As a nurse practitioner, I've had at least seven years of additional schooling, so that makes me almost-the-doctor. I see patients, do physical examinations, do patient assessments and diagnosis, write prescriptions and made decisions that affect the lives of the individuals I see. However, I'm always confronted by "where's the real doctor?" "I don't want to see a girl." "What makes you think that you're qualified to (whatever)" Everything that I do is authorized by the doctor in the end, but if there is a question about a diagnosis or outcome, we staff the case. Science has pretty much eliminated guesswork out of medicine. If a lab test indicates that someone has a fatty liver, I take it from there and tell the patient that he or she has to go on a diet if they want to live longer.

It took me a lot of years and hard work to get where I'm at today and I make a good salary, so it doesn't bother me when people ask for credentials. In fact, I encourage patients to investigate me, or whatever physician they are seeing for their problem. If they have to deal with HMO's or other managed care entities, they have a right to the best care possible (or whatever plan they are on).

I'm used to dealing with problems on a regular basis, and I make fast decisions. I have to. Someone's life might depend on the call I make at a specific moment.

If it's questionable, I always get a second or third opinion.

Perhaps I run my life the same way. I have always put one foot in front of the other, had a goal and got to the goal one way or another. There have been times in my life when I've had to take a detour to get to the goal, but that's all it was, a detour. My divorce was timed for mid-terms. Bad timing. Very bad timing.

I called the court and asked them to continue my divorce for another month, and I told them why I needed an extension. I got it, no problem. Sometimes you just can't deal with two or three major life events at the same time, and no matter how hard you try, you might find yourself down a notch. So do something about it. Make changes. If you can't change the situation, then change your attitude. Something has to give at certain times in your life.

On the more professional level, I am amazed at the amount of women I see with stress induced ailments: back and neck pain, migraine headaches, chest pains, colon problems, overweight, and/or eating disorders, inactive women who complain about sleep disorders, fatigue and depression. Men challenge me in my office. They want to know where I went to school, how come I'm not the doctor. Women fall apart. Once they sit down and we start discussing whatever physical problem that brought them in, we start getting to the heart of the matter. Nine times out of ten, I'm seeing women who are overworked, over-stressed, probably overweight and on the edge. First thing we do is a complete physical examination, do the pelvic and breast exam, play pokey fingers and make a determination if there *really* is a physical problem. Perhaps sugar levels are off, hormones could be off, those things we can deal with. I can write a script or two to take care of that problem, but I know next month, when I see them, the same environmental factors will be in their lives, without a bit of change.

I don't specialize in women's medicine, but a lot of the women I see, ask for me a second and third time, and they let me know that they are making changes in their lives.

I guess that I'm rambling on about my profession, when the topic of this paper is what is a bitch? Frankly, I don't know. I know that I have seen unreasonable women, selfish women who want to be seen first and fast, who want me to write a prescription for whatever, and move on out the door. Sorry, I take my time with every patient. I don't believe in rushed medicine. I sit and talk to people. Sure, there are interruptions all the time, but I have the ability to focus on the individual in front of me. I am warm and compassionate, hold hands with the person and look into their eyes.

When I see a patient who wants more pain pills, more tranquilizers, more of this and more of that, I take the time to find out why. When a patient needs a referral to the mental health services, I gently give that too.

Release Your Inner Bitch

This is a lot like obscenity. I know a bitch when I see one, but she's hard to describe. It could be me, or my sister, or my daughter.

Now that I think of it, it *is* my daughter. She wants to be an attorney, fine goal and she will achieve this, but right now, she's a bit bitchy about her GPA, which is 3.7 and brag-able, but she wants a 4.0 and will do anything to get it. She works hard, studies constantly and will stop at nothing to obtain her goal. I know that she will make a fine attorney, because she has always excelled at 'argument 101'. Even when she was five years old, she would wear MY hat in the rain, then argue that hers would get wet, and if the object was to keep her hat dry, then wearing my hat justified the end. She used the same argument with every other hat she ever had. She will make a great attorney. My daughter is a gutsy young woman and when we stand face to face in the mirror, I can see myself in her eyes.

I never told her "don't back down from your dreams or goals," but I guess my example of working and going to school, and basically, busting my britches, all those years made it possible for her to see that she has a future. I did it without child support, welfare or food stamps. I did it with old cars, used books, burned the midnight oil and maxed out every credit card I had. I took out loans, got grants and earned my degrees by myself. No one helped me pay the tuition or get through school, (although I am now in a position to pay her tuition, and gladly) because I want her to be successful.

I never thought of myself as a bitch, more of a determined woman. Maybe others see me as a bitch, (I've had three patients complain that they had to see that bitch..... oh well.) but if I am, then I can deal with that. I just might use this when I see other women and tell them that if they want to get rid of that migraine or back problem, maybe they should start being a bitch. Actually I would tone the language down to 'assertive', but I believe it means the same thing. Unfortunately, there isn't a similar word in the English language for a male.

* Janet's drive made her real to me. She and Jane, the Air Force officer, had the same things going for them. They both had goals. They set their sights on a career, and may have taken a few detours along the way, but they achieved their goal. That might be the problem with Teresa. No specific goal. Neither Jane or Teresa apparently *asked* anyone's permission to achieve a specific goal, they just did it. They had a plan of action, and they arrived.

So far, we have quite a few words to add to our list of bitchiness, or bitchdom. They would be focus, drive, education, determination, motivation, empowerment, self-determination. Each word brings with it a set of responsibilities. With focus and goal, you have to at least have an idea of where you want to go in life, a direction. You wouldn't get on a plane or train without a ticket with the destination clearly stamped on the ticket. Why would you go through life without a direction? It doesn't make sense.

Janet, Roberta, Rebecca, Marsha, Jane, Mary Ann and a few others all pointed out that education was a key element to achievement. They didn't let anything stop them from getting ahead in the academic world, and if you look closely, you will notice that they didn't let the lack of finances stop them either. They all seemed to borrow used books and drove old vehicles to get where they were going. They all worked full time while they went to school. They had their priorities in order, and on the surface, it might appear that their family (children) may have suffered as a result of their efforts. Quite the contrary. All of them seem to have children who now excel in life's challenges. The mothers set a fine example for their children. The children saw in their mothers hard working women who weren't afraid of a challenge. They saw strong female role models in their mothers, and I'm willing to bet that all the children of this group of women will achieve even greater heights as a result.

You can bet that the children of these women will be focused, goal oriented and outspoken.

***

Maria, age 29, receptionist at a car dealership.

You might have guessed from my name that I am Hispanic. OK, so I make a good looking receptionist. I have a good body, and the men like the way I look. I like wearing big gold earrings and gold bracelets, and lots of gold chains that hang just right on my breasts. I like the way I look in a tight skirt and jeans. I like my body, my eyes, my face and my jet black hair. I know how to flirt and I do it well. I am a bitch.

Some of the other women can't stand me. That's their problem, not mine. If they let themselves go, and get fat, then too bad for them.

I would like to sell cars. I know that I can do that. I know that I could sell to men easier than to women.

I have two children. I was a teenage mom. I would tell girls that they are messing up, but what's done is done. In my family we all had babies young. The grandmothers are the prettiest when they had their babies young. We are a close family, and if one thing happens to one, then it happens to all. The women run the family. We make the decisions. That's how it is. We decide what to wear, what to drive, when to eat, what to eat, where to live, and how to live. Like I said, I am a bitch. My mother and my aunts, we are all bitches. My little sister is a bitch. My daughter will be a bitch.

We have to be bitches. Sometimes the men we live with try to assert themselves. They abuse us, and we have to fight back. My mother took a knife to one of her husbands, and that was the last of that. He left the same night. No matter. She got another husband.

It wasn't always like this. We have a history of being abused by our husbands and men. Hispanic women are changing. The men have made a mess of things, and it's up to us to clean it up. They have gotten lazy, stopped working, stopped bringing in the money for the rent and groceries, so we have to be bitchy. If they don't like it, they don't have to come around. If a man isn't going to pay support, then he doesn't see the child. If a man won't make the car payment, then he can't drive the car. If a man won't pay the rent, then he's out. Vamoose. Adios. We don't look backwards. When a man screws up, he's gone. Sons, fathers, uncles, whatever. When they don't pull their weight, they have to leave.

I have one aunt, her husband was abusive. He beat her, he drank, he used drugs, he was in a gang and she wouldn't kick him out because she was afraid. So all the women in the family went to her house and kicked him out for her. He was a bloody mess when we got done with him. We took pots and pans, rocks, kitchen knives, tools (screwdrivers, hammers and an electric drill) and backed him into a corner, then he was able to leave, but not before getting a few marks on him. We hurt him bad. Then we changed the locks. He's gone. History. Now she can get on with her life.

I could go on about being a bitch. But in our language, we call it *perra* or *fuerrte mujer* or strong woman. White people call it bitch. We call it survival.

* Maria is an enigma. On the one hand, she dresses to appeal to men. She wants to sell cars to men. She smiles and flirts openly. Then she says that, basically, there is no room for men in her environment, but everything she does (clothing, jewelry, body shape, hair and make up) are done to appeal to men. She sounds like a scrapper, a fighter, a woman with a goal. But then, as she pointed out, Hispanic females have a tradition of being beaten my their men, so I would assume that this makes them distrust all males. It also makes them stronger as females, but it sends a double message. The way Maria dresses, and acts, it looks as if she wants a male. However, it also sounds like any man within ten miles of this woman would be dead meat. A black widow? Maybe. Perhaps there's a lot more to this young woman than meets the eye.

***

A bitch is a woman who knows how to get things done in the shortest amount of time. A man would be called a CEO. It's a matter of semantics. (Susan)

***

Eleanor, age 38, author, retail sales

"Don't give up your day job" is the first thing you hear when you say that you're an author. I've written two books, and I'm just beginning to discover how hard it is to get published. I thought that people would be camped out on my doorstep, but it's not so. Publishing is a man's world.

That's the thing that I want more than anything else in the world. I write, I would be happy to have me and the computer, but my home life isn't like that either. I have to sneak in writing. Steal time from the kids. My husband says things like "honey, be reasonable, writing is nice, but you just aren't going to sell. Why not be happy writing the church bulletin?" My mother says, "Well, writing is a nice hobby." (This makes me want to scream. No one takes me seriously.) My brother says, "Well, what else have you got going for you?" (I could kill him.) My father, bless his heart, hasn't got a clue that I write, and I wouldn't even mention it. Oh sure, I sneak in a class now and then, but most of the time I pretend that it doesn't matter to me.

Then I do the dishes, and the Saturday stuff (laundry, grocery shopping, throw in a movie, take the kids here and there, make love, do what everyone else does) when I really want to write. I've tried writing at the kitchen table (doesn't work). I've tried getting a small desk and working in the hall by the utility room (then I fold towels on the desk, and my writing gets buried under dirty socks). I get up in the middle of the night to write, but my husband thinks that there's something wrong with me. Maybe there is. It's a dream of mine and it seems that every time I turn around, someone is putting it down.

About my job, I hate it, but I can't afford to quit. We're like every other American, living on the edge of our paychecks. Just about the time we think that we have our heads above water, the car breaks down, or one of the kids needs braces. The harder I work, the more frustrated I get. I don't have two minutes to myself. When I get home, I immediately start supper. Then I do the dishes, or take the kids to practice of one kind or another, or throw in a load of laundry. By the time I get to bed, I'm too tired to even have a civil conversation with my husband. We have sex, that's it; on and off. I could time him at about four minutes, but he's as tired as me, so if it isn't that great, then it's because we're both working hard. He drives a truck (local) and has to carry stuff all day long and it's starting to affect his back. Neither of us can quit our jobs. We have a mortgage, a back yard, two vehicles, three kids and a dog, and every credit card in the world. We're in debt up to our wazoos. We also have a cat and two birds. Last time I checked, the goldfish were floating in the bowl, but I left them there, hoping that one of the kids would notice and flush them.

Am I bitchy? Yes, I find myself yelling and screaming when the garbage doesn't get taken out, or when there are shoes all over the living room. Little things are starting to bother me. I go along just fine for a few days, then I know that PMS is right around the corner. Thing is, I can *feel* myself getting bitchy. I would just as soon drive off a bridge as talk to anyone, and any little thing that anyone does makes me crazy. I have been known to throw things, break things, and once, in a totally bitched out mood, I drove the car over one of the kids' Tonka trucks that was in the carport. Don't ever do that, you will get a flat tire. You will wreck the kids' toy and you will hear about it for the rest of your life. AND you will have your flat tire, then you will have to get it fixed. Then you will have to explain to your husband WHY you ran over the damn truck in the first place.

But that's the point. I'm a relatively sane person. I didn't grow up to be a bitch, in fact, we all went to church and always were polite. We said "please," "thank you" and "may I be excused from the table?". We opened doors for anyone coming or going through at the same time, we smiled and learned to be nice. We were disciplined, sent to our rooms or had time out, when we misbehaved.

Now when I send one of my kids to his room, he flips me off. He'll go, but he mutters under his breath all the way. He's a teenager, a rotten, selfish teenager and there are times when I absolutely hate him. (Good thing my last name isn't on this.) He's already been in trouble with the law, and I had to take off work to go get his ass out of detention. It breaks my heart to see him as messed up as he is, and its probably my fault for not spending as much time with him as I should, but I'm so damn tired all the time.

I work hard, I clean up the house. I carry out the crappy papers from the bird and I empty the kitty litter. I clean the two toilets in the house. Seems that I'm forever cleaning up after (excuse the word) someone's else's shit. I'm tired of it. I want to run away with my computer and write. Is that so bad?

* Eleanor, as for the kid who flips you off, get in his face and tell him in no uncertain terms that you will not tolerate that kind of behavior. He flips you off because he got away with it once, then twice, and God knows how many times. He is your child, he lives in your house. You pay the bills. He needs to learn respect, right now, and your husband had better back you up on this one. If he doesn't, you'd better have a chat with the husband, and make them all understand that you, the mother, a co-breadwinner, are not to be abused in that manner. Put your foot down, and do not budge from your position. If the kid keeps it up, get professional help, and again, do not back down from tough love. If this kid isn't stopped now, chances are, he will be an abusive male later in life, perhaps end up in jail. A future wife will not tolerate this, why should you? His boss will never tolerate this. Again, why should you? You are his mother, you deserve better. Do not let this kid push you around. Not now, not ever.

Eleanor got to the heart of me. I have written 21 novels, and have battled it out with the publishing world. It is a man's world, dear, but you have to write so well that it doesn't matter whose world it is. You have to create a book so rich in texture that one cannot stop turning pages. You have to learn the craft so perfectly that no one, male or female, can dispute your work. You have a dream, and a goal. Go after it. If you don't do it, all the creative ideas will end up like the dust bunnies under the bed, they will get swept up and forgotten. Do it. Do it. Do it. Whatever the cost, find the time to write. It is that part of you that makes you dear to others, and when you don't write, you lose a part of yourself. An artist cannot stop painting, a sculptor cannot stop sculpting, and Eleanor cannot stop writing. She could sooner give up breathing. It's in her blood, and there is no cure.

Women authors are thieves. We steal time from our families, and like Eleanor, I was getting up at 3 AM to write, then I would go to work, dead tired, and fall into bed, totally exhausted. But I got up every day and wrote. It was the only time I had to myself. I had to let the dishes and carpets go, or learn to step over the housework. (Trust me, when the garbage gets so high, *someone* will take it out.)

What Eleanor has to do is to stake out her territory. She has to get a desk, a corner of the room, or perhaps even a whole room for herself, and make it known that this is her space. She has to allow herself the freedom to leave her work spread out on her desk, without other people dumping laundry or school books on her work. (Get a big bath towel and spread it over the work. Then all you have to do is lift the towel and begin the next day. God help anyone who trespasses.)

Then she has to make an announcement to her family (and stick to it) that she will write for an hour (same time, every day) or whatever amount of time she allocates, then do it. During that time, do not answer the phone. Do not talk to the kids (unless it's an emergency), put the dog out, and if necessary, put on peaceful music AND a headset, then write. She should not be discouraged, or become involved in anything else during that one hour of the day. Soon enough, her family will come to realize that she is serious.

Maybe she can't do anything about the finances or the job that she hates, but she can control the one environment that defines her creative ability. For her own peace of mind, this is something that she should never give up. When and if she gives this up, she will eventually capitulate totally, get lost in the shuffle for family and finances, and never realize her dream. For her, this is an important as the marathon runner, the mountain climber, the inventor, the person who builds a boat or plane in his garage, or anyone who has ever attempted the impossible.

All of the women before her in this book have had a dream. They have gone after it and seized it, regardless of the detours along the way. Write On, Eleanor. If you don't do it, no one can do it for you. The only way to see your book in the book stores is to *get it there*. Do not give up or give in. You must educate your family in this dream, and make them aware of your goals.

Why not? The kids see you at the ironing board, the stove, the washer, the vacuum cleaner. They see you going to work every day, changing flat tires, and making life manageable for them. Why not let them see you fulfill yourself? Let them see you at the computer, and let them see the results. Make them a part of that dream. If you don't have their support, so what? Do it anyway. Trust me, they will come around.

If the publishing industry won't let you in as a new author, try Publish on Demand Books. Look on the Internet and study the market. Then do it. If you don't, all the stories and books inside your head will eventually dry up and your dream is gone. Never. Never give up on your dream. (Go back and read Virginia.)

***

Dorothy, (pseudonym) age 56, prisoner

I'm doing 15 - 25 years for manslaughter. I could have gotten murder one or life, or death, but 15 years is plenty the way I see it. I killed my husband. There it is in black and white. I know what I did was wrong, but I reached a point where it was either me or him, so it was him.

We were doomed from day one. I should have seen it coming over and over, but I always did the right thing, and let him control me. He would sit in his easy chair, order me around. I had to clean his toe nails, wash his feet. He would drink his beer and make me do this and that; wash the windows immediately after a rain. Even if it rained in the middle of the night, I would have to wash the windows early in the morning, then get his breakfast; eggs and bacon. Not cereal. If the coffee was more than an hour old, I'd have to make fresh. Once he threw the hot coffee pot at me, scalding my face and neck. I went to the emergency room so many times that I can't even remember why. I knew the drill. I'd get beaten, go for the ice. If I needed stitches, I'd get them, and make some excuse for the doctors. I had a supply of butterfly Band-Aids at home so I could take care of them myself, but a broken arm is a little different. One night I killed him. I was watching him sleeping, passed out from drinking, so I stabbed him; then I waited until I was sure that he was dead, and I called the police to come and get me.

Rose Stadler, MSW

I wish that I had been a bitch and fought back. My kids visit me once a month and I'll wait out my time here. I do cross-stitch and make pillows. It's not so bad. I do wish that I could get a real haircut once in a while though, and wish that we didn't get fat off the prison food. We have to do 375 hours in the kitchen and all the women fight over their recipes. I was, still am, a good cook, and I wouldn't mind doing more time in the kitchen if I could cook, so I volunteer. I counsel other women now. I see a lot of women who have been abused, and I tell them, "don't take it. You stop it right away or it will go on and on, and never stop." I see women in here for drugs, prostitution, whatever, and I tell them to go back and pick up their lives. Me: I can't go back and pick up my life. My house was probably sold at an auction. All my stuff was probably sorted out by the neighbors right after my arrest. I have pictures and albums of the kids, and that's about it. I've lost everything because of my husband, but mostly, I lost me and any self respect I might have had.

Yes, I killed him and it wasn't even self defense. I confessed right away. I suppose I could get a new trial, battered wife syndrome, or temporary insanity, but I knew exactly what I was doing at the time, and I did it. There is no one else responsible for him, and yes, it was murder. I have dreams about the years of torture, and sometimes I wake up in the middle of the night, screaming, even now, after all these years, and I see him standing over me with a bucket of cold water, in winter, waiting to throw it over my head. Then in my dream, I am standing outside in the freezing cold, banging on the door, begging to be let in, and promise not to leak on the carpet. And he is there, laughing at me, inside the locked door, and I am shaking with cold. Or he is coming at me with his hands outstretched, ready to strangle me. Many times I prayed that he would kill me. I took pills once, and he found me on the living room rug, passed out. He took me to the doctor and pretended that I was mentally ill, that I did things like that all the time. Then he took me home and beat the living crap out of me. It was useless to call the police, because when they got there, he'd be reading a book, and tell them that I was unhinged. Or that I fell down the basement steps, or that one of the kids must have left the bike in the driveway again. I kept my mouth shut after about the sixth time the police came.

It doesn't matter because I just found out that I have uterine cancer. After almost bleeding to death in my cell, I had to have surgery, but I've refused all other treatment. Actually, some of the other inmates tell me that I'm a fool. I could be in a hospital instead of a prison but I welcome death at this point. I did tell the doctors that I would like a lot of morphine at the end because I've had enough pain. Right now I can't get pain pills because they're considered 'drugs', contraband.

If there's anything I can do in the meantime to help other women fight back against abuse, or not be abused in the first place, I will gladly do it. When I saw this flyer, I said, "yes, now's my chance." I should have been a bitch long ago. I should have kicked the bastard out, I should have got behind and kicked and shoved, or taken a shotgun to his behind. I should have done *something* to defend myself against his cruelty. But I never did. I took it and took it and then I killed him. See, the thing is, I *did* go to the police for help, I went to my church, I talked to my mother, but she said something like "you made your bed, now sleep in it." Or: "What did you do wrong? Go home and make it right." The notion that I did something wrong was always there, either from my mother, or in the back of my head. It *had* to be me. I deserved what I got, because the beds weren't made, or the soup was too salty. Then too, he always said that I *made* him hit me. He'd come through the door, and the television was on the wrong channel for him, or the curtains were 'not just right' then he'd smack me across the head, and say, "Look what you made me do." It was always my fault.

Later, there *were* shelters I could have gone to. I could have gotten out, but I never did. I always thought it would get better. But I can tell you now, once a man abuses you, it will get worse. It never gets better. After a beating, or a period of time that I can only call torture, we would make love. He would say, "I don't know what got into me." But it was always the same.

He was cruel from the very first day. The night before my wedding, my mother and I stayed up and made lace sleeves for my dress to hide bruises. That should have been my first clue, but it wasn't. I went through the wedding, feeling something in the pit of my stomach that wasn't right. But I was pregnant, and I *had* to finish what I started. I would say that he was always abusive, maybe a slap here or there, then months of nothing. Then it got worse. I would be a nervous wreck every time I heard the car pull up in the driveway, and I'd get that sinking feeling. Then I could tell just by looking at him, I swear to God his face changed. As the years wore on, the abuse got worse. Worse than that, he got downright *mean*. Once one of the kids brought home a stray puppy, a mutt, uglier than dirt; and he took it out and killed it. He didn't shoot it fast, but he strangled it in front of the kids. Then he made the kids bury it. That was mean. That was worse than him hitting me.

He did things like that. He'd take one of the kids' favorite teddy bears and hang in above the kid's bed because the child didn't do her homework, or put away her toys. He'd do mean things like that all the time, until one by one, the kids left home and it was just me and him. When the kids were around, I felt a little safer because as the kids got bigger, they'd protect me. They'd lie for me, say they did something so I wouldn't get a beating. By this time, I was totally numb. I bought rat poison once, planning to use it on him. Another time I bought a pistol at a pawn shop, but I didn't know how to use it. So when I finally did kill him, they called it premeditated. I was too numb during the trial to do much in the way of assisting the public defender in my behalf, so I got what was coming to me. I did it, I killed him, and I watched him die on the sofa in the living room, and I remember thinking that I never liked that sofa anyway. Strange, I mean I had just killed my husband, and I had blood all over me, and I was thinking "Now I can finally get rid of the sofa." While I waited to make sure he was dead, I cleaned out the refrigerator because I knew the milk would go bad and I didn't know how long I'd be gone. I took his pulse, and when there wasn't one, and his skin was cold and gray, I made the call, probably about four hours later.

Sure enough, the police came and when they went through the house, they found the gun. The judge wasn't very sympathetic, and frankly, I didn't expect any sympathy. I didn't care anymore. Jail was better than home. Now that you think about it, that's about as pathetic as you can get. When you trade a real dress for inmate pajamas, and you don't even feel the handcuffs on your wrist, or when you look at your wrists and you see that they're red and raw from the cuffs, and you don't care, that's pathetic. I was so desperate, and what I did was desperate. At the time, Hedda Nussbaum was making the news because she was a battered wife, so no one was about to give me the time of day because I had confessed. I said, "Yes, officers, I did it."

There wasn't a jury trial because I had confessed, just an arraignment and the sentencing.

I've given it all to the Lord now, but I know that if I hadn't killed him, he would eventually have killed me. It's over and done with now, but it doesn't have to be that way for other women. Don't wait until it gets so bad that you take a life, yours or his. Get out any way you can. Go, leave, take the kids and get out. Wait until he's sleeping and leave. Just go. Don't look back. Pretend the house is on fire and you can't go back for anything.

Had I been a bitch, had I done something to protect myself (and the kids) my life would have been different. I could have gotten out, I know that now, but at the time, I believed that I was useless and no good. I was worthless. I apologized for everything. I still flinch when someone brushes a piece of lint of my shirt or takes a piece of hair out of my eyes. I have nightmares about him beating me, or his favorite, locking me out of the house either naked right after a bath, or wearing a nightgown. If I didn't change my nightgown immediately when I got up, he'd follow me to the kitchen and as soon as he got the chance, he'd push me out the door. I'd be so embarrassed because I didn't want the neighbors to see me like that that I'd do whatever he wanted. Odd, but I have never had a nightmare about killing him. In my dreams, I still see him alive, always coming at me, and he's always laughing.

There are so many things that I would have done differently, beginning with NOT marrying him, but that's all history now. In retrospect, I should have taken the biggest kitchen knife to him the second time he hit me. There might not have been a third time. It's too late for me, but not for other women. Get out, never let a man hit you a second time. Never, never a second time. The first time, maybe you walked in front of his fist. OK, but never a second time. It's the second time that you sell your soul, and then it's too late.

* This is one of the saddest bitch stories that I've seen yet. Dorothy lived a hard life. As a woman, she was probably raised to give due respect to her husband, take whatever he dished out and don't complain. He sounds like a very cruel man, one who would abuse animals and children as well as his wife, a sadistic man married to a non-bitch. It appears that she was frozen with terror, afraid to leave, afraid to stay. Life must have been hell for her.

As a counselor, and as a social worker, I've talked to a lot of abused women, but I never heard it said that the second hit is the one that makes the difference. Many women have said that they would never let a man hit them twice, and that makes sense, especially after reading this terribly sad tale from Dorothy. Apparently Dorothy gave up on herself a long time ago. I've read this over and over and I don't think that Dorothy got much in the way of legal assistance. She folded much too easily, but she saw prison as a more favorable way of life than living with her husband.

She must have snapped, thinking not of the husband she just killed, but of the sofa that she never liked, and saw it as a good reason to finally get rid of the sofa. This is exactly the kind of thinking that the jury should have been able to see through had there been a jury. The fact that she confessed should have been secondary to the reason behind the murder. This is a woman who's sitting in prison, now dying with uterine cancer, who never had a chance at life.

Bitches don't get abused. Apparently she was abused early in the marriage, even before, but because she was pregnant, she didn't see any other options. This was probably back in the early 60's or late 50's. Having a child out of wedlock was considered a terrible thing. Also, there were no shelters for battered women until the 70's, then few and far between. It wouldn't have done any good to call the police in the 60's and 70's because they sided with the male. Not until the late 80's did police across the nation take a stiffer stance on domestic violence. By that time it was too late. She indicated that

Hedda Nussbaum was in the news at the time, so that has to put the incident at about 1986. Currently, there are more animal shelters than human shelters in the United States, which rarely have an opening.

In 1998, in Maricopa County, Arizona, 17,000 women were turned away from shelters. That's just one county in the United States. In the first six months of 1998, 7 women died in Maricopa County as a direct result of domestic violence. Multiply this by every county in the U. S. and you have a rough idea of the number of women who are still living in dangerous, life-threatening environments. In one week in October, 1999, two women died by the hands of their husband or live-in boyfriend in Phoenix. *Two women. In a single week.* Two women too many. Phoenix, Arizona. Maricopa County, October 18, 1999. Times have not changed. Read any newspaper in any city and you will see women dying at the hands of men.

My heart goes out to Dorothy. I hope that anyone who reads this and is in an abusive situation has the courage to get out. Abusers continue to abuse; that's the rule. Another rule is that it will *always* get worse. They do not change their ways, no matter how clean the house is or how perfect the children are. There is *nothing* the woman can do to please them, so stop trying. Get out any way you can. Like she said, pretend the house is on fire and you can't go back for anything.

***

Anon. no age.
My mother, the bitch.

I am 45 years old and I still can't talk to my mother without getting all worked up. She's the bitch. No matter what anyone says or does, its never enough. None of us can please her. We'd get her presents, say a pretty pink bathrobe, and she'd open the box, and say something like, "What'd you do? Shop K-Mart at the last minute?" We'd cook a fabulous dinner, and she'd say, "Not too bad considering the lumps in the gravy. (or the lumps in the mashed potatoes, or the turkey is a little dry, or the meat is a tad overdone...) Nothing was ever good enough, nothing was ever done right. I find myself talking to my kids like that. One day my daughter said, "Ma, you sound like grandma." Sure enough, I was starting to sound like my mother. It was a hard pill to swallow. I have to make a conscious effort to treat my children differently. I know my mother will never change. Nothing will ever be right for her. She'll bitch about the tombstone eventually. I need to stop bitching.

I guess I am a bitch after all. Maybe it's genetic. I don't know, but I do know that I don't want to pass on her bitchy legacy to my children and my grandchildren.

* It's amazing that this woman solved her own problems, or at least saw the dilemma that she's in. She recognizes that she's beginning to sound like her bitchy mother - - and needs to make positive changes. She can do it, and without sounding like Dr. Phil, it's not surprising that children emulate their parents. When you grow up with a critical parent, you become a critical parent. Constant criticism is a form of emotional abuse. It stays with a person, nags at them from the recesses of the mind, and surfaces when you least expect it. **Nagging Dragon** I call it. It loves chocolate, so when the Nagging Dragon comes calling offer it some emotional chocolate. Then release it, like sweeping up the dust on the floor, or taking out the garbage. Let it go. She can't change her mother, and no sense trying, but she can change herself.

***

Barbara, 54, Seamstress

I had to stop and think about what being a bitch meant. It always had a nasty connotation. To call a woman a bitch was in insult of the highest order. I became a bitch when I got divorced after 20-odd years of marriage. I had the house clean, did everything right, always had meals on time, kept the kids quiet when the husband was sleeping, pressed his clothes, in fact, I think back on the work that I did, and know that women never get a tenth of the credit due them. I worked my tail off for the marriage, but my husband was always between jobs, got fired, moved on, gone - - out of state, either looking for work, or going to school - - I never really got good reasons for all the jobs he had or the amount of time he was gone. In the meantime, I had to be the one to stretch the pennies, keep the bill collectors at bay and keep the house, yard and kids in reasonably good shape while he was gone.

Then one day he came home, after being gone for a year, either job hunting for *another* job or going to school. He didn't hug me, so I asked for a hug. But his response threw me for a loop. He said, "so this is about sex. If I want sex, I can get it on the street." That was it for me. The next day I hired an attorney, and when I saw the attorney was continuing the case for one excuse or another, I fired him and got another attorney. I was going to get a divorce and that was that. I've moved on, and know that I am stronger now more than ever before. You know, now I'm honored to be a bitch, and think of all the bitch sisters I know. There are a lot of strong women out there, and each of us had to come to terms with our own bitchdom in our own way. I don't have any regrets, except that I didn't do it sooner.

* Atta girl, Barbara. Sounds like the rest of us in the same age group. We were raised to think one way, when it comes down to it, being a bitch isn't so bad. Congratulations. Get this woman a bitch cup.

***

Paula, fast approaching the big 4-0, high school teacher.
I've been teaching high school for about 10 years now, and feel like I know bitches pretty well. Lots of kids think that they're bitches, some of them even have been gang members, tough girls who carry knives after school. They have tattoos and marks all over their bodies, and it makes me sick that the parents think that I, as a teacher, can do something with them.

Wrong, the damage is already done. Violence and gang related activities are not the way to succeed. Teen pregnancies and running away are also wrong, but these kids can't see the big picture. They live in the here-and-now, have no sense of permanency and don't care how they treat others. They think that they are invincible, that they won't get pregnant, or hurt in a gang fight. They live in a fantasy world. It's these girls who call me a bitch, and there is very little I can do to convince them otherwise. The truth is, they haven't seen a real bitch, or they would run like the wind.

We have some bitches on staff, burned out teachers, who should find another job, but there they are, battling with the youthful bitches. It doesn't make any sense.

Things used to be different. We could actually teach, but now we have our backs against the wall, finances and budgets are down, and we have to suspend kids when the administration says so. I disagree with this. There are times when I see a young girl, troubled, pregnant, in a gang, who really has a future, and there is very little I can to do to help her. I have to let her go. At times, I have suggested counseling, or special education, and a lot of times I actually meet with the girl to discuss her life; but that's not my job.

First of all, I don't get paid for the extra hours. Secondly, *it's not my job*. I almost lost my job for sticking my neck out for a young girl, I guess in hindsight, I stepped on toes. The girl was eventually dismissed, and I was maintained on 'administrative reprimand' for the rest of the school year. Very embarrassing and unsettling. I almost walked off the job, but I didn't. I hung in there.

Personally, I think that the principal is a bitch. She has a take-no-prisoners attitude; that includes teachers and students alike. It makes my job that much more difficult. It's one thing to work with people who are of a like mind, and have a similar goal, but it's another thing to constantly be working at odds with the very people who sign your paycheck. I've had to learn to be tactful, speak when spoken to, and politically correct at all times. This isn't necessarily me. I've always been an outspoken person, and now I have to tone it down because I need the money.

I have a family, house payments, car payments, and all the accruements that make life comfortable. So I'm stuck. I'm hoping to be able to transfer out next year, but in the meantime, I have to bide my time, bite my tongue and get along as well as possible. I try not to take the problems home with me, but I do. And yes, I get bitchy, but I get bitchy around the house, where I'm safe. My kids and husband understand when I've had a bad day, so they give me venting time. Mostly when I take the dog out. I run, and the poor thing has no choice but to keep up and run along with me. He and I have great conversations, and I feel better afterwards. He has a good run and stays in shape. We both win.

I've recently begun to enjoy making crafty things. This eases the tension a bit, but it isn't really me. The me I'd like to portray is a strong, intelligent woman, but the me I have to take to work is the history teacher, no more, no less. This is frustrating and unfulfilling. I need to blow off some steam once in a while, and there is no venting at work.

* Paula's frustration sounds typical of women who have to work to stay afloat. She might try to simplify her life by cutting back on the accruements of life, but I doubt that she will. Chances are, she has already set her sights on another teaching job or a less-tough school. I agree with her that there's no sense fighting back when the person who signs the paycheck is the bitch in command. Sometimes you just have to see the handwriting on the wall, and get out while the getting is good.

She teaches history, yet she seems capable of teaching young girls the fine art of becoming women in the truest sense. I have seen the same girls, the ones with tattoos and tear drops on their eyes, the gothic makeup and black attire that sets them aside. They have no idea of the consequences of their actions. They become easy prey to males, junkies, drug lords, pimps and gang-lords. They might find themselves abused, (sexually, physically and mentally) or worse, they might find themselves looking up at the lights in the morgue with a tag on their toe. Too bad for them, and too bad for their parents. Too bad for a society in which one million children killed or maimed each other in a ten-year period of time (1992-2002) and too bad for the babies that they bear. The children may grow up in foster care, drifting from one home to another with no stability.

I understand Paula's frustration. It's a tough job; the pay isn't enough and the hours are too long to accomplish what needs to be done. She can only touch one child at a time, and that, small as it seems, makes a difference to that one child.

***

Valerie, 42, banker

Of course I'm a bitch. I'm divorced. Divorced women get that title the first time they call an attorney. I didn't get everything I wanted in the divorce, but I'm educated, and I'm not afraid to go out and earn a living. I have three kids, two of them are pretty well grown, and I would have liked to tack on the college tuition to the divorce, but life has its limits, so they can work or get grants to off-set the cost. We do what we can to save, and all of us have a decent portfolio. That was part of the problem with the marriage. My husband drove us into debt three times, and the last time was the last straw. If he had a dime, he spent it. I was the one who pulled us out of debt, every time, by working an extra job - - you know the drill, you get up at 3 a.m., put on the coffee, drag yourself out of the house for a waitress job in the wee hours of the morning because the tips from drunks tend to be better than the tips from the dinner hour - - so it went. I worked my ass off, and hubby spent every last dollar in the checking account. I'd manage to save a little and he'd drain the account. He'd buy stuff just because it was on sale. He'd eat out three times a week before he'd pay any bills. Bill collectors were calling, so I got to the point where I'd let the voice message get it. He'd gotten the credit card debt up to over seventeen thousand dollars (for the 3rd time), AND he bought himself a motorcycle. He already had a boat in the yard, but it seems that he never grew up. He had to have his toys. I filed for a divorce.

The last time was just that - - the last time. Time to move on. So now I am stronger and more determined, more responsible than ever, and, if there is a next time, I want to see a firm financial spreadsheet in advance.

* Can't argue with that, Valerie. Most couples fight about money, sex and children, I'm not sure of the order. It sounds like the money fights got in the way of everything else. Sometimes you have to make grown-up decisions about money. Some couples can escape the money blues by having one person be responsible for the checkbook, bills and finances, but it's not fair. I generally advise that both people sit down once a week and go over the bills together, but it doesn't always work that way.

***

Diane, no age given, submitted by Judy P. (therapist)
Victim non-bitch

Diane is a young, attractive professional who has been a client for a little over one year. She has been married for about seven years and has a four year old daughter. Her husband (several years older than Diane) is an unemployed alcoholic who had his third DUI offense. Diane is a good, responsible person who stuck by her man, but things have gotten worse since I've known her. He parties with his buddies every day, all day, while she works. She takes her daughter to day care because she's afraid of leaving the child with him. He has taken money intended for rent which has jeopardized their home and most recently, he drove her car without her knowledge, wrecked and totaled it. Throughout, Diane has remained sweet, calm and hopeful, stating that he may change.

He is not changing. He has what Diane calls a 'temper' which is getting out of control. Lately Diane has been feeling threatened, physically, and fears for her daughter. She denies that he has ever hit her, but there is a hint that she may be covering up for him.

If he hasn't hit her, then I suspect that he might start hitting her (and the daughter). Over the past year, I have offered to assist in him getting employment, but he has yet to come in. Things are escalating. In a frantic call from Diane, she told me that he has stolen money from her again.

Well, enough is enough and too much is nasty, as my mother used to say. I have never tried to tell Diane - - or any other client - - what to do. I am not their judge. I provide information so they can make decisions based on choice and self-determination. I found myself in an extreme bitch mode and told Diane that for her sake and the safety of her daughter, she needed to leave him, get as far away from him as possible and start a new life. One without him where rent and grocery money doesn't disappear, or have him stoned or drunk out of his mind.

She actually agreed. She remained sweet and calm although I was anything but. She told me that she had known this for a long time, but no one ever said it to her. She needed someone to tell her what to do; she needed to hear it, and perhaps, have 'permission' to start a new life. It took her a while, but she finally left him. She's in a shelter with her daughter, the clothes on her back, but with the support of the shelter, she can begin anew.

* Diane sounds like any one of a hundred women I've seen as a therapist. Judy did the right thing by not telling Diane what to do, but any therapist will reach a point where things worsen, and sometimes you simply have to take the bull by the horns and say, "look, I've offered, I've listened, I've been there for you. Now it's time you have to make decisions for yourself." Sometimes you have to light a match under your client's behind to get them moving. This is empowerment or self-determination. Many times a person is so intimidated by the whole process of life, and the independence it offers, that they are virtually frozen and can't make decisions.

Diane sounds a lot like the sweet woman with two children in the front of the book whose husband tried to kill her six times, but she continued to pray for him. She, too, was a sweet woman, very sweet, sang in the choir with the voice of an angel, sang to her children in the shelter, sang in the shower, raised her voice to the highest level, but her husband still tried to kill her. Diane's husband continued to rob her and her child of a home, security, safety, sanity and the right to a reasonable life. Diane put her child in day care to keep her husband from abusing the child. Amazing. That should have been a huge red flag. Both women have a lot in common. I wonder, how many other sweet, calm, frozen, unempowered women are out there. Hats off to Judy, therapist, a very encouraging woman. Keep lighting matches where it counts.

***

Sidney, 39, Landscape professional, which is a glorified name for gardener assistant

Truthfully, I have a half degree in agriculture, but time and children made it impossible for me to go back to school and finish. OK, you asked for it. I am a bitch, I know it and so does everyone else. That's part of the problem, and part of the solution. My mother and father were married in the sixties, then divorced. My mother didn't believe in marriage when my sister came along, and didn't believe in marriage when my little brother - - the favored child in the family - - came alone either. So there are three of us, with three different fathers, and I never really paid much attention to biology and/or genetics until we all were practically grown up and gone. Of course, my brother was the caboose and the favorite child. He was the golden child, with blond hair and blue eyes, a winning child with a sweet personality. However, he got his way all the time, so my sister and I had to pinch him from time to time to bring him back down to earth. We had to take care of him when mother worked, so we decided that we didn't particularly like him. First of all, he was spoiled. We had to wait on him hand and foot. Cook his meals, change his diapers, pick up after him. Secondly, he came to expect that the world would take care of his needs as he got older.

I never understood why I had a quick temper. It was a flash-point temper and I was disciplined a lot for it. I got in trouble a lot as a kid, and my way out of it was to yell and kick up a fuss. It usually worked. I learned early on that I could have a tantrum and people did what I wanted to keep me quiet. It worked in the principal's office, and later, it worked at work. It worked in my marriage, and it has worked with my children. So I am a bitch. I am a loudmouth bitch, let's be clear about that. But I don't know when to keep my mouth shut. For example: my brother, the golden child, who is now a golden adult (married and divorced twice) and thinks that the world owes him a living, came to me, unemployed and looking for a handout. He has a bad habit of job-hopping, quitting or getting fired. I didn't ask what the last time was all about, with him you never know. So the last time he came around, we discussed parents. Turns out he discovered that his father is bi-polar. Duh? Could that be it for him?

Either way, I gave him two weeks on the sofa and tossed him out on his ass - - again. Then I become the family bitch - - again, because I wouldn't let him stay (freeload) for months on end. My sister, the middle child, is a wuss, she wouldn't complain about anything, and it seems that she is his favorite target. So I called her and told her that if she put him up, she'd be short-changing her kids. She lives from paycheck to paycheck and can't afford to feed him. But she has never told him that, so I told him for her.

So, one: I am the family problem-solver. Two: I am the family bitch. Three: I am the oldest child, so my sister and my brother both look to me to take over when things get tough. Four: my mother, now believes in marriage, won't admit that having three children with three different fathers was a little on the crazy side, so I have some issues with her. And I get bitchy. I get bitchy with my brother for taking advantage of us, and I get bitchy with my sister for not standing up for herself. So, when I put it down on paper, it seems that I get bitchy with my mother, and both of my siblings, but they still see me as strong. Go figure.

* Sidney might be a little hard on herself. Yes, she is a bitch by her own admission. She is the oldest child, and number one children have to pave the way for younger children. They are usually outspoken and assertive. They learn to be unafraid and are the first ones down the slide at the playground. Having the responsibility of caring for two younger siblings put Sidney in the role of mother-older sister, which could foster resentment because the years she should have been a kid were spent doing adult things, like cooking and cleaning. She doesn't say it, but I suspect that in the 70's mom was still out partying, and that could be a neglect problem with the kids. That put additional responsibility on Sidney. I would imagine that when the siblings got in trouble, it was she who came to the rescue, not mom. I would imagine that it was that way all the while she was growing up. So when the brother gets in trouble (again) she would bail him out, until the last time, when she finally got tired of it and kicked him out. I hope she sent him to a therapist or doctor to determine if bi-polar runs in the family. I would assume that the middle sister also comes to her with problems. It sounds as if Sidney is still taking care of her siblings, but I would suggest that she tone it down. She doesn't have to be a megaphone to be heard. She can learn to be soft, gentle and sweet, but that might be asking too much. Some bitches need to be heard at a higher octave to make a point. I don't know, but yellers and screamers and those who have tantrums in public are immediate turn-offs for anyone in a five hundred foot radius and they tend to get kicked out of stores.

***

Sarah, 43, single by choice.

I do not like men. Actually, I am afraid of men. I hated dating in high school, hated having anything to do with men. I just don't like them. I know it goes back to my father. He had the drill sergeant mentality. He'd yell at us as soon as he walked in the door. "Who left their shoes in the living room?" "Who left the plate on the table?" He was hard on us. He'd make us get up in the middle of the night to do the dishes "right". He'd stack up all the dishes from the cupboard in the sink and make us wash them over and over. Same with cleaning the house. If there was a speck of dust on the carpet, we'd vacuum it until our arms fell off. He'd make us stand at attention for hours.

If we didn't get A's on our report cards, he called us names, made us write sentences a hundred times over and over. I am still terrified of him, but now that I'm an adult, I have as little to do with him as possible. I don't call him, and if he calls me, I don't have to answer it. I don't have to be in the same room with him and I don't have to do what he says. But.... and here's the clincher. I am terrified of all men. I don't hate them, I just don't feel right with them. Even if I'm on an elevator with a man, I tend to duck and cower in the back, thinking that I'm going to get hit. I know it's stupid, and I've seen a therapist for years.

* Sarah might be missing some wonderful adventures by being so terrified of men. Her father was abusive, and downright mean from her description. It's a good thing that she's seeing a therapist. All men are not bad, and it's too bad that her father, who should have instilled a trusting relationship with his daughter, taught her instead to cower in the back of elevators in the presence of men. This woman is not a bitch; she needs to learn how to be one, or she will be 60 years old still cowering in the back of elevators. She will duck in the presence of half the world's population without ever having been loved the way she was meant to be loved, and respected. Get yourself a bo-bo doll and punch the hell out of it, get back the person you should be and have a right to be. Good luck.

***

Jen, (short for Jennifer) 25, part time receptionist and student for Developmentally Disabled Children / teacher to be.
Two years ago I was a terrible bitch, rude and inconsiderate to a lot of people, but that might have been my age. I was young and feeling the world for the first time, and I thought it was my place to exercise my adulthood. Then I was in a major accident, broke both ankles and had a head injury. I have so much metal in my legs that I set off metal detectors at airports. I have given up my high heels and there are times that I find myself short-tempered from the

frontal lobe injury. The doctors didn't think that I'd walk again, but I said, "you watch me." Within a year I was back on my feet; now the turtle is my totem. Slow and steady. The car accident was the best thing that happened to me because I'm sure angels stopped me from putting my entire head through the windshield. My belief in God is now much stronger, my attitude has been adjusted so I am not rude or inconsiderate anymore, and I know that I am confident, stronger, and able - - not disabled. Capable of doing different things. I probably won't run again, certainly won't play basketball or jog, but I know that I am capable of living a life to the fullest, regardless of what comes my way. I've been through the worst, and have the rest of my life ahead of me. My major is developmental disabilities, and I think because of my own experiences, I will make a more dedicated teacher for children with disabilities. I understand them now, and "know" their needs.

* I met Jen at a wedding, and commented that her shoes (cute white sneakers with the heels cut out which she wore with a charming yellow long dress) looked to be the most sensible shoes at the wedding. She told me her story and when she mentioned the word "bitch" in past tense referring to herself before the accident, I asked to have her story for this book. She has been there, done that, but isn't a bitch anymore in the negative sense of the word. She is a strong, capable young woman who knows where she's been, (a windshield, rehab for a year, several surgeries, challenging physical therapists to a new step or a few more feet, doctors, doctors and more doctors.) She learned about herself from a hospital bed, grew spiritually, feels that she is one with God, and will never be rude or inconsiderate again. She feels that God had to teach her a hard lesson, that perhaps she needed an extra cosmic two-by-four to fully understand her potential and purpose, and now that purpose has been defined. She will teach disabled children how to live. I wanted to wrap my arms around this beautiful young woman, because, I too, have been there and done that with the physical therapy, but more personally, my grandson has Cerebral Palsy, and I hope that one day

their paths cross, as Mikal will benefit greatly from Jen. She is a marvel. You go, girl. I hope we meet again.

***

Joan, age 32, photographer

I take great pictures. I'm a good photographer and my work speaks for itself, but breaking in with the 'big boys' is a lot more than taking great pictures. When I first started, I had dreams of being a photo-journalist to rank with the top in the field. But no, it hasn't happened that way. My work has won awards, which is something that is demanded in this field. But.....

So I've had to take jobs as film-roller on small sets, that's the person who always makes sure the camera is loaded, and the film is ready when the director says "shoot." It hardly paid the rent, and I was working ten-hour days for three months, then I was out of a job. I suppose it looks good on a resume.

Here's another problem. I'm married and have a child. Now I'm not free to travel like I used to. And: the biggie, my husband supports the fact that I have a great hobby, (but it doesn't pay the bills), but he won't support me going away for a shoot if it means leaving for more than two or three days. Photography means that you have to go where the action is. You have to be willing to hop a train, plane or get in a helicopter on a moment's notice. Now I love my little lamb, but the conflict within me is enormous. I want to stay home and be mommie, and get tons of hugs and kisses from the person most dear to my heart; but I want to be able to grab my camera and tripod and head on out the door, with my vest (full of film, batteries, bug repellant, disposable poncho, Band-Aids, etc) and do a shoot.

I've taken a minor job with a local paper, but it isn't fulfilling a bit. I feel like a prostitute when I have to take nice pictures of weddings and nursing home people celebrating their 100th birthday. I'd rather be in the middle of a war zone.

My husband says that I will never be satisfied with my mundane, middle class life, and that we might have made a mistake when we got married. But then he was full of zest. He enjoyed living out of the back of the camper for a week. Or at least it seemed that he did.

Here's the dilemma. We do love each other, and our child is the most precious person - - and has that kid got pictures - - but I'm not happy. I want more; I want to be running in the rain shooting a tornado when it touches down; I want to photograph train wrecks and exploding buildings. That means you have to be *there when it happens.* I want to live on the edge of deadlines and action. Somehow, cleaning the sink just doesn't cut it for me.

Then I get bitchy, have a tantrum, go off by myself and shoot a couple rolls of film, or lock myself in the dark room, and feel better. However, I can only go to the dark room when curly-top is sleeping. That's the last place I'd want her, not with all the chemicals and toxic fumes. That time is limited too, and I keep the door locked at all times because of her, so even when she's awake, I can't take the chance and sneak in for a quick processing.

It was my choice to have a child. My choice to have a husband and a marriage. I even made the choice to buy the white leather sofa and love-seat, that now has peanut butter & jelly smears (but it's washable) and it was my choice to become a photographer. It's the thing that I wanted to do since I first held a camera at age three. Now I'm frustrated because I feel like a part of me is sitting dormant. By the time I get around to dusting me off again, maybe I'll be too old to even take a crack at greatness.

* Joan's frustration at not being fulfilled is certainly understandable. Just about every woman who has accomplished anything great (writing, being an attorney, being a doctor, pilot etc) has had to weigh the values of family against career. Many women gave up their careers, because they also know the value of being a parent. Raising children is the greatest and toughest job one will ever have.

Way back when, I had to terminate a job (drug store cashier, wow!) because my baby-sitter called me in the middle of the day and said "come and get your kids, I quit." She never gave me an explanation, and I was out of the piddly job that didn't pay squat, but it left me feeling like I had very few choices when it came to child care. My children were my primary responsibility.

I also understand the need to be where the action is, to live on the edge of excitement. This is what Joan craves more than anything else. She also likes to see her work presented as a professional. Nothing wrong with that. She will just have to be patient a few more years, and when the child is five years old, she will have a small camera and go along with mommie on a few jaunts. I suspect that the husband will come around, especially after he sees that Joan is bringing in more than her share of the finances.

In the meantime, Joan, why not take that energy and create something from your home. With digital computers, scanners and any number of other high tech equipment, she could be creating web sites for others or with the instant gratification of digital, she could be teaching her child the love of photography without the chemicals in a dark room. Lots of things that she could be doing from her base environment, and it may not be as exciting for a while, but it will be worthwhile. Hang in there.

***

Susan, 33, Jill of all trades, mistress of none.
I didn't go to college, I didn't choose a career. I bounce from one job to the next, not really bouncing, but about two-and-a-half years is the average for each job. I take opportunities and expand my horizons with each new job. Each new job pays more than the last one, so I guess you could say that I'm always looking for a new challenge.

I've done retail sales, office work (hate it), working in a car parts store in the back room doing inventory and stocking, worked in a pet supply warehouse, drove a forklift, trained as a telephone repair person (and decided that I didn't like that at all), went back to office work (hated it even more) and moved on to cable installation.

I like working with my hands, doing things, connecting this wire to that wire and making things work. I hate sitting in an office, looking nice and acting sweet, when I really want to be on the road driving a truck. (I did that too, 18-wheeler, not for long, but I did it.) I don't like working around other females, and I'll tell you why. They whine about broken fingernails, and a bad hair cut. They whine about bad marriages and kids that are out of control. I tell them, "you know, complaining won't fix the problem," and they look at me like I have two heads.

I was married for a while (pregnant at 16), it didn't work out, and am dating a very nice man now, but if a light bulb needs changing, I know where the ladder is. I can fix the roof, change the oil in the car, do just about what a man can do. I lacked the upper body strength so I trained at a gym with weights. OK, so I have biceps. So what? I also have a 26-inch waist and 34DD chest. Not bad for a girl. I grew up with four brothers. Need I say more?

I am the mother of two sons, and yes, I get bitchy. Being a woman doesn't mean that I have to take s--- from people; it doesn't mean that I have to stand around and be cute, or that I have to pretend to be stupid to get a date, or look at some guy likes he's God's Gift. I have always gone out and gotten what I've wanted; car, job, date, whatever.

If my sons ever hit a woman they will answer to me, personally, over hot coals. If they join a gang, they are dead meat at home. If they lie, cheat, steal or con to get ahead, they will also answer to me on that. I was raised to be honest, hard-working and civil; but there ARE times when a woman just has to be a bitch. I can do that. I can open the first couple of buttons on my blouse and bend over so the black lace on the bra shows, and I can get my hair and nails done, wear a skirt with a slit up the side and five inch heels. I can cross my legs like Sharon Stone and I can be the best damn bitch this side of hell in bed, *and* I can shoot the gonads off a gnat at 50 paces. I should have been a cop. There's still time, I might try that next.

* Wow, you certainly have to admire a woman like Susan. Get this woman a Bitch Woman Cup!

Rose Stadler, MSW

***

Bunny (nick-name) fast approaching the big 5-0

I'm Bunny, the carrot-top kid who always did things right. Married, had kids, worked hard to make the marriage work, then wham! he up and leaves me for a bimbo he met on the Internet. Suddenly, he says that I can't do laundry right (I've been washing his clothes for 27 years), can't cook, wouldn't know a potato if it bit me, I'm overweight, overbearing, loud and aggressive, when in fact, he has always used mental and verbal abuse on me as a method of control. Now he wants his freedom! The Bimbette is half his age, the age of our oldest daughter. She left her husband for my Internet Idiot.

Well, this bitch is gonna fly. I've put up with so much crap in my marriage, that I thought I would go insane. There were so many times when he was right, when he had to have his supper on the table at a certain time, when he wanted to make love, when he controlled the remote..... well, no more, I've nailed him in the wallet, and baby, this is like when the dentist gives you a shot in the mouth. "This is going to hurt you a lot more than it hurts me."

I'm a little confused right now, and maybe looking for love again too quickly, but I think that this is a phase that will pass, like gas. I can't wait to see what the next part of my life will bring. If he thinks that I'll go quietly so he and Bimbette can have a happily ever after, he's dead wrong. In fact, here's one he forgot about: I purchased a life insurance policy for him, and I am the holder, no one has purchased the policy from me so only I can change the beneficiary on the policy. He has a bad heart, so I hope that Bimbette gives him a crash course in bedroom 101, literally.

* Well Bunny, you might start by changing your name from Bunny to Rabid, then do what you have to do to get right with your life. You aren't the first to be left and you won't be the last. Cyberspace is fast becoming lover's leap. It seems to be a ridiculous way of dating and courting, but I guess people who are looking, will look in all the corners of the hard drive. Don't worry, you'll be fine.

Learn a new dance step, kick up some dust and get on with your life.

Avoid long term relationships for at least a year because the first year after a separation is when you are the most vulnerable. There is a difference between being alone and being lonely. When you are alone, you get to listen to the music of your choice, when you are lonely, everything sounds like a scratchy old love song. When you are alone, you get to put your pictures on the wall. When you are lonely, all the pictures scream at you of times past. Get your own pictures on the wall, and toss out his choice of music. When in doubt, give yourself a facial. It takes at least a half hour, forces you to relax, and gives you thinking time.

And stop referring to yourself as the carrot-top kid. Stop thinking like a child. You are a woman; you have arrived at your own time in your own space. Enjoy it.

***

Doris, 61, retired sales clerk

I specifically remember the day I became a bitch. It was at my first husband's funeral twenty years ago. He was a good man, but we had our differences. He had been married before and had two children from the previous marriage, but he didn't see his children much, and when we had the kids there were times I thought I'd tear my hair out by being the step-mother. When he got sick, his kids were suddenly "interested" in their father, mostly because of the insurance I'd get when he died. The day he died, I did the right thing and called his children. They showed up at the funeral and first thing out of the oldest one's mouth was, "How much did he leave me?" It was very difficult, being a widow in my early 40's, with my own children, and now his kids, who didn't have time for him when he was alive, wanted money. That was all they wanted. Later, when they had the potluck in the church basement, I said, out loud, for all the world to hear, that they only showed up for the money. In truth, there wasn't that much insurance after all the bills, but I never let them know. I didn't tell them that their father didn't have a specific amount set aside for each of this children. I let it drop. They didn't get a dime. I might have given them something but I didn't think they deserved it. I haven't heard from them since the funeral and I could care less.

* Doris, it sounds as if the children were selfish and inconsiderate of your needs, your grief, and their timing stunk. It doesn't sound as if you lost anything by losing the relationship(s). I wouldn't call you a bitch - - in the negative sense of the word, but I would say that you appear to have some guilt associated with the incident. Stop beating yourself up. Besides, you were the surviving spouse so you were entitled to everything you got.

***

S. E. M. age 32
The day I became a bitch.

I'm one of those people who has been abused all my life; by my adoptive parents, by live-in boyfriends, and by the father of my child. I used to make jokes about being abused as a child, and thought that it was a way of life. I was abused by everyone I knew, including myself. I thought that it was love.

It was just after my daughter's first birthday. Her father (my ex) had just been released from prison and was stalking me at work and at home. At the time, I was living at a shelter for homeless women and children, and I was completely beside myself. I was tempted to use (drugs) again, or drink, but I knew that I couldn't. I was just beginning to get in touch with myself, and the reasons for my escaping, but I couldn't function with him stalking me. It was hell going to and from work, trying to hide on a public bus, walking down the street with a stroller, thinking that he was watching me.

Finally, I walked into the director's office and told her what was going on with me. She immediately called my ex's parole officer and I pressed charges. He couldn't understand what kind of bitch

I had become. I told him that I had become the kind of bitch who knows what love is, and abuse isn't love.

Something changed in me that day. I had never really stood up for myself until then, and now, weeks later, people are asking me what's the difference. They can actually *see* the difference, and I'm making a lot of progress with therapy. I quit smoking, don't use drugs or alcohol anymore, and feel like a different person. It was the day that I became a bitch that made the difference. I stand taller, speak more clearly, and know that I love me and my daughter. I don't need abuse in my life. I certainly don't need a stalker or a man to beat me. I think that I've just had one of those light bulbs over my head.

* The great Ah-ha light bulb! Being a bitch doesn't just happen in one day, like a flash of lightning. It's a process of learning to stand up for oneself. It's a growth spurt that happens in an instant.

It's that one moment, sculptured in time, when you are no longer willing to take one more minute of abuse, (mental, physical or spiritual) or stalking. In this case, SEM decided that she wanted to live her life free of this man. "What kind of a bitch did you suddenly become?" was the man's reaction. She obviously surprised him (and probably herself) with her action of pressing charges. "The kind of bitch who truly knows what love is." An excellent answer. Of course, he was stalking her. Makes sense. He had beat her in the past, and thought that things were going to get back to normal after he got out of jail, but things had changed. SEM was no longer his whipping girl. She's on her way to making other important changes in her life, but *the day she became a bitch* stands out for her. Something clicked that day. It was a pivotal or turning point in her life. Nice going, SEM.

***

Christine (Chris), 44

I do a ton of paperwork every day, I have to be responsible for huge sums of money coming and going, and payroll is just one of my functions. Every week, someone doesn't turn in the right paperwork, and generally the paycheck is shorter than they expected. I pay on the amounts I see in front of me. I don't track down the paperwork, or baby-sit the employees. If they haven't got the paperwork turned in, that's too bad for them.

Lots of people refer to me as a bitch. I do my job and expect them to do theirs.

Usually, a one-on-one with me will help clear things up, but it takes *them,* not me, to make the effort. It's their paycheck, not mine. I don't pocket the extra money, and yes, they will have to wait two weeks for the extra funds to show up. Maybe they won't make the same mistakes twice. And *don't* show up in my office wearing perfume or after-shave. I'm allergic. The minute I get the allergy headache, you're out the door, whether or not the paperwork is done.

I guess I run my house the same way. I have no husband - - we separated a long time ago - - with one child who attends college classes, and I am perfectly willing to pay the tuition as long as I see a decent grade report. If he works hard, then I will work hard for him. If he screws it up, then he leaves, get himself a job and an apartment. Very simple. Do it my way and we get along. No dogs, no pets, no carpeting. Allergies again. Stark environment.

If I'd have to expand on this, I would say, "Yes, I am a bitch." However, when I look in the mirror, I see a lonely woman. I haven't had a date in eons, and haven't had sex (what year is this now????) a long time. I haven't been out to dinner with anyone other than my son in ages, I haven't been to a movie with a friend, and frankly, I guess I don't have too many friends. When I want to be entertained, I go skating (alone) or go to a movie (alone) or rent a video and watch it (alone). I haven't even been on a good shopping spree with a friend in years, when I need something, I go to the mall (alone), buy what I need (alone), come home (alone) and try it on (alone.) I guess I need to get out more.

Writing this has made me sad and frustrated. I was fine, thinking that I was a bitch at work, then I realized that I have to get out and get a life! I honestly don't know how.

* Chris is in a rut. She may be a very capable employee, indeed it seems that she has people tiptoeing past her office door, and she likes it that way. But by her own admission, she's lonely. She lives in a stark environment, clearly alone. I don't think that she likes being alone, and I doubt it's the allergies. I believe it's a convenient excuse to avoid any human contact at all - - there are plenty of good prescriptions on the market now that don't cause drowsiness, etc. She needs to discuss the allergies with her doctor, but it seems to me that she's hiding behind them to avoid intimacy at all costs. If I would see this woman in my office as a therapist, I would confront the allergy issue and the reason for the alone-ness. I would want to know why she's hurting so badly that she has to have a life devoid of pets, friends, and perhaps even a teddy bear (it would have dust on it no doubt). I would dig deep until she knew the reason for shutting the door on everyone.

I would be hard pressed to say that this woman has been sexually abused, or physically abused, because I don't know her or her history, but when someone goes to such extreme lengths to avoid humanity, there is generally a pretty good reason. The loneliness is something that she will have to eventually deal with when the son leaves home. Right now, he's still there because he's no fool. He knows that his mother will pay the tuition, and it appears that he has a pretty free ride with mom. (She didn't say anything about him having a job or paying rent or helping out with the groceries.)

When that day comes, she will be so hungry for companionship that she might have to confront her issues. Or, she will follow her son forever, lashing him to her with bribes (?) of more tuition payments, rent, etc. She may invade his life, failing to have one of her own. God help the poor woman the man marries. She will have the mother-in-law from hell. God forbid the future woman has a child and a puppy, and the puppy licks the child's face. Can you see it? I can. Chris would come unglued.

She would be totally and completely unhinged if the smallest dust mold threatened her existence. Enough said. Chris is not the bitch she thinks she is. She is a little girl wanting to be loved.

Rose Stadler, MSW

***

Harriet, 55, professional woman
On the job bitch

In my line of work, there are three kinds of women: secretaries, administrators and top-notch professionals. The last one would be me. I've had to learn the art of hiring and firing. It's not pleasant, but now I have it down pat. When I have to be bitchy, I am - - but I usually try to be nice first. When I say I want something done, I want it done immediately, not next week or next month. When I have to discipline a person or write a performance report, I try to be fair, but sometimes, you have to say, "you screwed up. This is the first and last time we'll have this discussion. Next time, if there is a next time, you're history." Then I have to stick to it. The people above me expect me to do a good job, and I do. I've banked a lot on my career, and I won't let it go for people who won't, or can't, do a good job. I'm hired to do my best and I expect it from my front line people. On the home front, I'm a lot easier to live with - - or so I think. I take off the high-powered suits and put on jeans and tee shirts like everyone else, but I'm still a bitch when I need to be. I don't cut people off in traffic, and I tip well in restaurants, but when someone cuts in line at the grocery store, I don't hold my tongue. I tell them, "sorry, I was here first." So, if that makes me a bitch - - I can live with that.

* Harriet sounds like a professional, no-nonsense kind of woman. She apparently knows her value. I've always said that "humility is knowing one's worth." If that means you can type 100 words a minute, you have an obligation to say so. No one else is going to toot your horn for you. Harriet knows this. Obviously, she didn't get where she's at by being at the mercy of others. She doesn't say what profession she's in, or her educational standing, but I'll bet that she set a high standard of success for herself from the time she was ten years old. I would like to meet her.

***

Mavis E. 68, doctor's wife

We have a nice life, we can afford everything that we need and all the amenities. We take trips, spend time with the grandchildren, have put children through college, and can do what we want with our life. But we earned every dime of it. When my husband was going through med school, it was hard, very hard. Our first child was born prematurely, and it was a constant struggle to make ends meet. I almost never saw my husband in the first three years of our marriage (except for a quick hop in the sac, and got pregnant every time - - two more children). With daddy gone to his residency for a year, and me and the kids left behind, I was robbing Peter to pay Paul. It was always one thing or another, hard times and old shoes, my mother used to say. But we got through it, together, so I'm not a bitch - - I was at my husband's side all the way, but I felt like I had to sacrifice my own dreams for his career. I would have liked to do things too, but a doctor has to have a nice place to live, has to entertain, has to have good clothing, has to have children who behave in public. A doctor lives in the public eye, and so does his family, so the children and I were always clean, dressed well, and drove clean vehicles. We didn't stop at Dairy Queen because the children might get dirty on the way to visit daddy in his office - - and we didn't always take our vacations when we thought we could because of some emergency. So I was the doctor's wife, and I kept busy with the children and house. Eventually, the children grew up and I found myself still the doctor's wife, but now the doctor was having himself a little fling on the side. That's when I became a bitch. I had given up my identity for him, given up all the dreams and desires I had so I could present a nice picture of what a nice married couple we were. I knew about the little fling, and knew that I would never divorce him because while I didn't really work outside the home, I worked my butt off inside, with the gardening, cooking, entertaining, cleaning and raising the children, and I deserved everything that was mine. So I took an extended trip. I told him that he would have three weeks to wrap it up and get back to normal, and if I ever (*ever*) got wind of another affair, I would get a divorce, but first, I would have every single asset put in my name. We don't discuss it at all, but we're still married, and now that he is winding down, we're finally spending time together. I'm glad that I didn't divorce him then because I would be a very bitter woman now.

* Interesting, Mavis put her occupation down as a doctor's wife. Sounds like she knew when to hold and when to fold. It must have been a full time position, and I can understand a woman putting all her dreams on hold for her husband. Why not do something with those dreams after the children moved out?

***

Pat, 42, auto repair.

I don't work in a woman's field. I'm a better mechanic than half the men I know but I know how hard it is to work in my field. I get dirty, I smell like motor oil, and most of the time I look like hell on the job. People come to the garage, and I give them an estimate of what they need done, and nine times out of ten, they'll say, "well, I really wanted the mechanic," or: "when the mechanic comes in would you tell him..." I tell them that I *am* the mechanic and I get all kinds of rude comments, like: "what are you? A lesbian?" Frankly, I'm sick and tired of all the comments. I'm a damn good mechanic. I got into this by accident, I guess you could say, but I was good with engines from the time I was sixteen years old. When my father had car trouble, he'd come to me. I could fix anything. I never had the desire or inclination to go to college - - like my sister, who is the family goodie-goodie, - - or my brothers, but I like what I do, and I make sufficient money to feed and clothe my children. Yes, I am divorced, yes I am a female in all respects, and yes, I am heterosexual. No, I am not a lesbian, but I feel that I always have to prove it to other people. Once in a while, to rattle a few chains, I show up for work in short-shorts and a halter top. I also ride a motorcycle. By the way, I'm five foot seven, weigh 120 pounds and have muscles, but I am also very feminine, when I want to be, when it counts. I suppose I could pat my eyes (for about twenty seconds) but who needs it. I am what I am, and not ashamed of myself at all. But I do wish I could get the dirt out from under my fingernails. I get a manicure once in a while just to keep in touch with the feminine side, but I generally break a nail before the day is up. So, that's it. I'm me and proud of it.

* Bravo, Pat. I'm sure you can change your tire in record time. You wouldn't be standing on the side of the road looking like a damsel in distress with a flat tire. I'd hire you in a heartbeat to fix my car. Get the woman a bitch cup. I'll bet you get more exercise in one day on the job than most of get in a week. Five foot seven and 120 pounds sound lean and mean to me.

***

Emily S. 57, sales

I have no idea how to title this, but I know my feet hurt from wearing uncomfortable shoes when I was younger. You know, the pointy toed high heels that would kill you if you tried anything like walking down a flight of stairs. So now I wear sensible shoes, nice looking black pumps that go with my conservative business suits. Know what I'd really like: some Grateful Dead tie-dyed, sandals and loose cotton shorts. I am sick and tired of having to put on a show every day of my life to make a living. I am considered successful and professional, but in truth I am weary of it all. I would like to run away, take a three month break and write a really sleazy romance on some desert island someplace. I am tired of picking up the pieces of my kids' lives - - three children, seven grandchildren, whom I love dearly, but would like a break from them too. I am not the traditional grandmother. I don't bake cookies or knit booties. I work darn hard. When one of the kids needs something I give it freely, but just once, I would like someone to take care of me. I have worked all my life. Heck, I worked when I was in labor with my third child. I didn't have sense enough to take a break even then.

By every standard, I am a success. I keep telling myself that I have it all. The house, the nice car, the new carpeting, and landscaping that I've always wanted. Yes, I have it all, and by God, I earned every penny of it. I was widowed too early - - my husband died in a car accident, and I got a very generous settlement, but not enough to quit working, not enough to take that Italian vacation I've always wanted. But enough to help out the kids when they needed, enough to put them through college, and enough to add a room on to the house when the middle child moved back with two children, but not enough to quit working. I guess I'm just tired and ranting.

* Emily, sounds like you are very weary, tired and exhausted. Have you seen your physician lately? Maybe it's time for a check-up. It also sounds like depression, where you keep putting one foot in front of the other, walking by rote, living without really living. Take that vacation. I'm sure somewhere in your financial package you have enough money to take time for yourself. Go ahead, wear a tie-dyed tee shirt and cotton shorts, and sit on a beach. If you don't write, then read. Get a little hammock therapy.

***

Jeanette, (pseudonym) 62, retired
When I heard the title of this book, I wanted to shout, "Finally, someone has done what I've always said." I am a sweet Southern Woman, that's a category all by itself. We know how to bitch in the sweetest manner. We can bat our eyes, smile and say, "Why, darlin' I am tellin' you should see the devil before the day is up," and keep smiling, blinking and doing whatever we're doing with our hands. It's very important to keep your hands occupied.

Our mothers were bitches, our sisters are bitches, every female born to Sweet Southern Families will grow up to be a bitch - - but I can see that the younger generation has lost the tact and diplomacy that we were taught. I can honestly say that I am a bitch, but I still have the intelligence, finesse and charm to be sweet about it.

However, when that fails, (and it has) I can always resort to my granny's mountain up-bringin' and say something like, "now yo-all git that pig away from the table before I kill it," referring to my grandson's girlfriend, who is one of the young Southern women that I generally call trailer-trash. Of course, she will never hear it from my lips. But I swear, if I have to go to a wedding in the near future, I will be forced to change my will. (At the very least, have one of my fainting spells...)

* Whew. Jeanette, or whatever your name is, you certainly have mastered the art of bitchiness. But being a true bitch is a process of self-discovery, but you probably identified yourself as a true bitch when you were about ten years old, and went on to refine the art all your life. As for trailer trash, a lot of very fine people have resided in mobile homes, and do not define themselves as trailer trash. That's a slam, but you probably already knew that. I'm sure the grandson's friend already knows that she's not welcome in your home, so save the fainting spells for something really important, like a broken fingernail.

***

Mary Ellen, late-40-ish
I used to have different meanings for the word "bitch". I was a victim for much of my life, wife, or more like it, "Property" of a husband; then I got divorced, then I was surprised by pregnancy in my late thirties, and wouldn't' you know it? The guy took off. I thought, "I can do this," Hell, I *had* to do it. There were no options. Then I got myself into an abusive relationship. That is the worst thing a woman can do. She stays, regardless of the beatings and bruises, and thinks that she can make it right. It gets a little better, but it always gets worse in the end. Finally, when you are so battered and bruised, and you don't know which way is up, and the neighbors are calling the police, and you have pictures taken of you in the hospital, and people are asking if you want to press charges. Then,

you get the hint. There is something wrong with this picture. So you start to make changes, but think all the while, "OK, he'll be in jail for a little while, and things will be better. He won't do it again." Or make excuses, "He was drinking, he couldn't help it. He didn't know what he was doing."

Eventually, it got so bad that I ended up in a shelter for abused women, my child and I were homeless, and my ex was in prison. I had to learn how to think of myself all over again. This time I wasn't going to let anything or any one come between me and my son. I had gone back to school, gotten a decent job, and generally learned to get on with my life. I was running in place, not really getting ahead.

My life changed one day when I was coming home from work, a typical day; thinking "I'm tired, want to get the panty hose off, what am I going to make for dinner?" I didn't know that a crazed gunman was stalking the city in the very place I would be driving. I went the way I had always gone, down 15th Ave, then across the shortest route. I had driven into the very spot where police had cordoned off a city block because the gunman was there, shooting everything in sight. But this time I saw a man with long hair, ten feet from the car, with a gun pointed right at me. I didn't know if he wanted to steal the car, or shoot me. I saw his eyes, and for a split second, I thought, "Oh not this time buster. Not me. Not again." I turned the wheel of the car sharply and found myself instantly surrounded by policemen.

They all started to yell at me; "get out of here, go that way." I don't know how I managed to drive away from that awful scene, but I did. I didn't start shaking until I got about three blocks away, and thought. "My God, that man had a gun. He was going to kill me." I shook so bad that I couldn't drive another foot.

Three people died that day, and police eventually shot the gunman, but that was the day I decided that I would never be a victim again. I have lost about 20 pounds, died my hair red, and have made significant changes in my life. When I think about being a victim, or an abused woman, I think of that man and the fear that he drove to my soul. I could have been one of those people who died that day.

So now I am stronger because a deranged killer pointed a gun at me.

Maybe; maybe not, but I know this: no one will ever make me squirm again. I will never be a victim, weeping like some simp at the hands of a man, and never, never will I take single parenting for granted. I could have died that day, then what would happen to my son? Something snapped in me that day, and I can't go back to being the wimpy little old person I was.

You could say that was the day that my inner bitch was released. I know the difference between being a bitch, like a pms-bitch, or when someone takes credit for something that you did. This time, I took control, and that makes all the difference in the world.

* Mary Ellen hit the nail on the head with that one. Being in control of one's own destiny is the key to everything. Up to that point, Mary Ellen was at the mercy of others: from her husband, to the father of her child, to the man who abused her. She now knows that she could have taken control at any time in her life, but it wasn't until she was looking death square in the face, did she make that sharp turn, literally, from victim to survivor. Hats off to Mary Ellen. She has achieved a sense of empowerment, direction and her own destiny. Everything in her life is going along nicely now, because she is in the driver's seat. She knows exactly where she has been, where she is going, and how she will get there. Her son should be proud of her.

***

No name or age. Submitted by a male self defense instructor.

Can a guy get in here? I teach self defense classes to women, and I see women of all walks come through the doors. Most of them have issues with men, they are either afraid of men, were abused or something else. I teach them to be bold, attack first and never stop attacking. I tell them to use their fingernails, kick where it counts, spin and run, crouch and duck. By about the third class, or sometimes, even at the end of the first class, I see a change in the women. They become strong, not physically, but mentally. Yes, men are bigger than women and have better upper body strength, but women can be just as dangerous when they have to be. It's about having the courage to fight back, the spirit inside you, not the amount of muscle on your body. You have to be quicker, think like a snake, and do whatever you have to do to survive. I'm probably the only male in the book, but I have seen a lot of women over the years, and survival depends on two things. First and foremost; quick thinking and the ability to react. Not act, react. You have to be fast and dependable with your stance. You have to make a split-second decision, and if you can't do that, then you'll be a victim. If you have to go for the eyes with your nicely manicured nails, then do it. If you go for the nose, be prepared for a full frontal re-attack in the next second. Take classes, do whatever you need to do, but don't ever let anyone attack you or abuse you.

* Thank you for this submission. No address or name. It's a shame because I would be the first to pass out your business cards. You are right. Women do not have to be abused in the first place, but once the attack is underway, fast reaction has to be the front-line defense. I highly recommend that every woman take a self-defense course, and know how to do the dirty street fighting. It may save a life.

***

Jolynn (pseudonym) 34, research assistant, AIDS activist

Everything about my world changed when my little brother died of AIDS. He had gotten it through heterosexual transmission, so we don't have to live with the gay stigma; but there are those who still say that AIDS is a gay disease. They don't know what they are talking about. They have their heads in the sand to avoid the truth.

My brother was my world growing up. If there was anything to be done, we did it together, even if we were sneaking off to McDonalds or Dairy Queen on a Saturday morning when we were supposed to be doing chores. We were probably latch-key kids, but so was everyone else on the block at the time. We lived in different times. If we got in trouble, we could go to a neighbor, now a neighbor would probably shoot us for breaking and entering.

Billy and I were joined at the hip in all things. We loved each other and did things together, even though I was girl. We had snowball fights, went sled riding, went for long hikes, made picnic lunches in the park, rode our bikes at breakneck speed down "dead man's hill" and taught each other how to dance. When I went to the prom, it was Billy who was standing at the bottom of the stairs when I came down in my dress, and it was he who took the pictures.

I was about 12 years old (and Billy 10) when dad left. I never really figured out the reason, until I was older, but at the time we thought it was a case of dad wanting his freedom and mom wanting a new car. They never should have gotten married. Billy and I were allies when they were fighting in the middle of the night, and we would huddle together listening to the yelling. We would hear things banging around, and more than once I have seen my father hit my mother, but I was always sent from the room.

Billy and I tried to protect mom, and once Billy took after dad with a plastic baseball bat. Dad just held him at arms length and laughed. We were all glad when dad left, and mom didn't have to have an ice pack in the freezer all the time. Now that I'm an adult, I can see spousal abuse for what it is. I can still hear the glass breaking and still hear her screaming, running down the street in her slip, the street lamp picking up the whiteness of her legs against the snow....... bad dream, me looking out from my upstairs bedroom window, then trying to get back to sleep, and the two of them pretending that nothing happened....

Mom and I have had lots of discussions about physical abuse. She thought that she had to take it. She had made her bed, and she had to lie in it. That's what her mother would have said. Then I found out that my grandmother was also abused. Women are just now starting to talk about abuse, and mom, bless her heart, just finally admitted out loud, that she had been abused. She had been taking the shame as her own, taking responsibility for my father's acts. She always felt that she either had it coming, or that in one way or another, she caused it. Mom would lie about it and cover it up, saying, "well, there *was* too much chili pepper in the chili....."

Dad disappeared from our lives for a number of years, then he re-surfaced, apparently having failed two more marriages. By that time, mom was involved with someone else. I saw a moment of weakness in her, but it passed. I was terrified that she would go back with him, but now there wouldn't be anyone to protect her as both Billy and I had gotten our own lives.

Billy went to college in an Eastern state and we didn't see each other as often. We spoke on the phone a lot, in fact, one of my boyfriends accused me of having an affair with Billy. Stupid man, I didn't bother explaining that a brother is a gift from God.

Bill met a young woman and was planning to marry after he got his degree. Obviously, he played the field, and so did she. But they had unprotected sex, and he got AIDS and died. But it's not that simple.

First there is the physical wasting. You could see the pants hanging off his hips when he'd come home between semesters. Then you'd see the gaunt hollows in his face, and the fatigue. He thought it was the flu, or a cold that he couldn't shake. He promised to see a doctor when he got back to school, because then he could use the student health services at no cost.

He called me before he called mom. "It's HIV," he whispered. My heart stopped when I heard that.

After that, things went downhill pretty fast. Pneumonia set in, followed by everything possible. I moved Billy in with me and my family. First of all, I know that you can't get AIDS from having dinner at the same table, but I did make concessions with the bathroom. I gave Billy the upstairs bathroom and had a bottle of bleach on hand at all times. I learned how to live with someone with HIV/AIDS and more than that, I learned how to love a dying brother. I watched him lose weight, need help getting up the stairs, have difficulty breathing, and finally, I watched his hair fall out, watched him lose his grip on life, and watched him as the candle burned out.

I am a strong activist in the AIDS campaign. This is a deadly killer, and we have to stop it. I never thought that I would be addressing large groups of people or writing articles. I was an average, run-of-the-mill woman, not necessarily a take-charge person. Now I go into high schools and give lectures to kids on safe sex. (Abstinence is the only safe sex there is.) This has become my mission, my passion and the reason for my endurance. When Billy died, I felt like I lost my left arm, and half of me. He took me with him. Now all I can do is sit by the graveside and talk to him. Sometimes I pull up a lawn chair and sometimes I leave a good book on the grave. He knows I'm there, and he's feeding me the strength to continue the fight. Every now and then, when I'm talking to a group of kids or parents, I think I see him out of the corner of my eye.

I have no idea if this is what you wanted with the bitch assignment, but here it is. I couldn't stop the flow once it started. Here's to you, Billy. Love, your sister.

* Jolynn's heart-rending story is one of family commitment, love, devotion and dedication to a family member. Jolynn indicated that she didn't have personal strength until her brother died of AIDS, then something changed in her. The word bitch isn't anywhere in here, and that's just fine with me. It took a lot of courage to face AIDS, to move her brother in with her, to hold him and watch him die; but it took a lot more courage to address groups of kids. Hat's off to Jolynn. We need more women like her, women willing to take a stand against something, then DO something about it. She's not just talking about the spread of AIDS, she's actively doing something. Is anyone listening? Has this touched even one heart? If so, do something.

** I'm still trying to figure out why a woman as out-spoken as Jolynn is didn't put her real name on this. Is she afraid to be known as a bitch? Actually, this seems to have been a common theme for several of the contributors. Relax, ladies, you're in good company. It's OK to be a bitch. It's no longer a threat or an insult. It's a compliment of the highest order.

Rose Stadler, MSW

***

Rachael, (pseudonym) 43, (occupation, unk)

I didn't learn how to be bitchy until I was in my thirties. As an abused child, I lived my life in silence, desperation, and total fear. I was hit and whipped with whatever weapon was handy; belts, hairbrushes, wooden spoons, fly swatters, shoes, rulers, cords, sticks and anything that could be an extension of my mother's hand. She was a screamer, a raver, so the smallest thing would set her off. She was either flat on her back, on the sofa, demanding quiet because of her 'headaches' or she was in the bedroom, flat on her back, sleeping or pretending to be dead.

There were three kids in the family, I was in the middle. My older brother took a lot of abuse for us smaller kids, until we were able to handle it on our own. He left when I was eight, (he started a fire in a neighbor's garage and was put in foster care - - why the state left two smaller children in the same house is still beyond me......) My protection went with him. From then on, it was me and my smaller sister. We became targets of spontaneous combustion on a whim. My father either didn't care or didn't do anything to protect us, saying that it was between our mother and us. He always took her side. Sometimes she would deliberately break a dish then say we had done it. Then she'd wait for him to come home to administer the 'official' spanking. I preferred getting spankings from him, because there wasn't any hate involved. We got the required five slaps with the belt across our butts, and he was done. We could tolerate that. (Sometimes we couldn't sit afterwards, but I think that he was gentler, and didn't use as much strength. He did what she set him up to do.) When she beat us, it was anywhere, head, face, arms, legs; it didn't matter as long as she struck skin. Sometimes she'd pull our hair, then slap us if we cried.

I could go on and on, but my therapist says not to dwell on the bad memories.

At 15, I hooked up with an older man, got pregnant almost instantly, and thought that things would be different. He dumped me (he was married) and left me to fend for myself. I had no choice but to go back home. My father bailed about the same time. Once there, the abuse of me stopped, but my mother took over the care of my child, never letting me near my baby. This went on for about 6 months, then I moved in with a friend. I have never been home for more than 3 hours at a time since then.

I was terrified that I would abuse my child, and did everything to keep my child from crying. I fed my child constantly to make sure that she didn't cry. When I was 18, I had another child, a boy, and this time, not only feeling like the world's biggest slut, the love of my life abandoned me. My mother laughed at me when my son was a day old, saying "what did you expect, you whore?"

From then on, I withdrew. I got a small apartment, got a cheap job ($1.10 at the time) and tried my best to maintain my sanity. Later, it was welfare and food stamps. Another child later, I learned that I had inherited my mother's abusive traits. Instead of dealing with an issue, I would find myself yelling and screaming. I have abused my own children. Sadly. I will regret this to the day I die.

When I was in my 30's, child protective services were called on me because I was so abusive to my children. I was still on welfare, by now selling the food stamps to make ends meet, and lying to everyone about everything.

My children were placed in foster care. That was my turning point. I never realized that I had become my mother. I said I was disciplining them to teach them right from wrong, and that I had to lock them in closets to make them behave. I honestly believed that I was doing the right thing.

Wrong, wrong, wrong. I was using all my mother's scare tactics for parenting. CPS sent me to parenting classes. Then they sent me to a counselor. It took months and months of therapy, at taxpayer's expense to get my head on straight, but I did it. My kids were returned home after about a year and a half, but in that time, I had to go before judges, work with case managers and review boards. All of them wanted to keep my children away from me, and one case manager wanted to sever my parental rights. You have no idea how much I cried during that time.

I've had years of therapy since then, and have learned that there are triggers that send me up the wall. But I know how to recognize them, but I could be an MPD (multiple personality) and maybe the bitch comes out when I'm not looking. Some of the doctors I've seen said I'm bi-polar, others have said that I suffer from a genetic mental illness (paranoid schizophrenic). I've been hospitalized twice because the stress was so high that I honestly thought that I'd be better off dead. I tried suicide too, but all it did was make me sick, and locked up for 30 days. I've had spaces of time that I've blanked out, months; a few years. (I can't remember my early 20's.) I'm on medication for severe anxiety and depression, and probably always will be. There are days when I can't leave my house for fear that someone will attack me, and I can't ever go in to a dark room. I have lights burning all night long.

I don't think that my kids will ever forgive me, and I know that they still keep a distance, but my oldest child is now 27 years old and a parent. I haven't let my kids go anywhere near my mother in about 20 years, (she still can't figure it out.). Now she wants to see her great-grandchild and we all say "no way". I live three states away from my mother now and would never go any closer.

My little sister has been arrested for prostitution and drugs so many times that she has forgotten what alias she has been arrested under, and made the mistake of using the same name too many times. She's in prison doing ten years. Her kids have been removed. They have been adopted out. We both have sad histories which might have been prevented if my mother hadn't been such an abusive bitch.

My father is dead now, but I had the opportunity to talk to him a few years ago, and he apologized. I know he suffered too. We all suffered at the hands of an incredible bitch, abusive bitch, who cared more about herself than she ever did about any of us kids.

Sorry to run on so long, but it seems that I couldn't stop once the words started coming out. The bottom line is: I was an abused child, in turn, I abused my children. I have a mental illness, and my mother probably did too, and it may or may not be genetic, but all I can say is that children learn from their parents. I learned how to be abusive from my mother, and I taught that same abuse to my children. The cycle repeated itself. I can only hope that my children can learn to break the cycle.

* Rachael's story is a stunning example of the old environment vs. heredity argument. I've worked in CPS, and it could have been me removing Rachael's children 13 years ago because I saw the same type of women - - over and over - - women who abused their children because they were abused, and didn't know any other type of parenting. It's very hard to put a family back together once it's been separated.

The truth is, if Rachael hadn't done the work to get her family back, the children would have been placed for adoption. Maybe when her children were in foster care, they got lost, got separated from each other, and had poor experiences there as well. Maybe they stayed in the same stable environment for the duration. Whatever happened, the family was reunited because of Rachael's hard work and commitment to herself and the children. I applaud her efforts to remain in counseling and work through the abusive issues in therapy, and hope that one day she will find the peace and tranquility that she so deserves.

She's right to avoid her mother. If the woman never bothered to take responsibility for her actions, and continued to make other people miserable, then she deserves to be alone in her old age. No one has the right to abuse others, physically, mentally or sexually. Every child has a right to be raised in a loving environment (not necessarily a wealthy environment, as homes with dirt floors can still be rich in love) and every child has a right to be fulfilled as a human being. No child should ever be abused; I cannot think of a single reason why anyone would take a shoe or fly swatter (or any of the other weapons) to a child or to any other human being for that matter. People are not to hit. Period.

Good luck to you, Rachael, and to all the other Rachaels who are trying to put the pieces of their lives back together after years of abuse.

Rose Stadler, MSW

***

Gail, 43, dog trainer and stand-up comic

I was born bitchy. I grew up bitchy, I threw tantrums to get my way as a child, and once I figured out that it worked on my parents, I used it on boyfriends. Some of them didn't stick around to see the real me, but I figured, "what the heck, if they can't stand the heat, get out of the kitchen." I've been married twice, and both husbands called me a bitch - - and the second one, the one who is still standing, still calls me a bitch. And I am: there's no cure for it, I am a bitch, that's the way I am. I don't apologize for it, and don't make any explanations for the way I am, but I have learned to tone it down. I have a sharp tongue, and that's always been both my downfall and my victory. I can do stand-up comedy, and am always 'on' - - and sometimes it bites. I don't mean to be a bitch but I come across that way. If I mean to say the bread is good, I end up saying "not bad for a cheap joint," which is generally an insult.

I don't mean to live my life by insults and comments, but I can't help it. I remember people and places, so when I have an opportunity to get on the stage and make people laugh, I do, and often it's at the expense of someone I saw at a flea market - - the fat, whiskered flabby man with a chunk of belly fat hanging out from under a gray tee shirt, with optional teeth, and I use it as a one liner on stage (not the name - - I've very bad with names and never use names in my routine), but I know that somewhere in the audience, there might be a fat man with flabby belly fat hanging down towards his knees, and he might take it personally. It's both a gift and a curse. I love to make people laugh, and I laugh at myself because one leg is shorter than the other and I'm a big girl. No size five here - - no, I could do commercials for Just My Size panties and it would be more like selling hot air balloons. I could go on and on, but the one-liners either bring people to their feet or at my back. What can I say? I am a bitch, and now, come to think of it, I can use this in my act. (And it takes a bitch to understand dogs, so that's what really pays the rent. I'm a good trainer, and it may be the bitch in me that makes dogs behave. Husbands too.)

* Gail uses her dog training methods on her husband, but I suspect he uses them on her as well. She's a very funny lady, and when you listen to her, your face hurts from laughing. She's not really as much of a bitch as she is a comedian. She is not deliberately hurtful, (it slips out in the most innocent of ways) however, she could think before she speaks. But not when she's on the stage, because she makes a living at skillful talking, and she is a funny lady - - a young Phyllis Diller or Rodney Dangerfield. Hand the woman a microphone, and she can handle a whole room with one command, "Sit," (and they do). Underneath it all, she's a gentle, tail-wagging puppy.

***

Pamela, 40ish, un-bitch until recently.

I'm not a bitch. Or never thought I was. Of course, my soon-to-be-ex thinks that I'm a bitch, and has frequently called me one. We've been married for over 20 years, married young, right out of high school. I was pregnant, the oldest story in the world. So we got married, and everything was all right for the first ten years, or so I thought. Three children later, I discovered that he wasn't all right with the "we" in "wedding". There was him, his buddies, his hunting trips, his den, his remote, his car/truck/van or whatever we happened to have at the time. His vehicle was always new, and mine was always a used junker. It was a *second* car, so why did it have to be new?

We cut corners on everything, the kids and I shopped at thrift shops and the Goodwill, and his suits were over the five hundred dollar tag. He was the chief bread-winner. He had to look good for his clients. His shirts were new, my blouses were used. I never really took a good look at the finances while I was working, raising kids, cooking, cleaning and doing all the home-front duties while he was off at this training seminar or convention. Yep, sure, right. Was I a fool or what?

One day I happened to see the bills for the credit cards and sure enough, there were expensive restaurants in town (and out of town), department store purchases (perfume? - - not that I ever got), motel expenses (in town - - boy, was that a slap on the head) and more. Then, still not believing the obvious, one day when I was doing laundry, I noticed new underwear, red silk boxers on a man in his forties. He had been working out. Red silk boxers. Perfume. Motels. My breath stopped in my chest. Literally, I couldn't breathe. I was dizzy and had to sit down. No one was home at the time so I went through every nook and cranny in the house, found more invoices, found a ring with a card - - hidden in the hidey-hole in the staircase - - that read, "To my love. It won't be long now." I took the ring box out (with the card), took the red underwear, took the invoices, bills and other evidence, and immediately went to see an attorney - - actually, not the right attorney, but a family friend who happened to be a real estate attorney, but he put me on the right track. Turns out that the family friend knew about my husband's affairs all along. Good friend. Wow, if I ever need someone to keep his mouth shut for me, I'll see him first. No, in truth, that cleaned out that friendship for me as well. I was blind and stupid for 20 some odd years. The clincher! The affair happened to be the real estate attorney's wife. What justice!

I had the locks changed when he was out of town. I left a pile of his fancy suits in the front yard and turned on the sprinkler. I egged his car - - a beautiful new Lexus that I never got to drive. I cut up his underwear, threw out all the left shoes (he never could dance with me, but apparently he could dance with others), cut holes in his socks, and literally cleaned him out of my life while he was gone. When he got back, he was served with divorce papers in the driveway in front of the neighbors.

I got another attorney, and am in the process of taking my husband to the cleaners, just like I took all his fancy suits to the cleaners year after year.

* Well, Pamela, been there done that. I can understand the kind of wrath it takes to bring one to their senses, and it sounds like you were a little slow on the uptake, but once you got the message that the *we* in *we*dding (I like that, by the way, and may use it in the future

with your permission) wasn't the happy picture it started out to be, you acted quickly and decisively. It's amazing what infidelity can do to a nice woman. I hope you still like rummaging and shopping at thrift shops because you can find some really neat things, but I hope you don't *have* to. I hope you have your choice of stores and I hope it's on *his* dime. I have a picture of Bette Middler in **First Wives Club** here with a little vengeance. Get that woman a bitch cup, and raise it to her good health. She will survive.

***

Thelma, age not provided, housewife

I have never done anything like this before. People always say I should write my life story, but I don't. I can't. I got to the 8th grade, and that was it. My father, especially my father was very cruel, abusive, sexually and physically. He abused us in the worst ways. All the time, my mother must have known. Anyway, I ran away as soon as I could, hooked up with a guy who was 28 years old to my 15. We had a few kids within a few years, and one day when I was working at a factory, two cops came and told me that my husband had strangled both of the boys. We buried the kids separately and he went to jail for a long time. I still had two girls and didn't know what I was going to do. To make a long story short, it felt like I was sleeping. I guess I had been in a mental hospital. When I woke up (five years later) the girls had been adopted out. I married again, this time to another abusive man. An alcoholic. He beat me and the kids - - this time I had three children. I don't really know what happened. I heard he was sexually abusing the girls and beating the boy. Anyway, the one girl, Angie, ran away when she was 14 years old, and damned if history didn't repeat itself. The guy was older, and he killed their baby. Angie had three kids by the time she was 19 years old. CPS has all of her kids, which is probably for the best. It's been a hard life, and many days I don't know which end is up. I've been hospitalized about 27 times in 20 years, with all kinds of mental illnesses, and so has she. I'm on all kinds of medication, and it seems that I can't tell one day from the next. It seems that when I tell my story to social services, all they do is shake their heads.

* Thelma's story is so sad. She was an abused child, had two of her children strangled by her husband. Her daughter had a child murdered. This family begs the debate about hereditary vs. environment. Which has the most influence on a child? I don't know, but I certainly wouldn't say that Thelma is a bitch. If anything, she has been a victim all her life. Apparently, she couldn't stand up to her father as a child, and as an adult, she found herself involved with two abusive husbands. This could be a prime example of early programming, because it impacted the rest of her life. She couldn't protect her children either. She never said what happened to the rest of the children, but her daughter is doing 15 - 20 years in prison for failure to protect, and in fact, might have helped kill her baby. I don't know if the daughter is also mentally ill, but if she's in prison, she must have been determined competent to stand trial and assist in her own defense. The sins of the grandfather will haunt this family forever. Thelma assured me that she continues to receive good mental health services, but she lives from one small SSI check to another, digging through Goodwill bags and eating at homeless shelters. She carries her medication around in a paper bag with her at all times.

***

Elaine S. 58, grounds keeper and general maintenance.

My husband and I were grounds-keepers and general maintenance for a mobile home park. We were not hired as a husband/wife team because we weren't married when he got the job, in fact, he had been on the job for four + years before we even considered getting married. His mother was getting free lot rent for his services, and that, in addition to barely above minimum wage was all that we had. I worked at another place, totally unrelated. They were very bad to him, forcing him to work crazy hours at all hours of the day, holidays and weekends, without a raise. In the meantime, they hired me to clean the community room, do the pool, wash windows, etc, and I would get free lot rent for my space. When his mother had to go to a nursing home, the free lot rent stopped, but they didn't compensate for the difference in wages. So he looked for, and found, another job. They were very angry that he left them, but I assumed I still had a job. Then one day I was in the community room so I asked the manager/owner "Do I still have a job?" She said, "No, in fact, you have to come with me to sign something. We hired you on as a husband and wife team...." That's where I turned into a raving bitch. No, they did not hire us as a husband and wife team. I started yelling, "who would work for about $7 an hour anyway?" What I signed was a letter of resignation that I didn't even read because I didn't have my glasses on. I called my other employer and asked to get more hours, and with my husband's income, we did just fine. But that was a turning point. It wasn't so much about my husband working for next to nothing with no benefits, or the hours, or the fact that they took advantage of his good nature, or that we *offered* to help out in a pinch. It was a ruthless employer and finally I had to let them know what I had been thinking all along. He should have quit long ago, and I should have never let them walk all over us. We both should have stood our ground.

* Elaine is a rather outspoken person, so it surprises me that she held her tongue for so long. She did because her mother-in-law was in poor financial straits and needed the free lot rent to stretch her money. When she finally let it rip, she didn't hold back, in fact, she made up for lost time with her raving bitch moment. It was a turning point, she would never work for another employer who didn't have things spelled out in writing again, and would never be in a position to let herself (and husband) get stepped on in the future.

***

Grandma Betty, 73
Memoirs of A Bitch Personified

I am 73 years old, old enough to be considered a bitch. In another country, I would be a Grand Dame, the matriarch of the family. As it stands, now I am on Social Security, a pension and some savings; and I don't really give a damn that my dog dug a hole under the neighbor's fence. I have cancer, and time is of the essence. I'm on the countdown and I know it. This is a magnificent opportunity to say what needs to be said before I go.

My three daughters and my two sons and all of their wives and children will fight over the clock, or the pictures, or the stamp collection, and I could care less. Here's my story, take it or leave it. However, my will is all made out and the funeral arrangements have been made. All I want is the white dress hanging in the hall closet, after that, dead is dead.

I was raised in the Depression, married when WWII broke out, and had three children before I could blink an eye. We didn't have welfare or relief programs back then, so if times were tough, you just added more water to the soup and toughed it out. We didn't have food stamps or microwave ovens. If we wanted bread, we baked it. We canned our own vegetables, had a garden plot and took care of our own. We didn't rely on the baby-sitters or day care centers to raise our children, and the women did what had to be done. Some of us worked outside the home but you can see that with five children in the 50's, I didn't have much time for working outside the home. My husband supported us - - not always in the best manner, but we got by. He was abusive by today's standards and he drank too much. He'd hit me once in a while. You know, I wouldn't put up with it now, but I did then, and there's no going backwards. I got even in my own ways. Once I peed in one of his bottles, then watched him drink it. I never told any of my kids about that, so if I'm still alive when this comes out, we can all have a good laugh over it because he's dead now.

In the 60's I went to work. All the women were going back to work in the 60's and 70's and I was no exception. By that time we were mortgaged to the hilt, had credit cards and lawn furniture. Back when I was growing up, if we wanted to sit outside we took a chair from the kitchen and put it outside, then took it back in when we were done. No one would have thought about going out and buying

Release Your Inner Bitch

patio furniture, but we did, because the neighbors did, and so on and so forth.

Now let me tell you about the damage that was done in the name of women's lib. Because so many women were working, day care centers had to open so someone could raise the kids. My kids would have been latchkey kids but they were old enough to take care of themselves. But women then had to have their own cars (you financed it) and women had to have different clothes (you opened charge cards at department stores) and pretty soon you were up to your eyeballs in debt, but you looked good and drove a new car. You also had new lawn furniture, and probably new living room furniture. You probably got a new stove and refrigerator, then you got a bigger house. Then once you started working, you couldn't stop because of the bills.

My husband died in the 80's and left me a pretty good insurance policy. He also left me with two illegitimate children I didn't know about. They were adults when they contacted me, you know the old story, "just trying to find out who our real father is". That was BS as far as I could see, and the woman of the two was a real bitch. That's what I'm getting at. She had me convinced that she was my husband's child, and therefore entitled to about half of the insurance policy.

Over my dead body! My mother didn't raise no fools. I called the Attorney General's office and had the woman arrested. She was a scam artist. It turns out that she and her partner, really her husband, not her brother at all, were in cahoots with each other and they did this every time an obituary turned up in the paper.

All I had to do was go along with them for a while, pretend that I needed the money myself (I really did, because my retirement wasn't so hot, because back when I went to work, women made a hell of a lot less than men even though we worked just as hard.) and then, because I felt sorry for her (and the 'brother'). I would give them half.

I had to go to the bank and get cash like they said and take it home with me. They really wanted me to give them the money at the bank, or right outside in the parking lot, but I said that I couldn't do

Rose Stadler, MSW

that because I had a bad heart. (I lied.) They didn't want to meet me at my house, but I told them that I was afraid to go out with so much money on me. (I told them that it was over half a million dollars. OK, so I lied there too.) I had the 'money' (newspapers really) wrapped up in brown paper, with a binder on, so they wouldn't be able to count it right away, or find out it was newspaper. I was really afraid of what they would do to me if they found out before they left the house. They came over and the police were waiting for them in the dining room. I had French doors between the living room and the dining room and the fools never even saw the policemen. We had a tape recorder going in the corner of the living room. My heart was beating so fast that I thought I was going to hit the floor, but I kept on. Maybe I *would* have a coronary after all. When I handed over their 'share' the police arrested them. Later I had to testify against them. That really felt good.

When I think of it, it's not the bravest thing I've done. The bravest thing I've done is drive a tractor over wet ruts on a farm when the bull got out and was coming after me. The tractor got stuck in mud and the bull got closer. So I got out and ran, but that was a long time ago, and it seems like a different person. My youngest son was killed in Viet Nam; now *that* was hard. (I want my son's flag in the coffin with me; that and my husband's wedding ring.) I think of my son every day and wonder what he'd be doing now. Watching my husband die was hard, watching my kids grow up and leave was hard, now watching my grandchildren and great-grandchildren is wonderful. I have lived a full life, and been blessed with a sense of bitchiness and survival. I wouldn't have had it any other way. I guess I'm getting ready to go because I keep telling the truth about the past. No sense lying now.

* Impending death has a way of bringing out the truth of one's existence. It will happen to all of us sooner or later, so the idea is to live each day as if it the last day, and to be honest in all things. We all should be packed and ready to go. God speed, Betty, and thank you for your contribution.

***

Cheri, 40-ish, professional
GRAND ECCENTRIC LITTLE OLD LADY

I never use the term "bitch" in relationship to myself, although I'm sure that from time to time other people do. I refer to myself as an "old broad." Being over 40 is one of the great events of my life. Those people who like me, still like me. Those people who've never liked me, still don't like me. The difference is that I no longer care. I'm established in my field; I am who I am and the rest of the world can accept it.

I'm heavy, really heavy. I've played the yo-yo game for years since I was 16. I'm a professional woman in a profession where women are expected to look like fashion models. I came to join the profession in the years when a book called *Dress for Success* was the manual for young professionals throughout the nation. My classmates and I took it extremely seriously, but once in a while we did feel that there was overkill. *Dress for Success* advised all young women to wear wedding rings regardless of their marital status. Our conclusion was:, wearing a wedding ring only put one in a position where people, (instead of thinking that you were young and flirtatious), thought you were married and cheated.

As 25 years in this profession has progressed, again and again image has been proclaimed. I've never done very well at image. When you're heavy you don't fit the image to start with, never did very well with image through my personality, so this has always been a point of contention. Recently, a professional association started to give business development lessons. One of the meetings and lectures was on image and importance of image and the importance of professional image. This is the kind of place where women say they dress up to a parent-teacher conference because they represent the profession. I, quite frankly, have never cared whether the teacher knows what profession I'm in. Anyway, after an hour-and-a-half concerning this image (which, of course, included stockings, skirts and suits and I'm sure no one is overweight), I called a good friend of twenty-year standing with whom I graduated from law school and was in charge of the forum. I told her that I didn't do image well, had never done image well, but I finally decided what my image was. My image is that I'm eccentric and I'm so damn good, I can get away with it. There were peels of laughter on the other end of the phone. In the midst of this giggle, she gasped, "It took you twenty years to figure that out?" I rightfully replied, "No, it hadn't taken me twenty years to figure it out, but it sure had taken me twenty years to get comfortable with it." Whatever they call it, I like it and I'm on my way to the ultimate position in life - - being a GRAND eccentric, little old lady.

I have a close male colleague whom I work with frequently and who respects me greatly. He says my problem is that I'm confrontational. I said, "But I'm never nasty about it, I'm never angry about it, and I'm always polite." To which he agreed. However, he said men in the world just do confrontation well. I said I just ask the questions that have to be asked and it took me years to train myself to do this. He said the problem is "you always directly ask the questions that no one has answers for."

Is that the definition of a bitch?

* Cool. A heavy woman can be just fine, know herself and do a great job in any profession. Weight is one of the things that is often an identifying point with a person. The first impression, so to speak. I see a lot of women who are very dissatisfied with themselves. It might be weight, body size and shape, wrinkles, hair color (gray) or sagging muscles. If it's a health issue, do something about it, but if you are in good health, feel good and accomplish as much as any other human being, then don't worry about it. It's a shame that women have to live by the standards set in the magazines, on television and by Hollywood. We all can't be a size 5. We come in all sizes and shapes, some of us are tall, some of us are short. Some of us have blue eyes and some of us have brown eyes. It's a matter of DNA, hereditary and individuality. Good for Cheri for accepting herself the way she is.

A woman can look good at any age or shape. It's when a woman becomes sloppy in her appearance, or has poor hygiene, or has health issues that it becomes a problem. As a therapist, I have more concern when a person "has let themselves go", has stopped washing their hair, stopped bathing or taking care on the personal level. This is frequently associated with depression, or a sense of giving up.

***

Edna, age 71, grandmother.

Actually, I'm too old to be considered a bitch, and right now, I don't really care what people think. I say what has to be said, and that's the end of it. I will tell you a time that I was really a bitch, and my granddaughters are proud of me. My husband, a drinker and mean to boot, was a farmer most of his life. Then we went to the city to make a living, and that's when things got really bad. His drinking got so bad that he'd pee himself. We had five kids, and the kids had to take over, put him to bed and generally be men, when the man of the house was in bed sleeping or hung-over too bad to go to work. I couldn't work because I had the kids to take care of, besides, what kind of wages are we talking about here? Women were only making about eighty-five cents then, so it wouldn't have helped all that much. I had the kids to see to.

One day, he was in bed, so drunk that he was hanging his head over the side of the bed, puking his innards up. I had all I could stand that time, so I dumped a pitcher of cold water over his head. He got up, madder than a wet hen, and I was ready with the hose. I hosed him up one side and down the other, mindless of the water on the bed or the floor. I didn't care. I just kept hosing him down with cold water. I told him that if he didn't get his ass out of bed and go to work, I would take a whip to him. I meant it too. I would have. After that, he never got drunk again, that is not to say that he didn't drink. He still did, and died because of it, but he never got mean with us again, and he worked every day of his life until he died of liver problems. I don't know what would have happened if he hadn't made me so mad at him, he might have kept up with the drinking and getting mean. I think I changed the out-look of our future because I held my own that day. There were other days that come to mind, but that one day stands out because I had reached the point where enough was enough.

* Edna sounds like she had had enough all right. (See Diane). Enough is enough and too much is nasty. It must have reached the nasty limits the day Edna hosed her drunken husband down. It takes all kinds of courage to stand up for yourself, and your children, and it sounds as if Edna was at the end of her rope. Good for her. Get that woman a bitch cup.

***

A. J., age 28,

I've been selling myself since about fourteen years of age. I ran away from home because my step-father was molesting me. That had gone on since I was about ten-years old. When I left, I honestly thought that I could make it on my own. Boy was I wrong. I found out that life on the streets was harder than at home. I suppose that I could have turned myself into foster care, but I knew of other kids who were in foster care, and it didn't seem like it was much better there. So, I did what I had to do. I began a life of prostitution. I looked a lot older than I was, so I got along.

By the time I was eighteen-years old, being a hooker was getting a little old. I had been at it for four years, missing school, and missing all of the teenage things that everyone else was doing. I have had my jaw broken, my left arm broken, my shoulder dislocated and several punches to the gut. I've tried different drugs, thinking that it would help, but it never did. I'd wake up, still me, sore and wondering if I would die before the next week was up. It was a hard life, harder than I ever thought.

I've met every possible type of man in my line of work. It doesn't matter what they're wearing, once they strip down to their skivvies, they're all the same. A lot of them have been brutal, thinking that I was nothing. They treated me like scum. They think that because they paid for sex, they could treat me like dirt. That's when I became the bitch. I've ripped off a few clients because of that, (not that many, but a few); and once I had to fight for my life. All the while the guy was trying to strangle me, he was calling me a bitch. Then I became one. I carried a knife and gave him a few mementos. I was afraid to go out for about a week. But we had to eat too.

One day I was standing waiting for a walk-don't walk light to change and I caught a glimpse of myself in a store window. I looked old and tired. There were rings under my eyes from not sleeping, and I was gaunt from all the speed I had been doing. I looked like hell. I thought, "What the hell are you doing? You're not trying to get back at your family. They don't care what you do. It's not about money or drugs." By then I could get all the drugs I needed and very rarely paid for any of it. The johns bought it for me. It wasn't really about money, because I had more than enough. In fact, I had a pretty decent bank account by that time.

I had several 'dates' that night, and all the while my pager was going off, I kept seeing the girl in the store window. It was me, old and skinny. A bag of bones just waiting for some john to kill. They would find my body in a dumpster. It's a dangerous profession, and you have no recourse if you get beaten, raped or held at gunpoint. You just figure that it won't happen to you. I knew that I wasn't doing it to get back at my step-father any more, but I still hope he rots in hell, and I hope that my mother gets the hot seat next to him, because I still think that she knew what was going on, but I had this gut feeling that if I didn't stop, I would die.

It was that simple. I had seen just about everything, and done a lot of things that other people only think about, but I knew for a fact that I was going to die in exactly two days if I didn't give it up.

So, I quit. I had two dates that night, (of the four that I had scheduled), then I threw my pager in the garbage. I took all the money out of my bank account, got in my car and left. Just like that. I left most of my clothes and my stereo in my apartment. I had a roommate, and said good-bye to her, but that was it. I drove like the devil was after me. I didn't have any problem getting a motel room with stolen credit cards and I doubt if anyone ever checked. I just kept going. I didn't slow down for about two weeks.

When I finally parked the car, I took a look around and found myself in the Rocky Mountains. I have never seen such beauty, really seen beauty. I had been to the mountains before, with a one-nighter, but I had never seen the mountains by day. The trees were turning colors and it was the most wonderful feeling I've ever had. I knew that if I spread my arms out, I would be able to fly. I got my GED and enrolled in a local college, thinking that I could change, but when the money ran out, I was tempted to get back into it. I think back now and think that I was addicted to the danger of prostitution; not the sex, or the drugs, or the money, but the adrenaline rush knowing that any minute you could get killed or arrested. It was a roller coaster ride all of the time, staying one step ahead of the law, and the danger. I was an excitement-junkie. In hindsight, it was like looking at myself from the top of a ten-story building; it wasn't really me. It was someone who *looked* like me, but honestly, I don't have times and dates to recall. It was as if I blanked out for months at a time. I sold myself to survive.

Anyway, when I finally stopped the car and got an apartment, I found a roommate, a goodie-two-shoes to help pay the rent, but she turned out to be a real church-goer. She'd talk me into going with her, and because I had invented the perfect family in the Midwest, I told her that I went to church all the time. (Ok, I forgot the words to some of the songs...) but it was after I had been going to church for a while that I thought, "It wasn't the devil after all, but an angel." One day in church, I absolutely wept for the teenager in me who lost her innocence so young. No child should have to go through that, and even though I still think that my mother knew what was going on, I have forgiven her if she had anything to do with it. I'm not so sure about forgiving my step-father. What he did was wrong.

An angel must have been watching over me all along, because I had never been arrested, never OD'd, never been beaten so badly that I couldn't get along, and never got killed. I am especially grateful that I never got a STD (sexually transmitted disease), HIV or AIDS. I have never asked about any of the people I knew then because

I'm pretty certain that they're dead by now. I'm still not sure about all this religious stuff, but I know for a fact that I am alive today because an angel gave me a warning ten years ago. That angel said, "get out now or in two days you'll be dead."

I *used* to be a bitch. But then it was a matter of survival on the streets. You have to stay one step ahead of everything and everybody to stay alive. And I *could be* a bitch, or revert back to some of the old knife-carrying prostitute ways when I have to, but I have a different job now. I'm a mommy. Two days a week I take my son to day care, then I go to school, where I'm working on a degree in speech pathology. Who would have ever thought that it was possible? Just the other night I was up banging away at the computer instead of banging away.

Now when I look in the mirror, I see a twenty-eight year old woman, still firm in all the right places, not bad to look at, and even better, I'm smiling. And yes, my husband knows all about my past. He has never brought it up to me, not once; not even when I smashed the car.

* A. J. told a heart-breaking story that involved incest, probably physical abuse, life on the streets and selling herself for four years. I'm sure that a lot of people believe in angels after reading this story. A. J. had been in a life-threatening situation, but she managed to turn herself around. Congratulations, A. J. You've made it.

In every story presented we have seen some sort of trauma that triggered a belief in one's self and the ability for self determination. I have no doubt that A. J.'s strength had a lot to do with her survival methods. I see her as gutsy and motivated, and pale at the thought that she might not have survived. Her letter indicated that she had never written about prostitution, seeing it as something that someone *else* had done. This is not surprising following abusive situations. It's not uncommon to blank out or lose tract of time when everything seems hopeless. I applaud her for sharing her story, and hope that anyone who sees this, and is in a similar situation, will find a way out. (I cannot respond to A. J. as there was no return address on the letter, but I wish her continued success.)

***

Crystal, 38,
You bet I'm a bitch. I've been divorced, so that automatically makes me a bitch, but I think that I've earned the title. I'm not insulted when someone calls me a bitch, but I make sure that they get the name right. I've had a pampered childhood, good education and a decent degree, so when my husband failed to provide (what I thought he should), and I had to work, I rebelled. I didn't mind working at first, but when the kids came along, it got harder and harder. My husband didn't provide for me and the kids in the manner that I thought he should have, so I divorced him. Now I work hard, all the time, being both the mother and father, I have to be on my toes all the time. But.... and I know that this makes me sound even more bitchy... I can always depend on my parents for money if I need it. I like nice things and so do my kids, so when the grandparents come around, or ask me what I need, I tell them. Dad bought me a new car last year and the year before that they took all of us on a very nice vacation. It doesn't bother me that they gave me twenty thousand for the house, or that they built an addition on to the house for the deck and pool. I have a nice life, and that's the way it is. I don't have to explain or justify anything to anyone.

* Crystal, how nice for you. Sorry, but you sound spoiled to me, or maybe there's not enough information to go on. Let me get this straight. You have a degree, a good educational background, and you don't want to work. You have wonderful parents to give you whatever you need, but what happens if the buck stops and you have to depend on yourself? Could you make it on your own?

***

Olivia, (pseudonym) age unk.
Bitch in a Bottle
"Hi, my name is Olivia, and I'm an alcoholic."

Three times a week I say the above phrase, and three times a week I thank God that I am alcoholic. I have come to understand that by saying it out loud, I have been able to look back at the past and know where I have been, and where I am going.

About ten years ago, I was fat, obnoxious and drunk most of the time. It didn't start out that way. I started out the same way other people drink, a glass of wine here, a bottle of beer there; socially. Then something crossed a line, and it was two or three drinks before dinner, another couple of drinks before bed. I remember once my husband and I threw apart the sofa pillows looking for stray quarters and dimes, and before the corner store stopped selling beer, he made a fast run for a cheap bottle of something.

We fought all the time, physical fights; he'd say something, I'd snap, and before you knew it, we were trying to kill each other in the kitchen. We always thought that the kids were sleeping. Boy were we wrong! They were either hiding under the blankets or had their ears glued to the door. Our fighting affected them all their lives, and one of my daughters has had to go to counseling for an anxiety disorder - - I admit guilt here.

We'd look at the mess the next day, promise that it wouldn't happen again, but before you knew it, we were back at it. He had a few DUI's. He crashed the car into the neighbor's house. The car always had a new dent on it. There was always a garbage can in the carport that got run over, or a missing headlight. We were going to stop drinking, but we couldn't. We were both hopelessly hooked on the bottle. We never did drugs, in fact, we were righteous enough to condemn other people who did drugs.

Then it got bad. We were a mess, physically, mentally and financially. We were two steps away from bankruptcy. He lost one job after another. The kids were in terrible condition. I don't mean hungry or anything, but when I was drunk, I doubt that I did much cooking. Mostly peanut butter sandwiches and noodles. They ate, but it wasn't the best. And I was a good cook too. Sometimes, when things got really bad, I would cook and eat, and cook some more. By the time he'd get home from work, I'd have a ten-course meal ready, cold, but ready, and then I'd be in the sauce and didn't want to eat.

To make a long story short, it's important to say that we both came from families where it was perfectly all right to drink, and if you could drink someone else under the table, then so much the better. It wasn't all right for a woman to be a drunk, and some of the relatives told me that I was going over the edge. Did I stop? Obviously, the answer is no.

I kept drinking until I was hospitalized with an acute case of alcohol poisoning. The doctor told me in no uncertain terms that I would be dead in five years if I didn't get my life together. My liver was about shot. He wasn't telling me anything that I didn't already know, but it was never enough to make me stop.

I tried to stop on my own, saying AA was for sissies. My husband would sit in the living room with me, slapping back his 5th beer and say, "aren't you gonna have any?" I'd say, "No, I have to stop." and he'd say, "Ah, come on, one won't kill you." So I'd have one more, then two more, then three more, and before you knew it, I was face down again.

I hated me more than anyone can ever know. I desperately wanted to stop drinking, but by now I couldn't. But because everyone was on me about it, I stopped drinking in front of people. I started hitting the grocery store on the way home from work and stocking up on those little bottles. I had them everywhere in the house. Behind the towels, in the cupboard, always one in my purse, in the glove compartment, two or three behind the files at work. Years later, after I sobered up, I found a few bottles in the house, in places I would never have thought to look, but there they were, starring me in the face, daring me to take a sip. Just one. I couldn't get rid of them fast enough. They burned my hands just being there.

I'm getting ahead of myself. Our marriage was doomed to fail because he was catting around while I was trying to stay sober. He couldn't stand me not going to a bar with him, so he went alone. It never crossed his mind to stay home with me. I can't remember exactly what happened the night reality hit, but he was roaring drunk and I was sober. I saw him weaving in the carport, a bottle in one hand and hanging on to the support beam with the other. He was heaving his guts out and I was just standing in the kitchen, watching, wondering, "My God, what's happened to us?"

I wanted him to come with me to AA, because if I was going to stop, he had to stop too. Of course, that wasn't on his agenda; so one day, after a major fight, a friend dragged me to one of her AA meetings. I sat and listened to all the other women talking about themselves, and in the back of my mind, I was thinking, "that's me; she's talking about me, drinking alone, hiding bottles, drinking vodka with the morning coffee." When it came my turn to talk, I promised myself that I wasn't going to say a word, just pass the hat, move on to someone else. But the closer they got to me, the more things I heard that described my life. My children were moving farther away, my communication skills were nil, we only had sex when one or the other was out of our mind, drunk as skunks. We both cheated on each other. I was a bar slut, picked up cheap fixes for the night, passed out in the parking lot of bars; my husband got VD twice (sure, from toilet seats!) and everything about us was a lie.

Finally, when I was supposed to say something, I couldn't. I was numb. Tears were running down my face and I couldn't talk. But I did manage to blurt out, "My name is Olivia, and I'm an alcoholic." I choked on the words, and cried like a baby. It was the first time I had ever said the words out loud. *Alcoholic, alcoholic, alcoholic.* It was like seeing the movie, **Hunchback of Notre Dame,** where Quasimoto couldn't stop ringing the bells. It was a horrible echo.

That meeting was ten years ago. My husband has moved on. I saw him recently at one of the grandkids' birthday parties, and he looked like hell. Thin and gaunt, balding, pants hanging on his hips. I just shook my head and walked away. I've lost weight, walk three miles a day, actually go to church, got my spirit back and plan to live another 20 or 30 years. I've remarried, but three times a week, I go to AA, and say, "Hi, my name is Olivia, and I'm an alcoholic."

* One has to pat Olivia on the back for her courage in getting her life back. Nowhere is the word bitch mentioned, but over and over, we have seen that becoming a bitch is a process of growth. Olivia has obviously grown from her experiences, and I assume that if she attends AA three times a week, for ten years, she's now helping others stay straight and sober.

Congratulations on your continued sobriety. You have taken responsibility for your behavior, done something about it and gone ahead with life. You were able to pick yourself up, spread your wings and fly. I have a mental image of a caterpillar becoming a butterfly. The metamorphosis is complete. Life is good when you make it good. It also makes sense that you haven't engaged in unhealthy guilt. What is past is past, the history is over and done with.

***

Sparkles, stage name: real name; Teresa, stripper or exotic dancer

I take my clothes off for a living, I do lap dances in a "gentleman's club" (there are no gentlemen in there at all) but the money is good. No touching the girls, that's the bottom line. I dance, slide around a pole, take my clothes off, do whatever I have to do for the money, but no sex. That's extra, and only with condoms. I make a good living, and pay the bills on time, but my parents think that I'm still going to school. I moved away a long time ago, couldn't stand the small-town thing, and when I got to the big city, I thought I'd be a star. I'm pretty, and keep my body in good shape, but I'm not a star. That's the fairy tale. I tell myself that I'm doing this for my son - - see, here's the basic equation, kids eat, they need new shoes, and daddy bailed the first time he changed a diaper. My son is bi-racial, and that's a problem. No white man wants me now, so I take my clothes off for them, for the money. It's revenge. White men call me a slut and a whore (because I slept with a black man and had his child - - it was love - - then he took a walk and I'm branded). So I charge a white man three times what I charge a black man, and I'm rolling in money. Call me a slut, or a whore, or a stripper, or a lap-dancer. Whatever, I don't care. Yes, I'm a bitch. But let me tell you something, the men love it, they want more, and they pay very well. As long as I can, I will keep doing what I'm doing because the money is good, and since no one else is going to pay for my child, (and I sure as hell don't want welfare), I will do what I have to do. Not going to be trailer trash with a kid hanging off each hip. No thanks.

I'm a bitch on several fronts: my parents have accepted my child, but there is definitely underlying tension from my father - - a good old boy from the South, who is prejudiced as the day is long, and a weary look in my mother's face, a long-suffering Baptist who wouldn't say shit if she had a mouthful, and my good Christian family, who are so two-faced that it makes me sick. Yes, I have a beautiful biracial son, and he is tall and proud, and wonderful in every way, but he is still black, and my family members are still white. I don't go home very often. And a bitch on the other front, the one that pays the bills. I'm a private dancer, like Tina Turner's song, I dance for money. As long as the body holds up, I figure I can do this for another ten years, then I'll go back to school and get that degree I keep talking about.

* Teresa, you're fooling yourself. It's time to get real with your ambitions. I'm not putting you down for being a dancer or a stripper, in fact, dancing is a wonderful cardio-workout. But stop the lies and get rid of the anger. Your child is more valuable than all the lies you tell your parents. It might be time to confront the prejudice in your family, or in your own heart. The man who walked away from you did so because he was a wimp when it came to fatherhood, don't blame all men. Why not start on that degree you've been lying about and get on with your life? Your child is your inspiration, do you want him to see you swiveling and undulating your hips for strangers? I don't think so. You didn't say how old he is, but I'll be that you don't go to school when it's parents' occupation day and tell the truth. You're living a life of lies, starting with the name "Sparkles." Any occupation that requires a false name is no occupation worth having. (That's just my opinion - - I could be wrong, but when I write a book, I want my name on the front cover.) Teresa, you are worth something, you are a valuable human being, start seeing yourself in a different light. Believe it and let go of the anger. Humility is knowing your

worth. That worth is not wrapped up in skimpy dancer's g-strings; sooner or later the flesh will sag, gravity will take over and you will have to dance in granny pants or thermo long-johns. Change your focus and I'm willing to bet your dance partners change.

***

BITCH: Bringing In The Changes
(Bronwynn)

***

Cathie, age 44,
    This was a tough thing to write, I thought about it for about three weeks before being able to put anything down. Being a bitch is like being a cat. You get the picture of a woman with claws, snarling and tearing her way across a room, or to the top of an organization, with an animal-like quality. You think of words like *revenge, vindictive, angry, malicious*, but after closer inspection, I don't think that's the way it is. That's an image of a bitch. A bitch is someone prettier, smarter, richer, or in a better position than you. Someone who walks all over people, leaves a trail of ex-husbands and fearful children. Now I think that it's a woman who can stand up for herself, speak her mind and not be afraid of the consequences.
    As children, I think that almost all females were raised to be pretty little girls in ruffled dresses, sitting nicely with our hands folded on our laps. Dainty little things, daddy's little girl. Showpieces like the porcelain dolls on the top shelf. Too delicate to handle. Just look at it, don't touch.
    I used to get mud on my dresses. My mother would roll her eyes, then she'd take me in the house and let me wear my pants. I'd hang upside-down from the swing-set in the back yard in dresses, my underwear hanging out. It never bothered me, but I guess it bothered my parents. They'd say, "she'll get over it."
    I never did get over it. I still wear pants more than dresses, hate panty hose, hate high heels, hate the way a woman has to feel about

her body. If the bra is a bit snug, then you have to go work out, sweat, work out with weights and make that bulge go away. You have to drink 8 glasses of water a day. You get your period! You have to have your face 'made up.' You always have to be presentable when you're a female. Men will go to the store in their ratty old T-shirts; a woman would sooner die. Why is that?

I do know *bitches*; nasty, mean, rotten women who always have something snide to say about someone else. Bitches gossip, lie, cheat and change lanes faster than anyone you know. I was watching a young girl cut across four lanes of traffic the other day, and thought, "damn, if I tried that, I'd kill every person in the way." She made it with barely inches to spare, but she was driving a *red Camero* and I hated her for that. She was young, pretty, dressed up and dazzling. I called her a bitch.

Then I wonder how many people call me a bitch. I admit to getting bitchy (at *that* time of the month), but I'm not really a bitch.

But I called my mother-in-law a bitch many times. She was the meddling kind and had to have her say about every little thing; how I raised the kids, where I kept the cereal bowls, what shape the silverware drawer was in, how the towels were folded. You name it, and she meddled.

I called a woman at the store a stupid bitch (under my breath of course) because she was trying to pass off old coupons, then she had the audacity to write a check in the cash only line.

I called my boss a bitch, because she is. There's no other explanation for her sour face or finger-pointing. When she wants something done, she wants it done yesterday. She'll retire soon, Thank God.

My 18-year old daughter is a bitchette. She slams doors and changes the radio station in the car and doesn't put it back. She forgets to put more gas in the car after she uses it, and she leaves her wet towels all over the bathroom. She's sexually active with her boyfriend, and thinks that the world will have a place of honor for her when she finally gets her own apartment. (Which she thinks that she'll be able to afford with the $30,000-a-year job she thinks she'll get.)

My son's girlfriend is a little bitch. She's a spoiled brat who has to have her way all the time, she has my son eating out of her hands and she whines and complains like a puppy who isn't housebroken. I cannot stand the sight of that 'child' and leave the room every time I see her. Otherwise, I'd vomit, or say something really stupid, then my son would call me the bitch. Trust me; this one is a real piece of work. What's with the black lipstick! She has about eight earrings on each ear and the other day she was talking about getting her belly button pierced.

One of the women I see at lunch is frequently a bitch, but she's undergoing chemo, so we let that pass. Another woman at work is a bitch because she's going through a divorce. Another woman is a bitch because her father-in-law lives with her. Then there is the bitch at the gas station, the bitch nurse who told me not to push when I was having one of my kids, and the bitch sales clerk who remarked, "well, you *could* try Lane Bryant...." and the bitch waitress who brought runny cold eggs, and the nameless bitch at the IRS who told me that I made a mistake on my taxes.....

I suppose, in retrospect, I am also a bitch - - sigh - - and will have to face the fact that people probably call me a bitch behind my back. My son's girlfriend probably thinks I'm a bitch because I can't stand heavy rock. The nurse at the hospital probably called me a bitch because I insisted on pushing. Works both ways. I see bitches, and call them bitches under my breath, and they see me, and call me a bitch under their breath.

Yet some women are cold-hearted bitches, they get their way every time they inhale. And they smile, like snakes, little forked tongues darting in and out of their mouths; that's supposed to be sexual. I'm just as sexual as the next person, by God, and I can let my tongue slither around just as well, although I wouldn't do it in a meeting and I sure as hell wouldn't eat a cherry tomato like that! At least not in public.

I remember when I was young, in the seventies, and we explored with everything. Once we had one of those 'lingerie' parties and you were supposed to go try on a teddy then come back and sit around with other women wearing sexy stuff, then they passed out soup spoons and we practiced oral sex on the soup spoons. Fifteen women sitting in a room, wearing our sexiest stuff, sucking on spoons. What a waste of time! Of course, I bought three or four pieces of sexy lingerie, which on my paycheck was an enormous amount, then I went home and sucked on soup spoons.

I prefer the real thing and hiking boots. Not that I suck on hiking boots...... you get the point. Picture me wearing a teddy, *and* hiking boots, trying to tuck an extra piece of flesh under lace, *and* sucking on a soup spoon. (Hell, I'd go for the ladle!) Then call me a bitch if you dare. I'd beat you silly with that soup spoon, chase you down the street and cram it down your throat, and yell, *that's what women were supposed to do.*

* Sounds like that's the way we were raised; to be the *siren of the night*, servant during the day and keep our mouths shut the rest of the time. Tell the kid with the earrings not to walk through a metal detector.

***

Stacy, 33, Librarian

Just a few weeks ago I attended my much-dreaded fifteen-year high school reunion. After lubricating my tongue with some beer, I talked to a former classmate that I hadn't seen in at least ten years. Naturally he asked me what I was doing now. I told him, "I'm the high school librarian, which means basically that I'm the Head Bitch." The day after the conversation I thought about why I had described myself that way. I generally don't use the word to describe anyone, especially myself. Most of the time I am a typical, helpful, friendly, and mild-manner librarian.

If I am truthful about myself, however, I have to admit to a terrible stubborn streak, the occasional bout of I-gotta-be-right-itis, and a pinch of self-righteousness to boot. Not that these vices are always bad. Sometimes they come in handy. Hmmm. If I think about it in terms of action heroes, I guess you could say that my usual mild-mannered self is Claris Kent, (feminized) and to be painfully honest, not-afraid-of speaking her mind's self is SuperBitch.

SuperBitch appears when there have been too many hours between chocolate feedings; or when the computer doesn't work; or when the library budget gets slashed; or when the creditors use that tone of voice; or when her husband asks her if she's gained any weight; or when the car breaks down in the middle of Paducaville; or when a telemarketer calls just when she's expecting an important phone call; or when any foolish male makes the fatal mistake of commenting that it must be that time of the month.

Once SuperBitch arrives, things start to happen. Her X-ray vision eyes can look right through someone trying to feed her a heap of rotten baloney. Sensing this, the nemesis will usually start gibberish, beginning with the syllable, "Ummm....". Her silver tongue lashes out at the wicked, rendering them speechless. Finally, her ultra-powerful body language, (especially the look on her face) will seal the criminal's fate.

If all goes well, an understanding will be reached. SuperBitch will have made her point and the repentant villain will understand the world through her eyes. If all doesn't go as well as planned, the villain will at least know not to do or say that again. All SuperBitch really wants is to be understood, during her times of frustration, anger and hurt. Once this happens, she melts into a furry, purring kitten, full of love and contentment. It is a dramatic transformation.

So the next time I hear a teenage boy call forth the "Bitch" by name, I think I'll have him write down, "A bitch is a woman who needs to be understood." I'd make him write it about a thousand times, lest he ever forget the true meaning of the word. Come to think of it, that would be pretty bitchy of me. Cool.

* I think that we're starting to see a pattern. Being a bitch involves communication skills, speaking your mind, and making other people understand. It also involves change, as Bronwynn also pointed out. The changes can be minor, or major, as in the case of Rebecca, who had to take a drastic measure as to move across the country with virtually nothing to make her point.

If communication must involve bitchiness, it seems that our basic communication levels are a bit out of whack. Have we *all* been raised not to speak our minds, to let others walk all over us? I don't think so, but like John Gray (**Men are from Mars; Women are from Venus**) indicated, we probably need to learn the basics of communication. The fact that our DNA strands rotate in opposite directions is a strong indicator that men and women are different from the physiological standpoint. There had to be a reason for that difference. We compliment each other, beginning with the DNA dance.

Imagine the intertwined branches of the DNA strand, like a delicate vine, pulsating with life, all that comes before and all that comes after. Regardless of the genetic makeup of the individual, each person must make his or her way in life, and when people speak, other people should listen. That doesn't mean that everyone has to agree with each other, but respect becomes an issue.

It also seems that women go around speaking in half truths. "I want to go out." can mean a hundred different things. We expect men to be intuitive with our wants and needs, then we complain when they don't come across for us. They aren't mind readers. They are our mates, our husbands, sons, fathers and cousins. "I want to go out" might mean that I want to walk around the block, or I want to go to a movie. Or, it could mean, "If I don't get out of this house right now and take a 100 mile drive in the mountains, I am going to explode. Then you will have to scrape the brain and tissue stuff off the walls. You will feel miserable, and you're a crummy husband because you should know exactly how I feel." How are men supposed to know what a woman wants unless we clearly state exactly what we want? That's part of the problem.

Once honest communication has been established, respect follows closely. Communication should be talking, a dialogue with give and take, not yelling insults across the room. This works with some families: take the salt shaker. Whoever has the salt shaker in hand, has the floor. No interrupting, no shouting and no hurling snide remarks across the room at the speaker. Use an egg timer if you have to. Then give each person a chance to say (honestly, without criticism) what's on his or her mind. The idea is to have an exchange of ideas, rather than a one way discussion. Communication takes more than one person. The main concept with this is that everyone must agree to respect others in the room, to maintain privacy and truth.

***

Name withheld, age 33,

The whole Lacy Peterson case made my skin crawl, because it could have been me. When I got married, I honestly thought I had the White Knight in Shining Armor, with the perfect home, perfect environment and absolutely perfect, *perfect* setting. We never fought, we never argued, in fact, I thought everything was perfect until I got pregnant. We had discussed having children, but it was always me who brought it up, and I thought he agreed. The night I did the home test, he went berserk. I was excited, ecstatic. I was pregnant, we were having a baby. I wanted to dance on air. At first he sat on the sofa and didn't say anything, then very slowly, as if he were talking to a child, he said, "get rid of it." I couldn't believe what I was hearing, and made light of it. I thought he was joking. Later, when I was sleeping, he moved over to my side of the bed and punched me in the stomach. He didn't think I'd wake up, but I did. I couldn't believe it. Then he said his hand slipped.

I doubled over in pain, then I went to the bathroom, and locked the door. He knocked and knocked - - telling me that he was sorry, he must have lost his mind, it was the shock of us having a baby. I didn't know how to take it, but after a while I believed him. His hand must have slipped - - sure, with a fist! The next day I went to the doctor to confirm the pregnancy, and yes, oh, yes, I was pregnant. I was happy, exhilarated and almost (I say almost, but not really) forgot what happened the previous night. My stomach was tender for a week, but there was no bruising, so I didn't say anything to the doctor. In my third month, the abuse got worse. First it was a slap here or there, then a shove. I told him (begged) him to stop, then we'd make love and there would be a lull in the violence - - not really violence, but verbal abuse, threats, intimidation, shoving - - and no one ever saw it except me. In front of other people he was Mr. Charming, Mr. Happy-to-be-a-daddy, bragging about the baby stuff that was gathering in the spare bedroom (not unpacked because he said that it was bad luck to unpack baby things until it was there... and not knowing yet if it was a boy or girl, it was all yellow and green blankets and sleepers.) Then one day I came home from work early because I was feeling crummy, tired and exhausted, so my boss told me to take the day off. I walked in to find him opening the packages, and it seemed that with each blanket or sleeper he opened, he became more and more enraged. He was cussing to himself, throwing the things across the room, saying "that damn baby, she'd better get rid of if."

I heard what he was doing, saying, and I said something about the baby, and it started an argument - - loud yelling and shouting. He scared me to the very bottom of my skin with that yelling, no shoving or pushing this time, just backing me to a wall, a lot of finger pointing, telling me how inconvenient a baby would be, the timing was bad, we couldn't afford it, he didn't want a kid, was it someone else's. It got worse by the second, so bad that I actually peed my pants with fear.

"Lose that baby or I'll do it." He said, more of a snarl than anything resembling speech. I was terrified, and fled the house. I got in my car and drove around because I didn't know what to do. My sister lived about fifty miles away, so I went there. We have keys for each other's houses, she was out, so I let myself in. I called her at work and she told me to move my car to the back of the lot that couldn't be seen from the street, so I went outside to do that, then I saw him. He had followed me, and was sitting in his car, watching me. Instead of moving the car, I ran back inside the house and called the police.

Of course, he said the whole thing was a mistake, that I must have gotten it wrong, and since there was no evidence of abuse - - no destruction of property, no physical evidence of any kind, nothing except my word; and of course, he said that it was my imagination, that I was hysterical and "pregnant" there wasn't anything to do except move in with my sister. I was so afraid that he would hurt me or the baby that I stayed with my sister for the rest of my pregnancy. Everyone thought that I was crazy when I divorced my perfect husband, "for absolutely no reason." This is a fairly small town so everyone knows everything about everyone else, and I am pretty much regarded as a nutcase, but I know in my heart, I did the right thing. My child is three years old now, and I am so glad that I got out. Who knows how much worse it could have gotten?

As a footnote, I have moved to another town and am involved in a very healthy relationship. Unfortunately, my ex has visitation, so I have to interact with him at least once a week, and he keeps telling my current boyfriend how insane I am.

* Wow, this is a serious one. Many women (I don't have the exact statistics right now) are abused during pregnancy - - this is an extremely dangerous time. Good thing this woman got out of a potentially deadly situation.

***

Leslie T., 41, divorced

My first total bitching experience came with the divorce, but I'll bet you've heard that story a million times. The second bitching time what when my father was dying. The nurses didn't want to give him morphine because it might make him addicted. "He's dying," I finally yelled. "How addicted can he get?" I wanted him to be comfortable and pain-free in his last moments, and didn't give a damn what anyone thought of me. That was a few years ago, before hospice and pain management became household words, but at that time, I had to fight for his right to die with dignity. I have no regrets, and would do the same thing today.

* Leslie, I wonder how many of us, in your shoes, would have reacted the same way. Seeing a parent, or anyone for that matter,

suffer at the end would be difficult. Of course, you want that person to die with dignity and without pain. You weren't a bitch, you were sticking by your father.

***

Lou, 60-something

I have a roommate with breast cancer. She's stage 4, terminal, and if you don't know what that means, it means she's dying. Maybe not today or tomorrow, but soon. She has a son who is always in trouble, running away from his family, or getting fired or demoted or whatever. Whenever things get too tough for him, he bails out, leaving his wife and three children. He usually drains the checking account and leaves town in the middle of the night. Anyway, as usual, he was in trouble, and this time when he called, asking for her to bail him out, (again) I didn't mince words. I said, "You're killing your mother. Why not just bring over a gun so I can shoot her and save you the trouble." That was just the most recent bitching incident, but I have a long history of being a bitch - - it started when my husband pulled a shotgun on me. I generally say what's on my mind, but this was the first time I interfered with her son. She needed her rest, and he had some nerve calling her. In fact, she can trace her bouts with cancer (or getting worse) to the stress related to him just like a calendar.

* I've heard that stress is a cancer trigger. It is highly inconsiderate of the son to call his mother only when he gets in trouble. He should be sending her flowers and taking her out to dinner on a regular basis, and certainly, showing her all the love that he has. The son is selfish, thoughtless, uncaring and insensitive. Lou said that she held her tongue more times than she could count, but this time, he was especially tactless, so she let him have it with both barrels. She does not apologize, and has no regrets, but wishes that she would have "cleaned his clock" long ago.

Rose Stadler, MSW

***

Teri Ann Bengiveno, Ph.D., age 34 (Assistant professor of American Studies at San Jose State University)

Releasing the inner bitch in the classroom.

It's a hot July morning at San Jose State University. It is the 1st day of the first week of a three week summer session course. There is no air conditioning in the classroom. The session begins at 11:15 A. M., and I start with business items and discuss the students' upcoming exam. We sit in a circle, and I can feel the sweat drip down my legs.

I decide to give the class a pop quiz to see if they read the assigned novel. I collect the quizzes and briefly glance at them. Five of the twenty students read the book according to the quiz. My blood begins to boil. My inner bitch begins to wake up. I stand, pick the novel and wave it in front of the class.

"Well, what shall we do for the next three hours?" I ask.

Heads look down or out the window. I grab the stack of discussion questions I've prepared for them to answer in small groups. I wave them in my other hand.

"What shall I do with these?" I ask sarcastically.

One student suggests the five who read form their own group while the rest of the class quietly reads.

"I don't think so. Sounds like the people who did their work would be punished and those who did not would get class time to catch up. This isn't grade school. This is college. Presumably you are all here of your own accord and are here to learn." I lecture.

"Well, we had a written assignment to turn in today. We didn't have time to read the book too," one student whined.

"Do you honestly expect me to pass you if you do not do the work? This is a sixteen week course condensed into three. There is no time to get behind in the assignments." I ramble.

Very few eyes meet my stare now. The few students who are brave enough to look at me don't say a word, but their faces scream out 'you bitch.' If I had been a male professor, to what would the

Release Your Inner Bitch

class have attributed my aggressiveness? They definitely wouldn't characterize me as a bitch if I were a male. That is a term reserved only for women.

I smile and think to myself, 'your glance just invited my inner bitch to join us.' Here she comes in all her glory. After all, in my mind bitch stands for you **Bet I'm Taking Control Here**. And take control of the classroom she does. For the next fifteen minutes, my inner bitch gives the class a verbal tongue-lashing. By the time she's done, all eyes are looking downward. The classroom is silent. She walks around the room, wildly gesturing, then she leaves the room. I'm exhausted by the time she's finished.

The next day the students take their exam. They do remarkably well in comparison to past classes. Could it be they did so well because they met my inner bitch the previous day? Or were their high marks merely a coincidence?

* Thank you, Dr. Bengiveno! Get this woman a bitch cup! How many women have pointed out the gender differences? When a woman acts in an authoritative manner, she's a bitch. If a man does it, he gets a pat on the back. I'll bet that her students remember her for a long time. When they see their transcripts, they will say, "Yes, she forced me to learn something."

One of the fascinating things in doing this book is the amazing cross-section of women who have come forward with their bitch stories.

***

(Anon. came off the Internet. Original author unknown.)
A man was walking along a California beach and stumbled across an old lamp. He picked it up and rubbed it and out popped a genie. The genie said "OK, OK. You released me from the lamp, ... blah blah blah. This is the fourth time this month and I'm getting a little sick of these wishes so you can forget about three. You only get one wish!" The man sat and thought about it for a while and said,

"I've always wanted to go to Hawaii, but I'm scared to fly, and I get very seasick. So could you build me a bridge to Hawaii so I can drive over there to visit?"

The genie laughed and said, "That's impossible. Think of the logistics of that. How would the supports ever reach the bottom of the Pacific? Think of how much concrete...how much steel!! No, think of another wish."

The man said OK and tried to think of a really good wish. Finally he said, "I've been married and divorced four times. My wives always said I don't care and that I'm insensitive. I wish that I could understand women ... know what they are thinking when they give me the silent treatment, know why they are crying, know what they want when they say 'nothing'...."

The genie said, "You want that bridge two lanes or four?"

***

Sylvia, age 62, retired, mother and grandmother

My husband was assigned as a squadron commander on an Indo-Pacific Island. To escape seemingly endless social functions required as his wife, I became involved in a local shell club whose members were men and women from several services and civilian groups. Only a few members knew of my husband's position. Club activities gave me an interest while he was on rotation for three to six week periods and when he was home.

Our three daughters accompanied us overseas. The oldest, 19, worked in the base exchange; the 17 year old, was a senior in high school and our youngest was 11 years old. The senior was dating a young aircraft mechanic who was becoming a family fixture, especially at mealtime.

Over the months, I became an officer in the shell club which necessitated some involvement during family time. This was never a problem, merely occasional phone calls to make or receive.

One evening as the girls, the boy friend, my husband and I were finishing dinner the phone rang. My husband answered it. The desk and the phone were within an arms reach. The call was for me from one of the young men who was club treasurer.

As I stood behind him making notes on club business, my husband kept laughing and kidding with the rest of the family loudly, which required me to ask the caller to repeat himself several times.

Irritation over this overt display of rudeness, based partly on unspoken and unwarranted jealousy, had simmered into anger throughout the call.

I am known for an even disposition and generally avoid confrontation. That evening I lost my temper. A water pitcher on the table about one third full caught my attention. Without a word, I reached for it and poured it over my husband's head.

Stunned silence ensued. My husband was not known for being an easy-going man. Everyone's eyes were wide open, awaiting the explosion that would surely come. I have no idea how he looked when the cold water hit him, or what kind of expression he had on his face, because I was behind him. But I could tell from the shocked faces of everyone else, that I had definitely made a statement. I expected full outrage.

Instead, he burst out laughing, the last thing that any of us imagined. He thought it was the funniest thing I had ever done, and to this day he talks of the water pitcher experience.

I've never thought of myself as a bitch, but that was definitely the bitchiest thing I have ever done, the thing that sticks in my mind as the day I decided never to let him control me with rudeness. It might have been one thing to be a squadron commander with his men, but at home, he was supposed to be a husband and friend. He had taken control of everything in our lives up to that point, and a lot afterwards, but that one day stands out in my mind as a crystal clear moment of my own control. I don't think that I've been the same since.

*Bravo, Sylvia.

***

Jackie M., 38, book seller

I see magazine articles about women all the time: how to be stronger, how to be financially secure, how to go-it alone, but I've never seen one for releasing your inner bitch. Well, here I am, responding to the call of the wild. I am a bitch. I'm not sure what kind of bitch I am, (super bitch: maybe - - naw, I'm not that good: maybe a beginning bitch.)

Seven years ago my husband and two sons were on a vacation when we were robbed of everything we had. We had gone to the pool for an afternoon swim, leaving everything but the key in the room. We trusted the motel to keep things safe. Opps, bad mistake. Our luggage was still there, but my jewelry, credit cards and extra cash was gone. Naturally, we didn't notice it until much later, when we went out to dinner, and wouldn't you know it, we stood there like fools, no credit cards in my husband's wallet, nothing in my purse. No cash except the change at the bottom of my purse. The restaurant wouldn't take an out-of-town check, but there were no other options. Thank God I still had my driver's license. (My husband's was gone.)

When we got back to the motel, they said that they weren't responsible. Of course, the first thing we did was cancel our credit cards. We couldn't do anything about the cash. We immediately filed a police report for the theft, (the jewelry eventually had to be written off on the insurance.) But here's the clincher. The motel wanted cash for the few days that we were there, but I didn't have any. Didn't have my debit card either. I had two checks left - - we didn't take our checkbook but we did have a few extra checks along, just in case something came up. They *knew* we had been robbed in their motel, they *knew* I had booked the room in advance with a credit card that I just cancelled, and they had the police report number in case there were any questions. You'd think that they would have taken some responsibility for the theft, given us the room free until we could repay it. The manager kept insisting that we pay cash for the room, but we didn't have any and no way to get to an ATM without debit cards. I got new credit card numbers right away, but they wouldn't take any of them - - they wanted cash only.

That's when I hit the roof, in front of God and everyone, I started yelling and throwing a fit, right there in the main lobby, with other people checking in and out. I was on a roll, and wouldn't be hushed by my embarrassed husband. Finally, the manager decided that hell hath no fury like a woman robbed, and decided to write off half the stay of the motel. In my mind it was a fair thing to do, but they should have done it without all the yelling and fussing, after all, it was their motel, and I don't care what kind of policy they had on not being responsible for personal property. It was their responsibility to make sure that no one could get in the room, or provide better security. When I got home, I wrote a long letter to the home office of the motel chain, and three weeks later I got a free pass for five days and six days at any motel (in any city) of my choice, PLUS a total refund for the days that I did pay for. I know that if I hadn't pitched a fit in the lobby, nothing would have been done. My husband would have handled it differently, and we still have debates about the best way to handle the situation but I was on my last nerve at the time. I could have been tactful and diplomatic, (I honestly tried that), but it seemed that the only thing left to do was give them the all-out bitch.

* Jackie, I'll bet you have other shining bitch moments that come to mind as well. I know that if I had been in your shoes, I might not have been calm either. Sometimes you have to make a scene.

***

Suzanne, 46, why did I stay?

I was in an abusive relationship for over 20 years, and I have absolutely no idea why I stayed. Looking back, it was totally insane of me to stay there, protecting him, making excuses for him, covering up the holes in the walls and pretending that there was nothing wrong. I lied to my parents, to my children, to everyone; to my co-workers about why I had another black eye. I remember one day when a co-worker followed me to the bathroom, shut the door and looked under the stall doors to make sure we were alone. "This is the third time you've woken up with a black eye. I'd see a doctor if I was you." Then I started to cry. She knew, she had been there too. I broke down like never before. I had always cried privately, thinking that he would change, or that no one knew, or that I did something to cause him to beat me. It wasn't always like that, but some of the times were worse than others; first a slap or a punch, then shoving, then the finger-pointing, the total unpredictability of his abuse, sometimes triggered by drinking, other times in the middle of dinner. It was always my fault - - I made him do it, I did something, didn't do something, the kids left their bikes in the driveway, the dog chewed a sock, it didn't matter what it was, but I was the punching bag. Mostly on my body where bruises didn't show, but sometimes he got my face, and that's when I told people that I didn't understand it, but I woke up with black eyes. If he was hitting on me, he'd break my good dishes, destroy pictures that I liked, (once he killed a batch of new kittens, and kicking the dog was common). Once I bought myself a new winter coat and the next day it was slashed to ribbons. He said that he had to do it to teach me a lesson in money management. I should have asked first. I never even got to wear it.

    I used to dream of killing him, but I never did anything. In my dreams, I would get on a roller coaster, behind the seat he was in, and when the roller coaster would go chug-chug slow to the top, I'd get the knife (or sometimes it was a gun) out of my purse, and when the roller coaster started down the fastest first hill, I'd slash his throat - - or shoot him in the back of the head. I always got out of the roller coaster before it came to a stop. I don't know how I got out, but when it came to a complete stop, I'd be at the end of the rail, screaming, "someone killed my husband."

    The closest I ever got to telling anyone about the abuse was once I asked for a prescription of Zanax, which I only took when my husband was home. The doctor never asked me why I needed it, but he gave it to me. I suspect he knew, but didn't want to get involved. I would take half before my husband got home from work, and if there was any yelling or ranting, I didn't have to really be involved on the psychic level. It was as if I could step aside. He didn't really beat me when I didn't react, so the Zanax helped, although, once I deliberately took an overdose so I could sleep. I wasn't trying to commit suicide, I just wanted to sleep for a few days. My kids were worried that time because I had taken so much that I was like a rag doll for days afterwards. I didn't do that again, because I needed to be there for them.

The day the co-worker followed me to the bathroom was the day that saved my life. She confronted me in a very gentle manner, let me cry, gave me phone numbers to call, told me to see her therapist. It took me a week to make that call, but I started seeing a therapist (on the sly, on my lunch hour, covered with my insurance only) and then it took another six months for me to get up the courage to call the police the next time he hit me. It was terrible, the whole thing, but once I was alone, I shook. Later I danced, alone in the living room with the stereo blasting. He spent a night in jail, and when he got out I had the locks changed. I filed for divorce as soon as possible. I have no idea why I stayed; I have no idea why I lied and covered up for him, I have no idea why it took me so long to see the light, but now that I'm out of it, I am so glad.

I could never go back to him; he's begged and pleaded. No, I can't. That part of my life is done and gone. The kids still have to see him, and every once in a while we have discussions about abuse. They knew. I wasn't fooling anyone. They heard the fights, the thumping and saw the black eyes and bruises. My parents knew, they saw. My boss knew. My friends knew and no one (NO ONE) ever interfered except the co-worker who followed me to the bathroom that day. We have become close friends and I can never thank her enough for caring about me that one day that changed my life.

* I have goosebumps with this one, Suzanne. People don't want to get involved, but thank God that someone did. Frequently, abuse goes on so long that everyone knows, and yet, like you pointed out, no one got involved. You must have been screaming inside, all the time, yet no one heard you. Why didn't you go to the police or a shelter? Why do women stay? I don't know, but in 2002, there were about 6 million women who reported being abused. How many don't report it? By way of comparison, Phoenix, and the surrounding areas, have about 4.5 million people in it, with the winter population changing year by year. We're talking about a major metropolitan city here. By contrast, the population of West Virginia is about 5 million people. So we're either talking about a very large, crowded city, or a small state. Of those women, over 70% reported that they had been abused prior to the time of reporting, and many of those had been abused at least three to six times in the previous year. Eleven percent of violent crimes are committed by someone who is intimate (National Center for Victims of Crimes statistics.)

According to Abuse Counseling and Treatment website (7/04) Why a woman stays: *fear, lack of resources, lack of finances or economic reality, children, feeling of guilt, promises of reform, sex role conditioning.*

Fear: According to the FBI, up to 40% of female homicides in any given year occur when a woman decides to leave the abusive relationship. This is a good place to attempt to explain why some women stay: See the websites for domestic violence. Quotations are used where appropriate.

Lack of resources: "Since one of the major components of abuse is isolation, the battered woman most often lacks a support system. Her family ties and friendships have been destroyed leaving her psychologically and financially dependent on the abusive partner."

Lack of finances/economic reality: "the economic reality for women (particularly those with children) is a bleak one. This is especially true for women who have not worked outside the home. Economic dependence on the abuser is a very real reason for remaining in the relationship. Public assistance programs have been drastically reduced and those that remain provide inadequate benefits.

Children: "Being a single parent is a strenuous experience under the best of circumstances, and for most battered women, conditions are far from the best. The enormous responsibility of raising children alone can be overwhelming. Often, the abuser may threaten to take the children away from her if she even attempts to leave."

Feelings of guilt: "The woman may believe that her husband is 'sick' and/or needs her help; the idea of leaving can thus produce feelings of guilt."

Promises of Reform: "As is consistent with the cycle of violence, the abuser promises it will never happen again: the victim wants to believe this is true."

Sex-role conditioning: "Most women are still taught to be passive and dependent on men. In addition women generally accept the responsibility for success or failure in their relationships: to leave is to admit failure."

The above is credited to http://www.actabuse.com/whyshestays.html. This is an excellent web site for anyone wanting more information. Check it out.

This is also a good time to point out the cycle of violence is generally the same. First the abuse takes place, the couple makes up, make love, or at least have dinner out, there might be flowers, and apologies all over the place, then when someone trips on a shoelace, the tension builds, leading to abuse again. Picture a circle, with three distinct points on it. Abuse, apologies (excuses, amends), tension, leading back to abuse. It's a circular series of events, not linear.

***

Anon.

A bitch doesn't walk, she *struts, prances, pounces, strides.* Her hips swirl from one side to the other, moving furniture and breaking hearts along the way. She is Jessica Rabbit. A bitch doesn't ask for anything. She never says "Please, thank you, I'm sorry, or have a nice day." More likely she'll say "Go hang yourself."

A really good bitch can get a same day doctor's appointment, get a hefty discount at a gold exchange and get her car serviced without waiting. She can get the shuttle service to take her to work, *and* pick her up, without charging, and she can get free meals when she complains about the quality of the food in the finest restaurant in town.

Rose Stadler, MSW

A bitch is a woman who takes advantage of sales, knows when to shop, when to hunt for prey and when to lay low. She is good at reading other people, and waits, like a panther, for a moment of weakness, then she attacks. A non-bitch never sees it coming.

The bitch is a master at verbal karate.

She's the ninja female in black leather, very soft, very expensive black leather. She knows your every move. Never cross a bitch. (Like, never walk under a ladder, or open an umbrella in the house.) You *know* she'll retaliate, you just don't know when or where. It makes you crazy wondering when she will strike. A good bitch can metastasize a grudge for years.

She is alive and well in all females. What God did was give the man a penis, and the world automatically knew his status. It was the Tower of Babylon, proud, erect. It was Kokopelli, the hump-back flute player impregnating all females. The penis has been displayed in art throughout time, beginning with cave drawings. All hail the penis. Freud had a thing about penis envy, and Karen Horney disputed that theory in record time, yet women continue to need, want and crave the penis. Maybe not envy it, but want it, embrace it; like a marble statue that will endure for all time.

Now, the lowly female, born without the penis, has no way of showing her strength, but she has a swift and cunning tongue. A really good bitch has done her kegles and can pick up a dime on cue. She knows what the penis likes. She knows how to make it beg, how to make it wither and go limp, how to stay erect. She also knows how to castrate men with a look, a glance and a flick of the finger. Lorenna Bobbit has her own fan club. Women all over the world were saying "you go, girl." Men shuttered at the thought that someone would actually take a whack at it.

* Why do women have to resort to drastic measures, to absolutely and completely lose one's mind, in order to accomplish something? I'm sure that Lorenna Bobbit had reached the level of complete frustration with her husband and his demands, but she could have left. She could have gotten a divorce and started over. Or maybe not. She might have been able to seek the services of a marriage

Release Your Inner Bitch

counselor or therapist, but keep in mind, that once a woman seeks help, she is admitting a weakness that furthers the frustration.

Men rarely seek help. Women seek the services of a professional about 90 times more often than men. One really has to wonder why. Is it because males, by the fact that they have a penis, were automatically given more responsibility and freedom as children, and as adults have learned to make choices and decisions (good or bad) much quicker than women? Do women weigh all the pros and cons of a situation, then make a move? Or, like Lorenna Bobbit, on a lesser scale, do women take it and take it and take it, until they reach a point where they can't take it one more second. Then they lose their minds, implode or go off the deep end.

Men are accustomed to women going on a mental binder, they expect us to rant and rave at least once a month, they expect that regardless of the situation at hand, it must be hormonal. Do we honestly have to preface everything with, "This isn't a case of PMS, but I really want the vacuum cleaner fixed." If she has waited for months to get the vacuum cleaner fixed, then she might at well shut up and do it herself. How many times should a woman ask to have the vacuum cleaner fixed? And how many times should she get "Yea, yea, I'll do it." before the vacuum cleaner gets fixed? Go get your own tool box and learn to use it.

As for women cheering Ms. Bobbit on after she took a knife to John Wayne Bobbit's shaft, it seems to me that a lot of women were experiencing their own frustration with sex. They might have been sexually abused as children or adults, been subjected to severe, horrible rape situations, or perhaps, they have never been loved by a good man. A good man wouldn't rape a woman, he wouldn't indulge in sexual (dis)advantage of children, and he wouldn't insist on sex when it isn't mutually agreeable. Sex between two people should be a loving experience, and taking advantage of anther person should *always* be considered wrong. When a woman says "no," it means no.

Had Ms. Bobbit become a bitch prior to the incident, she might never have come to the forefront (excuse the pun). Or, she could still be abused at the hands of her husband; and in order to survive, she *had* to do what she did in a moment of temporary insanity. When all reason slips away, the world hears about it. It's the process of becoming insane at the hands of a mistreating spouse that the world never hears about. It's business as usual. I would never advocate that women take up kitchen knives and take a whack at the men in their lives, but I would advocate for an acceptable level of communication, respect (mutual and personal) and empowerment with all women. Had she been self-empowered, she might not have had to resort to madness to make her point.

***

(Email from my mother when I was complaining about rejections from the 'big' publishers.)

Dear Rosemarie, You gave some good reasons why women bitch in your last email, saying that women write 80% material and men control the publishing industry. Men just need to dominate, while women need to bitch about it! They have greater strength, larger bodies, longer fingers, bigger feet, hold the best jobs, are generally stronger in every aspect, and in athletics, cannot be beaten by women. They are the gods of the universe, fought over by women, and put on a pedestal. Maybe Monica will put them to their test! Don't give up on the book. Love, Mother. (This in response to a note from me saying that the book had been rejected by comet force when sent to a particular publishing house. Absolutely return mail. Must have burned the hands of a male who opened the mail.)

* reference to Monica Lewinsky, mistress/lover of President Clinton; woman to bring down the presidency. Apparently he didn't get the name "Slick Willie" for no reason. Monica may be the presidential knee pad bitch. Specifically, one cannot blame the poor 24 year old intern who was probably told that if she got down on her knees (begging or praying position) in the Oval Office, she would be ensured a better position. As it stands, she has offers galore, but not for the reasons that she went to school or became a White House

Intern. Women have been put in the knee pad position since time began.

Imagine the caveman: If you want fire and a carcass to chew on, get down on your knees and beg, bitch! Cavewoman probably rolled up a piece of fur to kneel on.

Women throughout time have known the proper and effective way to beg. I can see knee pads selling in stores all over the United States. Rhinestone knee pads, fur knee pads, velvet knee pads, lace knee pads. It won't be long before *Victoria's Secret* and *Frederick's of Hollywood* picks up on the idea. We will see knee pads to be worn with high powered suits, to be worn while hiking, to be worn while cleaning the toilet, everyday knee pads, Sunday knee pads, knee pads with pockets and traveling knee pads. I'm sure the industry is just dying to make knee pads in different sizes and models, beginning with a navy blue little number called the Oval Office Knee Pad. It's a matter of time before we see them in *Just My Size* Knee Pads and *18 Hour* Knee Pads. Then before you know it, *Gitano* and *Levi* will embrace a new industry. Women all over the world will be wearing knee pads, then just as quickly, there will be a new revolution, in which women will get tired of wearing them and there will be a great knee pad burning.

Plastic surgeons could specialize in creating Lewinski lips; fuller, rounder lips that would gain in popularity to wealthy, sexually-addicted men. Or: *The Gap* could re-introduce the "little blue dress" with its own DNA stains on the front; or the makers of thong underwear would suddenly make a mint between the cheeks. Either way, Monica Lewinski has already, or will go down in history, as the dark eyed beauty who either ruined a president's term, or prayed for *reign*. Imagine for a minute if the White House had an intern by the name of Lorena Bobbit.

***

Gina, (not my real name) 36, Been there, done that.

My ex is a drug dealer. There are no excuses for that, but in my case, at first I didn't really know - - well, yes I did because I was using too. But it wasn't like we were in it together. I had a full time job and two kids so with the laundry and housework, I didn't really pay attention. I was pretty busy, so it wasn't surprising when there was a lot of traffic at the house when I wasn't there. I do know that there were places the kids and I weren't allowed to go in, or look in - - the garage, the attic, and the basement except when I was doing the laundry, then I could do the laundry and get right back out. I didn't really know until he was busted. I mean, I knew, but I didn't know. This doesn't make sense. When he said that he "scored a joint" I didn't think that he scored a ten pound bag. I used occasionally, but I didn't know he was dealing in the quantity that he was until he got busted. It was a scene out of some horror movie, with SWAT teams breaking up the house. I swear, I didn't know about the guns. I was face down on the floor, with a cop's foot on my back, (just daring me to breathe, or move). I was so scared and my kids were screaming, it was the worst thing I can imagine. I never knew it was so bad. You have to believe me, I didn't know how bad it was.

But when he was arrested, there were over 40 weapons in the house - - I only knew of two guns. He had a whole slew of them, rifles, shotguns, pistols, you name it and he had it. He had several pounds of marijuana, cocaine and stuff I didn't know what it was - - in baggies, some of it was wrapped up like bricks in newspaper, and some in garbage bags.

I must have been so stupid not to see what he had been doing. He was out of work, so when I'd ask, "how was your day?" - - Meaning were you out looking for work, or did you find something - - I usually got, "oh, you know, no one wants to hire me because of the tattoos (or the hair, or because he's white - - there was always some excuse not to find a job.) So I worked doing what I could, keeping a roof over our heads, and sometimes he'd say that he got a little pot, (and of course, he'd offer me a hit - - when the kids were asleep,) but never in my wildest dreams did I think that he was dealing big time - - guns, that made it a federal offense. Everything we owned was confiscated: the cars - - even mine, the house, and the kids ended up in foster care for a while. It was a mess, and I had to fight to get my kids back, prove that I was a good parent. It was horrible.

To make a long story short, he went to prison for a long time, and I got a divorce. I wouldn't touch a joint to save my life now - - and I know that I'm not blameless for what happened, but I sure was blind. And yes, there was abuse, but mostly he was a criminal, and that still pisses me off. I'm mostly pissed off at myself for not seeing what was so obvious.

* Gina, it might have worked for a judge, but it doesn't cut it for me. I'm much too realistic - - that's the reason I don't write romances. I've seen too much in the 20+ years of social work, including CPS, to know that you aren't as gullible as you're putting on. I can't believe that you didn't know what was going on. If you were smoking a joint now and then, you were deliberately blindsiding yourself. You had to know the pot was coming from someplace, and you had to be equally suspicious if you were told to stay out of certain spots in the house. If you were smoking pot (even when the kids were sleeping, which I also don't believe...) you HAD to know that things were not what they seemed to be. Your blindness was selective. I wish I could have more sympathy but I can't. Drugs are drugs. By smoking pot, you were jeopardizing your children's health, safety and welfare, and certainly you know the laws. You can't plead ignorance with me, but I do believe that you may have been browbeat into keeping your mouth shut. I do believe that you were working your butt off for a no-account cracker, but I don't think that you are totally blameless either. Consider yourself lucky and get on with your life. I hope you wise up a bit.

***

Barbara, 47, engineering
Thank God my parents raised me to be self-reliant and independent. My father insisted on a good education for his daughters, all three of us. One sister is a scientist, the other is an economist. I'm a civil engineer. I'm very logical and task-oriented, which means that I plan and organize everything before I actually do anything. I see it, then

I do it. However, that doesn't mean that my personal life has been mistake-free. My first marriage was a disaster. I should have seen it coming, but of course, I was in love, and love is totally illogical. My husband was a controller. He wanted things done *his* way. He wasn't necessarily abusive, but controlling is just as bad. You think: I'm an intelligent person, I have a master's degree. I can do anything. Sure: except when it came to the two of us. We were opposites, and yet, I tried to do everything for him, because of him, for him. He selected the vacations, the cars, the houses, and living room furniture. No matter what I did, it wasn't right, wasn't enough.

I started having migraines, bouts of dizziness that couldn't be explained through medical tests. I was stressed out, having IBS (Irritable Bowel Syndrome), insomnia, headaches and all of the things that I logically knew to be psychosomatic in origin and if anyone would have mentioned a bad (failed?) marriage, I would have been the first to argue. But one day, he was dominating me in a traditional manner, saying I didn't know what I was talking about, telling me that I was stupid and that I didn't have the sense to know which end was up. Perhaps it was the word *stupid* that got my attention.

I wasn't stupid. I knew that. I had gone through graduate school when I was pregnant with my second child. I worked full time even when I was dead tired. I was the financial force in the marriage, but I kowtowed to him in everything that involved the home and kids. It hit me like a ton of bricks. The headaches, the dizziness, the IBS, stress and now stupid! I waited until he went hunting with his buddies, then I moved his stuff to the garage and had the locks changed. The divorce was as ugly as it can get, but I realized that I had been a floor-mat for him. Maybe he had to demean and control me because I made more money than he did. As the divorce got uglier, he called me a bitch, and one moment, I smiled and said, "You bet I'm a bitch. You ain't seen nothing yet, buster." I have no explanation why I put up with it except to say at that time in my life, I was irrational and in love. I'm glad my father insisted on education for his daughters because I had to be both mom and dad for a few years, but I managed to buy and sell houses one step up each time, and learned a lot about myself as a single parent.

Since then I've never looked backwards. I've remarried and we have reached an agreement before we got married. I've given my children roots and wings, and an education. When they were little, they had to play one musical instrument and take one sport. They had to experience camps and puppies. Like my father, I insisted that they attend college. My son is struggling in a master's program, and my daughter is graduating at the end of the month with a degree in political history. I see my ex-husband from time to time at a family gathering, and it seems to me that he hasn't gotten on with his life. He never did get that degree he kept blathering on about when we were married, and now he's driving a truck and has bad kidneys from long periods of sitting and driving. He looks twenty years older than he should, and just recently, he said he was sorry. Too bad. Too late. I'm happy with my second husband, a logical man if there ever was one.

When there are disagreements, and there are, we are both rational and logical enough to have a sensible discussion. Emotions get in the way, so does fighting, so we let it cool, think about it, and wait a day before we discuss the details. It works much better for us, and I have no reason to be bitchy - - except for the hormone thing, and I'm working on it.

* Here again, communication and education seem to be key issues with the mature woman. This woman has the advantage of being logical rather than emotional. She is able to step back and see the big picture without the emotional baggage that gets in the way. By the way, she never thought of being a bitch as a good thing. Now she does and pats herself on the back for a job well done. She says that she is working toward her Ph. D., in bitchdom, but won't step on anyone to get where she needs to go.

***

Rose Stadler, MSW

Eunice, retired from social services
It's a man's world

I have never been a bitch in my life, not that I know of anyway. I have gotten a good education, gotten promotions that I earned, had to fight the male ceiling throughout my professional life, and had to be diplomatic, tactful and sometimes cunning, but not a bitch. However, there was a time when I was continually passed up for promotions with the state because some man who had less education or experience than I got the job I was going after. This happened about five times that I know of, but one time I filed a grievance, stated my case, and got the job. However, and this is a huge **but,** my salary wasn't anywhere near what they were paying the man who had the job before me. His grade was a grade 22 and mine was a 19, with a huge variable in the pay scale. I had to appeal again, it took about a year, but I finally won, with back pay to the day I started the job. I shouldn't have been in a position to have to argue about my qualifications, and it angered me greatly that I did, but in the end I won, and that's what matters. People saw me as a bitch after that because I (1) filed a grievance, and (2) had to appeal the salary and grade. It was an effort for me at that time because so many people said, "don't rock the boat, don't make waves, be glad you have a job." People should advance on skill, not gender. I fought and won, hopefully paving the way for another generation of females after me.

* Eunice, this isn't a new thing. It has always been a man's world and working women have fought to be recognized. You'd think in social services, where people are in the helping arena, things would be different, but alas, not always so. Your story is one a lot of women can relate to, so by telling it here, you have opened the door for other women to advance to a higher level. Enjoy retirement. You've earned it.

***

Sheila, 25,
Bi-racial relationship

I was the first in my family to have an inter-racial relationship. I was a late-in-life baby for my parents (my mother was 40 when she had me) so it was hard for her to accept my partner. My first child is five, a girl, and my son is four years old. The first prejudice I got was from my own family - - my brothers told me that it would be so much harder on me if I had a biracial child, that everything would be that much more difficult, that a white man would never accept me again. They have since come around, and my children are very much loved by my family, but it was difficult at first.

I've experienced prejudice in one of my jobs when I worked for a non-profit child care agency that provided care for low income families, with three different locations. I worked at the Central location, which was three blocks away from home, but they were going to transfer me to the South location because there were more Black people there and I was told that that "I worked well with those people." The distance in travel time was 45 minutes each way. I told them that I didn't think that it was right, and that I wouldn't tolerate it. I wasn't bitchy about it, but I was firm, so I gave a two-week notice. They still gave me my two weeks' income to avoid a lawsuit. I'm the kind of person who stands up for myself. I'm high on principles and standards. It made me angry that they would refer to *those people* who just happen to include my children and mate.

* There should not be any prejudice today. Ever. Under any circumstance. It simply should not be tolerated in any form. Period. End of discussion. Sheila has two children, a girl age 5 and a boy age 4; that's all anyone needs to know. The fact that these children were born of a bi-racial relationship should have absolutely no bearing on anything, including the mother's job. She was right to walk away from a job that had prejudice as a letterhead. If it had been me, I would have taken them to court in a heartbeat. Right on, Sheila! When we spoke, you didn't sound the least bit bitchy, but like a clean, level-headed young woman.

Rose Stadler, MSW

***

Shannon, 39, unsure

Shannon admits that she may or may not have been a bitch, but for 22 years, she's been married to an abusive alcoholic who has had several DUI's, in-jail and house arrests, probation, and other bouts with the law. Currently they have separated (3 weeks) but she is still unsure if she wants to leave him for good or not. He has promised to turn over a new leaf, not hit her anymore, and quit drinking. He has even promised to go to church. But she's asking herself if he will really change. If so, for how long? Is this another play at getting his way? I see it as an act of desperation on his part. He wants his mommy back. He wants her to do his laundry, cooking, provide for his sexual needs and be a battering ram for his rages. He keeps saying that his parents separated when he was a juvenile, and if she rejects him too, he wouldn't be able to live.

It's a pretty heavy guilt trip. There could possibly be a history of mental illness in his family, (bi-polar, schizoid tendencies, rage, violence, alcoholism) and if she leaves for good, she's no better than his mother. Then he says, "go ahead and leave, just like my mother did. You're just like her."

In the meantime, Shannon's enjoying her new freedom, living each day to the next, putting one foot in front of the other. She's uncertain about the future. Right now she describes her current living conditions as a dump. She has money in her pocket, but not much. She's afraid to go it alone, has four kids to think about, is afraid to take him back, afraid of what will become of her and is feeling old at 39. She feels all washed up, used and left over. On the plus side, she doesn't feel that she has to lock all the doors and hide in the bathroom, or constantly wait for the other shoe to drop. She can actually inhale and exhale without flinching. But she loves him. But she loves her freedom. But he needs her. But she likes it without him, she's at peace. But but but..... She could go on all day making lists of the pros and cons of a 22-year marriage. One of the big *buts* is that she firmly believes in a marriage vow.... a promise made before God and family.

* I told Shannon that it's all right to live in a dump - - a new coat of paint will take care of the walls, but she can't put a coat of paint on a human being and be guaranteed of any changes. She can fix the steps and put down carpeting, but she can't make the changes in HIS life. He has to want the changes for himself, not as promises - - that she doesn't believe because of the past - - and is scared to death of the future. Promises don't count - - she needs to see at least two years of sustained sobriety to be convinced of anything better. As for the guilt trip about him being rejected by the women in his life, perhaps if he treated her better, she might not feel the way she does. AND: he needs to grow up and move on. If he's in his 40's and still attached to his mother's apron strings, or lack of apron strings, he needs counseling on his own. He has to deal with his mother's rejection on its own merit. That is an issue that has nothing to do with Shannon, but he knows that when he brings it up, she feels guilty and returns.

She loves him: fine, but she might have to love him from a distance. Her man will have to change on his own, for himself, not for her, to be successful. They both have changes to make, but she can only be responsible for herself. In the meantime, I told her to hang on for six months, one day at a time, to breathe her own air and look at her own pictures on the wall. She needs to understand that she is capable at 39, capable of living out her dreams, and being her own success. One day at a time, Shannon. In the meantime, look in the mirror - - working up to five minutes a day, and say, "I love you" to herself until she believes that she is worthy. Right now, she's not sure of herself. She doesn't feel that she deserves a decent life.

It's amazing, all the women in the book had different reasons to stay in abusive relationships, ranging from "if you go I will kill myself" to "you're just like my mother" and "If I can't have you, no one can." Shannon's reason was a 22-year-long guilt trip. Both of these adults have to grow on their own. But she shouldn't have to stay out of guilt, after all, she is the one who was abused. This marriage is fraught with a ton of whatifs, shoulda's woulda's and coulda's. My opinion is if the love is real, it can wait out the trial separation. Give it two years of sobriety and responsibility - - or not.

It's a matter of *choice*, your choice, and how much you are willing to tolerate.

My mother, Fran, to whom this book is dedicated, used to tell me that "everything is temporary, even hanging. Sooner or later they have to cut you down." I love that. Consider the fact that everything is temporary - - even abuse. It would stop when you die. Do you want to wait that long? It's your choice. Life is temporary, you have the power, use it well.

***

Other comments about **Release Your Inner Bitch.**

"I don't remember a time when I wasn't a bitch."

"I'm a PMS bitch, but most of the month I'm pretty good."

"When are the tee shirts coming out? I want fifteen of them for my family reunion."

"Me, a bitch? You bet your ass."

"I'm not a bitch yet, but I'm working on it."

"Of course, I'm a bitch, all women have to be bitches."

"Absolutely, I'm a bitch, how else would women survive?"

"No, I'm not a bitch. My mother is a bitch, ask her."

"I'm only a bitch when I have to be."

"I've never been a bitch in my life, but I lie like a rug too."

"All women are bitches. It's the color of blood."

"Women are bitches, all men should know that. It's safer for them if they just understand that we get bitchy from time to time, do what we say, and get out of the way."

"Am I bitch? Yes, but I do it with a smile."

"I am a bitch by the nature of my ovaries."

"Me, a bitch? Is the Pope Catholic? Does a bear shit in the woods?"

"I'm a woman, of course, I'm a bitch. What's the difference?"

"I have a jar of bitch cream by my bed at night. It erases wrinkles at the same time it feeds the bitch."

"How many colors in an artist's pallet? That's how many different kinds of bitches there are."

"Bitches unite, that's my motto."

"I'm not a bitch, I'm a Methodist."

"I'm divorced, that makes me a bitch."

"I'm a wife, mother, lover, friend, and naturally, a bitch."

"I have a uterus, that makes me a bitch."

"Absolutely, without a doubt, I am a bitch. Proudly. I am a card-carrying bitch of the highest order."

"Ask my husband..."

"Of course..."

"Try me and find out."

"Yes, who wants to know?"

"That's a silly question. We're all bitches, just different sizes."

"I'm a bitch, my daughters are bitches, my mother is the bitch-master, and we all have whips."

"I have always been a bitch, but this is the first time I thought it was a good thing."

"Hey, I'm from New York, we're all bitches there. Gotta be to get a cab or a decent table."

"I'm a polite bitch."

"I'm like the poster that says something like 'I have PMS and a handgun, any questions?'"

THE BITCH	**THE NON-BITCH**
Speaks up with precision, stating exactly what she wants or needs.	Speaks in half sentences stating only a part of the package.
Knows where she has been.	Has no clue how she got to the other side of the fence.
Knows where she is going.	Travels willy-nilly through life, accepting whatever happens.
Makes decisions.	Rely on others to make decisions for her or freezes.
Handles or knows about her own finances.	Rely on others to make financial decisions for her.
Gets educated, whether its learning how to use tools or getting a Ph.D.	Has a sense of learned helplessness.
Has her own tool box..	Borrows a *thingamajig*.
Does not seek approval. Doesn't get permission.	Seeks approval, needs permission.
Has a sense of 'posture' and erectness. Gets taller when needed.	Slouches.

Has excellent eye contact.	Has poor eye contact.
Doesn't fidget.	Fidgets.
Is honest and direct.	May be honest, but has a problem with communication.
Has excellent communication skills.	Has poor communication skills.
Has a clearly established set of goals.	Has no goals.
Takes responsibility for her actions.	Avoids responsibility for her actions, passing that to others.
Doesn't take a 'victim' stance.	Is frequently a victim.
Doesn't hide.	Hides, locks herself in the bathroom or closet.
Is never invisible.	Is invisible a large amount of time.
Will NOT accept abuse or maltreatment by others.	Is prone to accepting abuse or maltreatment by others.

Will never allow intimidation to occur.	Allows intimidation to occur.
Will never be abused.	Is probably one of the 4 million women who report abuse annually.
Is empowered and self determined.	Is NOT empowered and self determined. Has a sense of learned helplessness.
Is willing to compromise.	Is on the receiving end of compromise.
Doesn't comply for the sake of complying.	Complies with everything.
Has a reason for everything.	Doesn't have a reason, but relies on others, or fate.
Is motivated and directed to success,	Is not motivated or directed toward success
Is a participator.	Is a spectator.
Doesn't accept her own excuses.	Has a ton of excuses handy for every event.
Optimist. Sees opportunities.	Pessimist. Sees burdens and ruts in the road.

Adventuresome, grabs life.	Avoids the non-routine.
Risk taker.	Not a risk taker.
Rarely has time for depression.	Does a lot of self evaluation, often resulting in depression and unhappiness.
Exciting, flashy, vibrant.	Dull, boring, routine.
Reads a lot. Learns.	Reads what is necessary or 'standard.' Avoids learning new material. Same-oh, same-oh.
Validates self.	Validates self through other's point of view.
Is strong.	Is weak.
Makes a grand entrance.	Uses the side door.
Knows when to hold and when to fold.	Doesn't know when to shut up.
Enjoys life. Laughs frequently.	Sees life as a drudge. It's all work and no play.

Release Your Inner Bitch

Is not over-committed. Knows it. Sets limits and sticks to it.	Is often over-committed, going in 10 different directions, starting projects and leaving them unfinished.
	High stress and/or psychosomatic illness may result.
Is not a fixer of the universe.	Must be a fixer to everything and everyone. A rescuer all the time.
Isn't a worrier.	Worries about everything.
Doesn't necessarily care what others think.	Worries constantly what others think.
Isn't impressed by the anger levels in herself or anyone else.	Is afraid of anger. Will not confront anger in others
Doesn't apologize to excess.	Apologizes for every little thing in the universe.
Doesn't blame self when things go wrong.	Blames self for everything.. Must be her fault that the train got derailed on the other side of town, and it must be her fault that it's raining on the garden party.

Rose Stadler, MSW

Has a sense of preparedness. (Keeps an extra thousand dollars in the bank, has a decent spare tire and an air compressor.)	Is frequently caught off guard.
Takes time for herself.	Never has any time for herself.
Does not engage in unhealthy guilt.	Surrounds herself with guilt.
Can take criticism. In fact, welcomes criticism.	Cannot take criticism. Will fall apart at the slightest provocation.
Isn't a perfectionist.	Must be a perfectionist in all things.
Can take a compliment very well.	Can't take a compliment. An oxymoron when one needs to be perfect and can't take criticism.
Has a good sense of self esteem.	Has low self esteem.
Is independent.	Is codependent.

Being a true bitch is being a woman who is self-assured, empowered, determined and honest to herself. This is a process of personal or individual growth, and each woman has a sense of knowing when she has *arrived.* Once that arrival has taken place, there should be no need to lie, cheat, steal or belittle others in a fashion that indicates the evil bitch from hell, but rather a firm voice, and an *attitude* of personal strength and courage.

Humility is knowing one's worth. Every person on the face of the earth has worth and value, but it is knowing the exact specifics of the value that makes a difference. Know your own worth and take it from there.

Rose Stadler, MSW

Glossary of various bitches:

Aggressive Bitch This bitch takes a warrior stance on everything. No matter what she does or where she goes, she is dressed for battle, wearing armor in the form of a 357 tube of lipstick. She is on the attack, ready and able to do battle at any time, with anyone for any reason.

Bimbo bitch This is a *Barbie Doll* bitch, an airhead on the surface, (usually with big hair, huge breasts, tiny waist and plastic brain) but watch out for the 9mm *thingamajig* under her skirt. Similar to the **Bimbette** who is not a full-fledged Bimbo Bitch.

Bi-polar bitch Often manic and demanding. This bitch accelerates from sweet and innocent to psychotic and vicious in a heartbeat, and God help anyone in her way. She is as unpredictable as a tornado, hurricane or tsunami; does as much damage as an earthquake, then returns to a subdued self in the blink of an eye, and will sweetly ask "how did this happen?" This bitch never accepts responsibility, and is frequently mistaken for the **victim** bitch. Her vast mood swings run from hilarity to bleak depression, seldom staying the same for long. This has been called the **borderline** bitch as well, however that term denotes a character or personality flaw. However, the bi-polar bitch does not think that she has a personality flaw, and will not accept responsibility for her behavior. It is the cut of her fabric.

Bitch	One who has learned the art of self determination, empowerment, knows how to speak her mind, is assertive and strong and will not take crap. The true bitch is goal-oriented, motivated toward success, independent, open to others, respectful and has 360 degree peripheral vision. She is strong, assertive, thoughtful and intelligent.
Bitchiness	Frequently related to PMS and hormonal changes, however true bitchiness is the finely tuned style that the bitch has achieved during her bitchdom.
Bitchdom	Liken to kingdom; the territory in which the bitch reigns, or like dynasty: the length of time the bitch reigns for a specific amount of time, or a sense of having *arrived*.
Bitchy	The art of being a bitch.
Bitch 101	Course in bitchiness. Can be given or taken at any time in life. The earlier the better. Required for Bitch 201 or higher. This is the basic course and covers the elementary aspects of bitchiness.
Catty Bitch	This bitch can't resist gossip. She frequently engages in petty put-downs of other women, in a small meaningless way, generally in front of an audience, but couldn't fight her way out of a box of sanitary pads. (Examples: Did you see the eye makeup on that one? Can you imagine leaving the house with *green* shoes? I'm sure she knows better, but having a blouse with stains on.... my, my.)

Consumer bitch   This bitch is only bitchy when consuming or purchasing products or services and wants the best deal possible. She is usually very proud of her accomplishments and will brag about them later.

Damsel in Distress Bitch
This bitch is *always* in trouble. In fact, she makes it a point to have car trouble just when an available target is leaving the office for the day. It doesn't matter if the target is married or single, if she needs him or his position, she will do whatever she has to do to get his attention, and/or a promotion in the deal. She is helpless, flirty and every bit the bimbo when she has to be, but always appears vulnerable on the surface and will go out of her way to look as dumb as possible. Watch out, her cleavage may be wired.

Drunken bitch   This is a bitch to be avoided. Her altered states of bitchiness are inconsistent with her world. She wants and craves attention, but like the **rude** or **obnoxious bitch,** her status of bitchdom is questionable, often leading to Karasoff's syndrome.

Eccentric bitch   This bitch is frequently seen wearing odd combinations of clothing, often seen with a camera or art bag slung across her shoulders. She is confident in herself enough to wear cowboy boots or comfortable sneakers with a formal suit. Usually highly creative and right brained. Often unaware of the comments from others. She is in a world of her own and if an insult comes her way, she probably sees it as a humorous remark. This bitch laughs frequently, seeing the energy of life.

Enabler Bitch This bitch is a type of controller, an enabler, the one who makes life miserable for the alcoholic or codependent person in the same environment, causing the individual to slip and fall, consume substances, or slam doors, then complains about it later. This bitch is a master of disguise, can wear a persona of whimpy and weepy (victim bitch), swiftly changing to cunning and deceitful (warrior bitch). Often mistaken for the **bi-polar bitch.**

Ex-wife bitch This bitch reserves vindictive, hateful bitchiness in a specific and directed manner, most frequently directed toward her ex-husband or the father of her children, frequently denying visitation and/or information about the child(ren) to the father. In this regard, the bitchiness is specific and generally not directed to others.

Hi-falutin' bitch This bitch runs with a pack of bitches and is most frequently seen at the most expensive hotels, restaurants, and lounges; has a case of credit cards in her briefcase and takes no prisoners. She does not associate with common bitches, does not wear polyester, and does not shop at Wal-Mart. She expects diamonds and gold to do her speaking for her and will dismiss the commoner with a flip of her hand. She ranks with **royal bitches.**

Hydra-bitch — Like the robo-bitch, the hydra-bitch operates in high gear at all times, has instinctive 'hydraulic' reactions and can respond in record time.

Junior bitch or **bitch-in-training** — This is provided to young bitches, or women who have only recently acquired the need for bitchiness; striving for bitchdom.

Mabitch — This particular species is male. The same attributes of bitchiness and bitchdom apply to men.

Menopausal Bitch — Commonly refers to a period of time in a woman's life, called the change of life, when the urge to nest ceases and the urge to fly the coop seems to be most prevalent. Side effects of a decrease of hormones can be controlled with medication; however, many women experience a sudden emotional or spiritual growth spurt during which they no longer assume the responsibility for each and every living thing on the face of the earth, and will frequently soar in her own right. Have wings will fly. Moreover, removal of the uterus at this time is a wise decision, getting rid of the crib and keeping the playpen. White underwear becomes a delightful option.

Non-denial, Denial Bitch. — This bitch is cat-like and cunning, using the reasoning: I didn't do it but if I did, I didn't inhale. (Catherine Zeta Jones in *Chicago* comes to mind. "I didn't do it, but if I did it, he had it coming. He only has himself to blame.") However, if I did it, I probably had a good reason, but I forgot, so I'm not responsible. (Like having sex with your clothes on, therefore it's not really sex. Runs neck in neck with there are no calories in broken cookies.)

On-the-job bitch Clerks, cashiers, secretaries, administrators, professional women who successfully divide their bitchiness between home and job. These bitches punch in and punch out with the time clock, arranging their bitchiness according to their paycheck.

PMS Bitch PMS: PreMenstrual Syndrome. This is a woman who is bitchy during that time of the month, and no other. Usually remedied by a quick chocolate fix, time spent alone, a good book, a hot bath and some candles. The man living with the PMS woman should slip her flowers, then leave the room. Unfortunately, anyone being bitchy is accused of having PMS, or that PMS is related to all other forms of bitchiness. PMS bitchiness can assume any or all of the bitch forms, but is short-lived and timely. Often accompanied by weeping or the desire to rip the head off a small bird.

Primo Bitch This woman has mastered the art of bitchiness to the queenly or royal level and does not associate with common bitches.

Queen Bitch This bitch rules in the land of bitchdom. She is the Queen of Darts. Liken to the beehive, there can only be one queen bitch in the hive at a time.

Quiet Bitch Like a lone killer bee, the quiet bitch stalks her prey and attacks when the opponent is unguarded.

Relative Bitches Title granted to a specific member of a family or kinship. The relative bitch is a grandmother, aunt, cousin, sister, twin or daughter-in-law. This can extend to ex-wives, but the ex-wives are more frequently in a category by themselves.

Right Bitch This bitch is always right, never apologizes and knows that there is only one way to achieve anything. It's her way or the highway. "Like it or leave it," is her attitude. She not open to suggestions, recommendations or solutions that do not have her name at the top of the letterhead. She is not a team player, works best alone or as a supervisor, and never releases her authority over lesser bitches.

Robo-Bitch This is a bitch supreme, one who is in overdrive constantly, armed and dangerous, wears armor at all times and is in high gear at all times. The robo-bitch doesn't sleep.

Royal Bitch This bitch has had a good life, starting with diamond-studded booties. She more than likely attended private, every expensive schools and learned the art of bitchiness at an early age. Upon entering bitchdom, she achieves favored status in youth. She does not tolerate the common bitch, wastes no time with them and will not demean her status by being in a confrontation with a common bitch.

Rude Bitch This is a bitch who has declared open warfare on the world and wants everyone to know it. She is loud and abrasive, has a personality like sandpaper. She can be easily subdued by the sweet bitch or the quiet bitch or the gentle bitch. The rude bitch is not welcome in most circles and rarely achieves total bitchdom, but because she is so loud and ruthless, she has no way of knowing that her status of rude bitch is really, **obnoxious bitch.**

Saintly Bitch A lot like the martyr bitch, or the victim bitch, these women either promote bitchiness on the saintly level or bring up past issues which make the victim bitches for the remainder of their lives. This bitch frequently indicates that things are brought about by Divine Intervention, therefore, it is not necessary to take responsibility when things go wrong. This can and does involve the hurting and maiming of others, in personal and professional relationships. When (not if) those relationships go sour, this bitch is quick to place the entire situation at the Lord's feet, thus eliminating the need for empowerment, communication skills, self-determination or any other process on the human level. When all is said and done, the saintly bitch is completely blameless, righteous, and once again walks in the glory of her sainthood, totally disregarding the needs, wants or opinions of others.

Rose Stadler, MSW

Seasonal Bitch   This bitch dresses for the occasion. At Halloween, her decorations can be seen for miles in every direction. She doesn't use last year's Easter candy, and wouldn't be caught dead in a polyester witch hat. Other holidays are okay, so-so, with flags and yard ornaments for the appropriate fanfare, but Thanksgiving and Christmas literally are *pageantry* in her home. The toilet tank cover matches the rug, which matches the shower curtain, which matches the toothbrushes, which match the towels and toilet paper. *All* details of her house are festive in matching, *expensive* holiday decor, and God help anyone who uses a hand towel that says, "Noel." It will be *God rest ye merry gentlemen* six feet under for anyone who crosses the seasonal bitch. The angel on the top of the tree is *exactly* in the center of the tree, or it is not an angel. This bitch makes everyone around her miserable with her merry cheer, insisting on happiness and good tidings to anyone within yelling distance. This bitch also makes snow angels, tinsel braids for the homeless, and peanut brittle for the toothless aged.

Stupid Bitch   This really is a bitch-in-training category. This bitch frequently embarrasses herself and others and has no concept of how or why she screwed up, continuing the bitchiness without direction or goals.

Super Bitch   This is a bitch who has arrived at bitchdom early and has made it a way of life in all things.

Supreme Bitch	This bitch has made herself a goddess, or a deity to rule over other bitches. Even the robo-bitch, hydra-bitch and the queen bitch bow to her supremacy, frequently seeking her counsel in matters of bitchiness, bitchdom or bitch attacks. Frequently seen in **Great Mother** bitches or the **matriarchal** bitch.
Sweet Bitch	This is the Scarlet O'Hara of bitches. She is sweet, like honey, and carries herself like a soft woman. Do not underestimate the power of this bitch. Those underwires may be made of C/4 explosives.
Total Bitch	This is a woman who makes bitchiness a way of life and has accomplished the aspects of all the bitches into a single, integrated personality.
Uppity Bitch	This bitch simply knows that she is better than all other bitches, so no matter how hard they try to compete with her, she is the best bitch in the world. The law of physics applies here: two uppity bitches cannot occupy the same space at any one time.
Victim Bitch	Generally speaking, this is an oxymoron, because by the nature of the victim-ness, this person is not really a bitch, but a whiner. This person uses past life experiences as a resource for everything that happens in the here-and-now. This person, male or female, is the type of person who goes about life in a fearful manner, ducking and flinching at everything and everybody, and complains about it later. However, this person can hold a grudge for

years and has a memory like an elephant, never releasing or giving up on the victim status, but wears it like a badge throughout life. The victim is Murphy's Law in action. If anything can go wrong, it will, and it will add the fuel to keep the victim's fire burning. The victim relishes disaster, and sees disaster in every waking minute of the day. This is the poor-little-me, who will get the biggest piece of cake because of the poor-little-me status without having done anything to earn the piece of cake.

Related bitch words: banshee, vampire, vamp, seductress, witch, slut, tart, vixen, tramp, trollop, call girl, strumpet, wench, paramour, courtesan, mistress, concubine, kept woman, prostitute, bimbo; goddess, queen, princess, lady-in-waiting, wife, mother, grandmother, daughter, mother-in-law, step mother, step daughter, cousin, step sister and second cousin twice removed; any female of the human species.

***

Codependent: This is a person (male or female) who relies on the values of others to exist or co-exist. This person if powerless, spineless, submissive, beaten (mentally or physically), insecure, could be an enabler in a relationship involving alcoholics and/or substance abusers. Cannot make decisions, is a worrier, fixer, controller and is frequently resentful. This person often carries guilt like a banner, is self-righteous and indulges in fearful emotions.

Empowerment: This is the direct opposite of learned helplessness. It is the finely honed art of being in control of one's self, being capable of making decisions and accepting responsibility. Keep in mind that the decisions made can be changed. The empowered person has the ability to keep going when things get tough, can see the big picture and is able to find strength in one's self. This does not eliminate compassion or compromise for/or with others, but emphasizes one's ability to make decisions based on historical events, logical analysis and factual data, rather than an emotional reaction to a situation. Self-determination and empowerment are often words that are interchanged, having the same or similar meanings. The sense of self-worth and self-understanding are essential ingredients in empowerment.

Fight or flight: This is an instinctive reaction in animals when confronted with a dangerous situation or event. This is adrenaline based, and found in humans as well. Some animals will rear up and face an opponent; other animals will flee. Humans are no different. Some will fight, some will flee. Some will form habits of flight in all situations, and others will form habits of fight in all situations. The battered woman who hides in the closet (flee) learns to fight back (fight), the scapegoat secretary who does all the work will learn to re-evaluate the job (fight), or quit (flee). Basically, this is a choice when initially confronted with a hostile and/or dangerous situation.

Freezing: Not making a decision one way or another. A person with learned helplessness freezes with decision-making, allowing the first person to come along to make decisions for him or her. Sometimes it is wise to freeze on making a decision, (example: Should I move to another state? Should I quit this job and become self-employed?), but freezing as a way of life needs to be avoided. People who avoid making decisions at all are people who live their lives in ruts, can't see a way out, and know no other way of survival. They scratch out their life with what they have available, rarely seeing opportunities.

Interdependent: This person is peaceful, or at peace with herself and the decisions she makes, is tolerant of others, reserves judgment, is proud of her accomplishments, is calm, assertive, forgiving, strong, loving, joyful and compassionate. This is a helpful, self-actualized individual who is confident and independent.

Learned Helplessness: This is a phrase commonly associated with psychology, sociology, counseling or social work. If a person waits long enough, does nothing to rectify a situation, something will change. Perhaps the situation no longer needs clarification or rectification. Maybe the memo that's been in the 'in' basket for a week no longer needs a response. Someone else took care of it. The person with learned helplessness knows that if she waits long enough on the side of the road *someone* will change her tire for her because she is blocking traffic. *Someone* will push her car off to the side of the road because they want to get through. This person doesn't have to make decisions, because *someone else* will take care of it. She probably doesn't have a watch because ten people around her will tell her the time. This person doesn't have to drive because *someone else* will give her a ride.

ON THE SERIOUS SIDE

Myths, Facts, and Stats (taken from **Domestic Violence: the Facts**, sponsored by Harvard Pilgrim, Health Care Foundation, brochure, 1997 by Peace At Home, Inc.)

MYTH #1 Domestic violence does not affect many people.

FACT:
- A woman is beaten every 15 seconds (Gelles and Strauss, Intimate Violence, 1988)
- over 2 million women reported being beaten (1997) that figure is now up to about 5 (+) million who report abuse, but that 5 million figure might also include verbal and sexual abuse in the home.
- Between 1.5 and 3 million children witness domestic violence annually (ibid)

- Females experience over 10 times as many incidents of violence by an intimate partner as males (Bureau of Justice, 1994)
- Women age 20 to 34 have the highest rate of being victimized by their intimate partners (ibid)

MYTH #2 Battering is only a momentary loss of temper.

FACT:
- Battering is the establishment of control and fear in a relationship through violence and other forms of abuse. The batterer uses acts of violence and a series of behaviors, including intimidation, threats, psychological abuse, isolation, etc, to coerce and to control the other person. The violence may not happen often, but it remains as a hidden (and constant) terrorizing factor. (Common Purpose, Inc. Jamaica Plain, MA.)
- "One out of five women victimized by their spouses or ex-spouses report they had been victimized over and over again by the same person." (Surgeon General Antonia Novello, 1993.)

MYTH #3 Domestic violence only occurs in poor, urban areas.

FACT:
- Women of all cultures, races, occupations, income levels and ages are battered - - by husbands, boyfriends, lovers and partners. (For Shelter and Beyond, Boston, MA, 1990)
- White, Black, and Latina women all endure similar rates of violence committed by their intimate partners. (Bureau of Justice Statistics, 1994)
- Approximately one-third of the men counseled [for battering] at Emerge are professional men who are well respected in their jobs and their communities. These have included

doctors, psychologists, lawyers, ministers, and business executives. (David Adams, "Identifying the Assaultive Husband in Court: You Be the Judge." Boston Bar Journal, July/August, 1989)

MYTH #4 Domestic violence is just a push, slap or punch - - it does not produce serious injury.

FACT:
- Battered women are often severely injured - - 22 to 35 % of women who visit medical emergency rooms are there for injuries related to on-going partner abuse (Journal of the AMA, 1992)
- One of four pregnant women have a history of partner violence (A. S. Helton, *Battering During Pregnancy: Prevalence Study in a Metropolitan Area*, 1985)
- Of the murder victims killed by an intimate partner, 70% of the homicide victims were female. (Bureau of Justice Statistics, 1994)

MYTH #5 It is easy for battered women to leave their abuser.

FACT:
- When leaving their partners, women are at a higher risk for homicide in the first two months of the separation. (Wilson and Dally, *Violence and Victims*, 1993
- There are nearly three times as many animal shelters in the United States as there are shelters for battered women and their children. (Senate Judiciary Hearings, Violence Against Women Act, 1990)

Some other facts might astound you. About six million women report abuse annually, but how many don't report it at all? This is probably not an accurate reporting number because some women might have reported several times during the year. Children who grow up in abusive homes are more likely to abuse other children, and/or animals, and many of them like to play with fire, literally. Male children who see their fathers abuse their mothers are more likely to abuse their wives. Women who are abused as children, are more likely to be abused as adults as well. Children who are sexually abused are more likely to be sexually abused as adults, in fact, almost 45% of prostitutes report being sexually abused as children. When I worked for CPS, I did an intensive study pertaining to adults, who as children were in foster care for two years or more. Those adults were almost 50% more likely to have their own children placed in foster care, which indicated that the parenting skills that they learned (or didn't learn) from their parents carried over to their own parenting skills, repeating the cycle of abuse.

If you are a woman who is in a domestic violence situation, you need to get help. But first you might need to get out. Most women leave when the situation it at it's worst, getting out with the clothes on their backs. A planned escape is preferable to running down the streets in your nightgown. The following is a list of some of the things that a woman should take/do:

For emergencies: Call 9-1-1
- **If there are any injuries, bruising, bleeding, torn clothing, etc, get pictures. A picture is worth a thousand words in court. Save the torn clothing.**
- **If you or one of the children need immediate medical attention, get it before you do anything else.**

For non-emergencies
- Examine the house closely, look for quick escape routes.
- Make a list of safe people to contact.
- Have change handy for a pay phone or keep your (charged) cell phone in your purse at all times.
- Talk to a friend or a relative so that in the event that you have to leave quickly, you have a place to go.

- Have an extra set of keys handy. Include the house key, car key, safety deposit box key, and any other keys that might be important later.
- Pack a change of clothing for you and each of the children. Keep the suitcase or backpacks located near a quick exit.
- Locate all the important documents that you might need. Make copies of birth certificates, medical records, school records, immunization records, names and phone numbers, Social Security numbers, employment records, etc and put that in with the change of clothing.
- Get extra toothbrushes, deodorant, soap, and shampoo etc, and put that in the suitcase. Travel sizes will do. Don't forget a supply of sanitary supplies for yourself and a week's supply of prescription medicine.
- If your destination is in another city or state, see what you can do about getting non-dated airline tickets. Keep these in the suitcase.
- Don't rely on domestic violence shelters to have an opening. Bed space is generally limited. Go to a motel or a friend if you have to. Beware, you will leave a paper trail if you charge the motel to your credit card. You might be better off paying cash if you suspect that your abuser is stalking you.
- Have a stash of cash ready. You can be traced with credit cards.
- Call the police and 1) get a restraining order, 2) press charges, and 3) be willing to follow through. This is one of the events that are often the most frightening, and women tend to be intimidated at the thought of having their partner arrested and jailed, especially if that partner is threatening and abusive in the first place.

Once you have left or are freed of the abusive partner, get professional help for yourself and the children. Change your phone number. If you have gotten a restraining order, follow through. Press charges if necessary. Change all the locks and code numbers to the house, garage, windows, security system. Vary your daily routine. (Example: If you had been jogging in the morning, change the route and time of your outdoor exercise. Or join a gym.) If you feel that you have to move to a new location, do it quickly. Have as many witnesses as possible when you move. Let people know about the abuse. (This may even involve your employer. He or she may be in a position to help by screening calls, refusing contact with your abuser, etc.) Take legal action: either press charges, get a divorce, take out a restraining order or an order of protection. This leaves a very good paper trail for your protection. However, you need to know that a order of protection, restraining order or even divorce papers will not stop a bullet.

Domestic violence is something that should never be repeated, however, many women make the mistake of either taking the perpetrator back (again and again) or finding another abusive partner, repeating the cycle of abuse all over.

HOTLINES AND INFORMATION
NATIONAL COALITION AGAINST DOMESTIC VIOLENCE
P O Box 18749
Denver, CO 80218
Phone: 303-839-1852
web address: http://www/ncadv.org

National Domestic Violence Hotline
1-800-799-7233 voice (1-800-799-SAFE)
or 1-800-787-3224 TDD

Violence Against Women Office
beampbel@justice.usdoj.gov
810 7th St. NW
Washington, DC 20531
202/616-8894
202/307-3911 fax

Rose Stadler, MSW

Center for the Prevention of Sexual and Domestic Violence
936 N. 34th St. Ste 200
Seattle, WA 98103
206/634-1903
206/634-0115 fax

Children's Defense Fund
25 E Street NW,
Washington DC 20001
202/628-8787

National Council on Child Abuse & Family Violence
1155 Connecticut Ave NW, Ste 400
Washington DC 20036
202/429-6695

National Helpline National Committee for the Prevention of Elder Abuse
c/o Institute on Aging Medical Center of Central Massachusetts
119 Belmont St
Worchester, MA 01605
508/793-6166

National AIDS Network
P O Box 13827
Research Triangle Park, NC 27709
National AIDS Hotline 800-342-2437
TTY 800-243-7889
Spanish 800-344-7432

WHISPER
(Women Hurt in Systems of Prostitution Engaged in Revolt)
P O Box 56796
St. Paul, MN 55165
612/644-6301

National Women's Political Caucus
1275 K Street, NW, Ste 750
Washington, DC 20005-4051

National Resource Center on Domestic Violence
Pennsylvania Coalition Against Domestic Violence
6400 Flank Drive, Ste 1300
Harrisburg, PA 17112
800-537-2238

Battered Women's Justice Project Minnesota Program Development, Inc.
206 West Fourth St
Duluth, MN 55806
800-903-0111

Health Resource Center on Domestic Violence;
Family Violence Prevention Fund
383 Rhode Island St. Ste 304
San Francisco, CA 94103-5133
800-313-1310

Resource Center on Child Custody and Child Protection
National Council on Juvenile and Family Court Judges
P O Box 8970
Reno, NV 98507
800-527-3223

National Coalition for Low Income Housing
1012 14th St. NW, Ste 1200
Washington, DC 20005
202/662-1530

National Clearinghouse for the Defense of Battered Women

Rose Stadler, MSW
125 South 9th St. Ste 302
Philadelphia, PA 19107
215/351-0010

Check your state or local directory for individual coalitions against domestic violence.

There is a lot of information on the Internet pertaining to domestic violence with information about local shelters and transitional housing facilities, but don't expect to get the locations of the shelters. They are confidential for obvious reasons.

Call 9-1-1 for emergencies.

When in doubt, get out.

ABOUT THE AUTHOR

Rose Stadler, MSW, is a glassy-eyed author by night and for over 20 years, a social worker in the trenches of humanity. As a therapist at a transitional housing facility for battered &/or homeless women and children, Ms. Stadler made the not-so-startling discovery that bitches don't get abused. It was a light-bulb moment that gave rise to this book. Instead of writing another self-help book that battered women would never read, she decided to ask for shining bitch moments from survivors. A transplant from Arizona, she resides in West Virginia where she is setting it on fire with her outrageous ideas.

Made in the USA
Las Vegas, NV
22 November 2024